Big Carp

·BIG· CARP

Tim Paisley & Friends

The Crowood Press

First published in 1990 by
The Crowood Press
Gipsy Lane, Swindon,
Wiltshire SN2 6DQ

British Library Cataloguing in Publication Data

Paisley, Tim
  Big Carp
  1. Carp. Angling
  I. Title
  799.1752

  ISBN 1–85223–341–9

Dedication

To Mary, who not only understands but catches bigger carp, too.

Typeset by Inforum Typesetting, Portsmouth.
Printed in Great Britain at The Bath Press.

Acknowledgements

Trying to find something original to say about each of the contributors to this book would put a considerable strain on my superlatives thesaurus – and they are all well enough known anyway. Significant though they are in their own right – as carp men and writers – the contributors haven't been selected because their names might sell a few extra copies of the book, they appear in here because they are no strangers to big fish, because they are specialists in the sphere they write about, and because their years of experience have given them much of interest to pass on. In addition I suppose I'm old fashioned in that I feel that how people write is at least as important as what they have to say. The contributors not only have something of interest to say but they know how to put it across. All have established themselves as writers through their articles in angling and carp magazines and books, and Rod Hutchinson, Kevin Clifford, Chris Yates and Elliott Symak have all had books published in their own names.

The chapters that follow cover a variety of aspects of carp and big carp fishing, and I'm grateful to the contributors – Rod Hutchinson, Elliott Symak, Kevin Clifford, Julian Cundiff, Brian Garner, Jan Wenczka, Chris Ball, Ken Townley, Pete Springate and Chris Yates – for the trouble they have gone to in passing on some of their experience, knowledge and emotions and helping make this book such a terrific read.

I would also like to acknowledge the considerable additional assistance given by a number of people whose help has been an essential ingredient in the putting together of this book: Steve Corbett, Phil Harper, Kevin Nash, Bill Cottam, Chris Ball, Ritchie Macdonald, Dave Charlesworth, Sandra Procter, Sarah Bacon, Steve Wilde, John Lilley, Ray Stone, Dave and Gary Morgan, Lee Jackson, Alan Smith, Rob Maylin, Dave (Kryston) Chilton, Jon Holt and everyone I have ever discussed carp with.

Tim Paisley

'There are some things which cannot be learned quickly, and time, which is all we have, must be paid heavily for their acquiring. They are the very simplest things and because it takes a man's life to know them the little new that each man gets from life is very costly and the only heritage he has to leave.'

Ernest Hemingway

Contents

Big Carp

My first book for The Crowood Press was called '*Carp Fishing*'. It was an attempt to convey to readers something about the whole spectrum of carp fishing; not just trying to catch them, but what it is about carp that makes fanatics out of those who fish for them, a bit about the history of this comparatively new pursuit, and even a bit about the family feel that encompasses the carp fishing fraternity. That the book was far from adequate for those who wanted the full chapter and verse on bait, tactics, presentation, and waters, I had no doubt at all, but when I was planning the book in my mind I was aware that I'd got one major difficulty that I couldn't get across in the space available.

The difficulty is that there is carp fishing and there is fishing for big carp, and the difference between the two is major – for at least the vast majority of carp anglers. I was so aware of this difficulty that there was some discussion about doing the original book in two parts. The concept was shelved, the idea being that if '*Carp Fishing*' proved popular a further book would follow, a book in which I could concentrate on big carp and the pursuit of them. This is that book.

I've got two bridges to cross before I go any further. First, why am I writing a book about big carp fishing when there are others far better qualified than I to produce such a work? Second, just what is a big carp anyway? I'll deal with both questions as best I can.

In 1912 Hugh Sheringham, at the end of an account of the capture of a carp of 16lb 5oz, had this to say: 'So much for what I know about catching big carp. In *fishing* for them,

however, I am somewhat better instructed.' I know exactly how he felt. In fact many carp men who concentrate all their endeavours to the cause of catching big carp know exactly how he felt. Whatever mistaken impression the weeklies may inadvertently give, the capture of a big fish is an event. There are a *handful* of anglers in this country who consistently catch big carp, 'consistently' meaning to the tune of more than ten a season. There are perhaps a score or more who consistently catch half a dozen each season. Perhaps there are as many as one or two hundred who catch one, or two, or perhaps three per season. Then there are the rest of us who occasionally get lucky. If I were one of the chosen few for whom big fish seem to fall into their laps I would perhaps think that big fish fishing is easy. Because I'm not, I don't, and I think that gives me a strong enough case to be forgiven for being presumptuous enough to put together a book of this type.

So what is a big carp? In 1974 I landed what I thought was my first double. It looked huge in the early hours' darkness and I hoisted it up on my brand new Avons, convinced I'd cracked 'the double' barrier. The fish weighed 7lb 14oz. It still weighed 7lb 14oz on another angler's scales when I went round to have the weight checked after first light. At the time it looked a very big carp to me, and it was almost twelve months before I landed a carp that did take the scales past the magical, but undeniably modest, one-o barrier. A double seemed like a big carp at the time, but it hardly qualified as one on the national carp scale then, and that is fifteen years of carp inflation ago at the time of writing.

I don't think twenty pounds is a realistic big carp bottom limit, either. No, that's not me being blasé. I still get a thrill out of any carp, a big thrill out of one over fifteen pounds, and an even bigger thrill when I land a twenty plus. They are all big to me, but I think that when we refer to big carp we are talking about something *special*, and I'm setting that special limit at twenty-five pounds for the purposes of this book.

Twenty-five pounds is an arbitrary figure, I know that, but I think it is a weight you have to be very lucky to exceed accidentally. By very lucky I mean that either your local water contains fish of that weight, or you go to a water and catch one that big against all the laws of likelihood. Most anglers have to work very hard, travel a long way, and then get a bit lucky to catch a twenty-five plus. I can think of quite a number of consistently successful carp men for whom I've got the greatest regard who have not caught a carp over twenty-five pounds. Some of them have caught stacks of twenty plus fish, but not a twenty-five.

That will surprise many of you: I hope it will encourage you, too. If you read the weeklies you can rather get the impression that every other carp man is banking whacker after whacker. It's an awful mistake to think that, and it's the wrong impression to have if you are starting out in the pursuit of big fish. When I consciously made the change from just carp fishing to chasing biggies I gave myself the target of one fish over twenty-five pounds from the season's fishing. I caught one, too, from Waveney D Lake early in November. From memory I caught three or four other fish that season, none of them big, but in a split second, five months into the season I moved from failure to success. If at first you don't succeed . . .

A realistic target is an essential ingredient in the recipe for big fish success. All summer you must know that your best chances are likely to come in October and November – knowledge that should keep you going through the inevitable periods of inactivity and unredeemed blanks. If your target is one biggie, and you have confidence in your methods and your bait, you can keep telling yourself that success is just a session away: just one more four-hundred-mile round trip could crack it. Just because it hasn't happened so far doesn't mean to say it isn't going to happen.

Venue is all-important in the pursuit of big carp, and we've included details of as many twenty-five plus waters as possible in Julian Cundiff's chapter (Chapter 4). Take the chapter as a starting point and search out waters unknown to the in-crowd if possible. I've done a tremendous amount of travelling in the cause of catching carp – particularly in travelling to distant big carp waters. Some of the waters mentioned in Julian's chapter are the best in the country for twenty-five plus potential, particularly the Darenth complex in the south, Tilery Lake in the north, Homersfield in East Anglia and Savay Lake in the Home Counties. These waters have waiting lists, but they are open to anyone provided they are willing to wait, and waiting of one sort or another is just part of the big carp game. The lakes mentioned are examples; there will be others with equal potential.

Big carp fishing is not exactly a leisure pursuit, it is a full time occupation, in the sense that it tends to occupy all your leisure time. If I'm not making bait, tying rigs, sorting out tackle or fishing I'm working. I have had the odd terrific big fish season, and I've had a number of singularly unsuccessful ones, but because I know that is par for the course I plod on. I know how other carp anglers are doing, and many of them are having similar results to mine. A season's blank in terms of twenty-five pound plus fish is no big deal, particularly if you aren't fishing one of the prolific big fish waters.

Tim with a Tip Lake fish of 26lb 12oz caught in 1985.

Don't get confused between carp fishing now, carp fishing on the first flush of the tiger nut tidal wave, or carp fishing in the early years of the bare hook rigs. Carp fishing is hard; big carp fishing is even harder. I hope the pages that follow help put big carp into perspective and encourage some of you to look on big carp fishing as a pleasure, not a cause for going on the valium. There are times when it hurts; there are times when it's a chore; there are days when you think you will never want to sit behind a pair of fishing rods again. We've all been through it a hundred times and more, but if catching a big carp wasn't an achievement it wouldn't be worth doing, would it?

There are areas this book does not specifically cover. In some ways fishing for carp and fishing for big carp have a great deal in common. There is little or no difference in the tackle, so there is no tackle section in here. That may be an omission, but I can sum up your big fish tackle requirements in two words: be prepared. If you don't understand enough about carp fishing to know what the tackle requirements are you shouldn't be considering fishing for big carp! But understand what I mean by 'be prepared'. When you travel to fish for big fish you are wasting your time if you get to the water two hundred miles away – or twenty miles away for that matter – and discover that the fish you are after are out of your reach. There is no implication there that big fish can only be caught at range, but if that *is* the case, you must be ready for the eventuality. I can think of a number of big fish waters where the fishing isn't long range, and a number where it definitely is. Casting over a hundred yards isn't difficult in these days of advanced carp fishing tackle technology, but it amazes me how many anglers just aren't equipped to cope with casts of anything like that distance. They are severely limiting their carp catching capabilities, and even reducing their potential to virtually nil on some waters.

On the other hand it has to be said that many of us can become too obsessed with fishing at range, and miss out on some obvious opportunities. I've done a great deal of surface fishing this last year, and soon realised what a lousy surface angler I am. I've got better, but nothing like as adept as I would like to be, or should be. That will take time. I've never caught a twenty-five plus off the top, but I did catch a twenty plus on floater this session. As we've been told many times floater fishing can occasionally be ridiculously easy, and I think that's because you are able to watch the reaction of the fish to the bait and adjust your tactics accordingly. Elliott Symak is a committed stalker, as his lovely chapter makes clear, and as carp get harder to catch we are going to have to take heed of what the stalkers have to say and work harder for our successes. Ken Townley's terrific contribution really emphasises the benefits to be gained from observing fish on the baits and his is a real eye-opener of a chapter.

I'll mention one other contribution in detail, and that is Yatesy's. Some of you will accept the workings of the sixth sense; others will be as sceptical about it as Hutchy, who claims Chris predicted he would have a big fish in the morning every night! I used to long for what Jack Hilton first described as 'that feeling' when I took up carp fishing. I had no carp fishing instincts then, because I wasn't tuned in. I later developed this instinct and it almost always manifested itself some time into a session, or in the course of a series of sessions on one water. It was far more than a built-in understanding of what the carp in the water were doing; on occasions it was an actual prescience of something about to happen, or the spot to cast the bait, or the swim to be in. It happened on the Mangrove and at Waveney, as the D Lake chapter bears witness. I wrote that chapter in 1983 and haven't altered it since. In fact I've only used it now because it emphasises a number of the main themes of this book.

If you are not succeeding in your carp fishing, don't be afraid of changing your whole approach. My first sortie into the big fish world was a week on Longfield at the end of the 1981/1982 season, which I describe in Ritchie Macdonald's book 'Ritchie on Carp'. I went to Longfield armed with a vague feeling that the capture of big carp was just an extension of carp fishing, and that if you did it for long enough on the right waters you would catch your biggie. I came away from that week rich in the knowledge that I had been under a misapprehension: you catch big carp by fishing for them. I also knew that the two major ingredients in the big carp recipe are the waters you fish and the bait you fish with. I made two changes after that week. I put together a high quality HNV bait, having seen that Ritchie was fishing with *a food source*, not a 'bait' concept, and I stopped fishing for myths. I had been fishing for two local monsters, the existence of which I believed in, but wasn't certain of. They haven't been caught from that day to this, as far as I am aware! I didn't know of many waters containing big fish at that time, but those I did know of I started visiting – and I started to catch twenty-five pound plus fish. Was it really as simple as that? Well I don't know that it was simple, but it was certainly far easier than if I'd stuck on waters with no big fish in them and had continued using a smell for bait rather than a food.

I started by quoting Hugh Sheringham, a man whose marvellous writing was a strong influence on the early carp catchers in the late forties and early fifties. I'll finish this introduction by quoting from Mr Sheringham again, on an aspect of carp fishing very few people write about at length: luck. We tend to accept our good results as rightful rewards and our bad sessions and seasons as unmitigated bad luck. If you look at it the other way round you will be far more grateful for any big fish that you do manage to land. I think what Mr Sheringham has to say is very pertinent to our theme.

'For practical purposes there are big carp and small carp. The latter you may sometimes hope to catch without too great a strain on your capacities. The former – well, men have been known to catch them, and there are just a few anglers who have caught a good many . . . So far as my experience goes, it is certain that good luck is the most vital part of the equipment of him who would seek to slay big carp. For some men I would admit the usefulness of skill and pertinacity; for myself I take my stand entirely on luck.'

I know how he felt! Good luck.

Tim Paisley
November 1989

1 Why Big Carp?

Kevin Clifford

The factors which affect the growth of carp and determine why in one particular water they grow to a very large size whilst failing to do so in another, are clearly known. Of these factors, the two most important are environmental influence and the genetic role played by selective breeding.

The environment controls the availability of food items and determines to a large extent when, and often how, feeding takes place. The carp is a warm water fish, classified as eurytherm, its ancestors evolving from the area around the Caspian Sea some 10,000 years ago. When other factors remain constant, carp show an increase in growth with temperature increase, up to about 27°C. Above this figure, growth becomes erratic and finally ceases. Clearly water temperatures of this magnitude are almost never achieved in this country.

Indeed, the mean air temperature (not water temperature, which is invariably lower) for the hottest month of the year, in the south of England, is likely to be in the region of 16–18°C. So, manifestly, carp are unlikely to achieve their maximum growth and potential size in this country. This is borne out by the existence of much larger fish in countries such as Spain, southern France, Italy and Africa where water temperatures are considerably higher.

Light rays do not penetrate far, even into the purest water, and we can assume that about 15 to 20ft will be the maximum depth of light penetration in the vast majority of carp lakes. This has a direct bearing on water temperature and at what depth aquatic plants can thrive. Although shallow water warms up quickly it also cools down rapidly, so an ideal fishery would have both extensive shallow water,

Carp and Temperature According to a Range of Researchers

Temperature(s)°C	Notes	Authors
32	final preferendum in graduated temperature apparatus	Pitt *et al.* (1956)
23–29	optimum for growth	Shpet & Kharitonaova (1963)
23–30	optimum for growth in cages	Gribanov *et al.* (1966)
33–34	growth greatly depressed	Korneyev (1969)
22	growth sub-optimal	Korneyev (1969)
29	preferred temperature in thermo-regulatory shuttlebox	Reynolds & Casterlin (1977)
28–30	optimum for growth	Adelman (1977)
29.6	optimum for growth	Adelman (1978)
28	optimum for growth	Aston & Brown (1978)
25–30	optimum for growth	Jauncey (1979)

being deep enough for fish to gain access, and relatively deeper water, no more than about 12 to 15ft. It follows that a large gravel pit, for example, where the margins quickly shelve off into deep water is only as productive as a much smaller, but shallower water. That is not to say that the large deep water cannot produce big carp, but it will not support the number of big fish, or more correctly, the biomass, that its size might suggest.

The basis of all food is plant life and therefore the fertility of any fishery is dependent, first and foremost, on the green plants within it. In turn, this depends on the interaction of other factors: the amount of energy gained from the sun; the physical and chemical properties of the water, particularly the amount of essential nutrients; and the nature of the bed of the lake or pond. Only green plants which contain the green pigment chlorophyll are able to utilise the sun's energy and manufacture complex high-energy organic materials. So clear water is necessary for good plant growth. Coloured water inhibits bottom weed growth, although algae can proliferate.

Aquatic plant life also requires access to the necessary nutrients, the same that are essential for trees or grass to thrive. The main essential nutrients are nitrogen and phosphorus and it is often the exhaustion of dissolved phosphate which brings to an end the seasonal plant production in an aquatic environment. Nutrients are provided in a number of basic ways. They may be naturally present in the substrata over which the fishery is formed. They may be introduced from the surrounding land by drainage, or perhaps from a much larger area by a feeder stream. (The amount of dissolved nutrients present naturally in that land may have been enhanced by the addition to organic and inorganic fertilizers). They may be provided by leaf-fall from surrounding trees and in some cases by feeder streams, which take the treated effluent from sewage farms. So fisheries rich in

Kevin with a brace of carp from the big fish water he helped to create, Hull and District AA's lake the Tilery.

aquatic plant life are often indicative of good fish growth. This is usually, but not always the case.

The carp is classed as an omnivore, which means it eats vegetable matter as well as animal life, such as fly larvae, shrimps, snails and other molluscs (which are probably the significant food item of big carp), zooplankton (by small carp), water beetles and crayfish. Of course the carp, like most fish, is very adaptable and will utilise any available food source, including temporary ones such as tadpoles. It has been suggested that because carp do not have the necessary bacteria in their gut for breaking down the cellulose wall material of which green plants are composed, they cannot derive

Kevin with a magnificent common from one of the country's original carp waters, Redmire Pool. Kevin was one of the most successful anglers of all time to fish the water.

any nutritional value from it. However, whilst it is true that carp derive only little benefit from the actual cellulose, their extremely efficient pharyngeal teeth can physically grind down the plant walls giving access to the readily digestible cell interiors.

Many water animals require another essential substance for their successful development. Calcium is necessary for bone and scale formation in fish and is normally absorbed in the digestive tract when food containing calcium is broken down. However, fish probably also have the ability to absorb some dissolved nutrients directly from the water via the gills. Many animal food items, such as snails and mussels, also require calcium to proliferate and alkaline water (where calcium is present in reasonable quantities, giving a pH over 7.0) shows the greatest diversity of animal species. Too high calcium levels may not, indirectly, be ideal for the growth of fish. Certainly in some snails the thickness of the shell varies according to the amount of calcium available in the water (WD Russell Hunter and associates – Syracuse University) and carp have been shown that they can be selective in choosing molluscs with the thinnest shells (RA Stein and JF Kitchell; *Journal of Fish Biology* 1975 391–399).

Some species of fish clearly compete directly with carp for the same food items and where large quantities of big bream or tench exist they usually have an adverse effect upon carp growth rates. Smaller species such as roach and rudd do not compete to the same extent unless they are clearly overstocked and stunted. Waters with a high proportion of predators, be they pike, perch, eels or fish-eating birds, can lead to a low overall stock density of prey fish and subsequently better growth rates for the surviving fish. Infestations of tapeworms, such as *Ligula intestinalis*, can lead to high mortalities of young fish and low overall stock densities in some fisheries. The life cycle of *Ligula* begins

Redmire again, and here Kevin poses with a lovely Leney linear caught in July 1975.

with the egg being released from a fish-eating bird and then hatching the first larval stage. This is eaten by a specific type of water flea, *Diaptomus gracilis*, in which it develops. If the water flea is eaten by a fish the parasite penetrates from the intestine and grows in the abdominal cavity. The length of the white worm can be up to 40cm and heavy infestation can form up to twenty per cent of the total body weight of the fish. Heavy mortalities can occur annually and the cycle is completed by the fish being eaten by birds. Once the fish reach a size where they stop eating water fleas and move on to larger food items they do not become reinfected. Stocking with carp over about two pounds reduces considerably the chances of them being infected because, regardless of what has been written in the past, big carp do not feed on daphnia.

Kevin Clifford happily smiles as he holds a beautiful Redmire common.

The selective breeding of carp for the desirable qualities of size, rate of growth, colour, resistance to disease and adverse climatic conditions, body shape and scale cover has been carried on in central Europe for some 500 years or so. The general term used in Britain to describe this form of carp is 'King Carp' and its original, and nowadays its principal, objective is the production of a more commercially viable food for human consumption. Twenty-five years ago, around the time when many of today's big carp in this country were being stocked for angling purposes, the total world yearly production of carp for food was estimated at more than one million tons. At its simplest, selective breeding constitutes the continuing practice of selecting, from the harvest on a fish farm, those fish which have the most desirable qualities, be they size, shape or whatever, and using them as the parents for the next generation. The realities are more complex. Inbreeding can depress growth rates and lead to genetic defects. Some times the improvement of one particular trait results in the weakening of another. For example, reduced scale cover, which renders the carp more attractive to the housewife, results in slower growth and reduced viability. Ideally, the King carp common would be the fish farmer's choice, offering the best growth and viability. Leather carp and Linear carp show generally much lower growth rates and viability, and so the Mirror carp, which breed true and can be bred with few scales and show almost as good growth rate as the fully scaled domesticated carp, is the compromise adopted by most commercial fish farms.

Selective breeding to improve the growth rate of carp mainly affects the willingness to feed and has only a minor effect on food-to-flesh conversion ratios. A fish that grows twice as big has to eat nearly, if not quite, twice as much. It figures, therefore that other things being equal, a carp that grows twice as fast ought to be twice as easy to hook. In practice, this is very often the case. The biggest fish in a water often get caught the most. So stories of uncatchable monsters, such as those which were often claimed to exist in Redmire, are usually just that – good stories. They sell newspapers and books but the reality is that the maximum size of carp in this country is around fifty pounds. For bigger fish, go south young man!

2 The Leney Legacy: Burton's Beauties

Chris Ball

There can be few carp anglers who have not now heard of Donald Leney and the Surrey Trout Farm, for this man's indefatigable work almost single-handedly changed the course of English angling by introducing into our waters the resplendent 'King Carp'.

Donald was the son of Douglas Leney who owned the thriving business and although the Surrey Trout Farm was involved in almost all aspects of freshwater life, it was Don who had a soft spot for carp.

Originally, there was only one species of carp – *Cyprinus Carpio*, but the intervention of man was to change that, with dramatic effect. The true wild carp was, until the last century, the only English carp you could catch, and though rarely attaining weights over 10lb could fight with fury and power. It is from the true wild carp that other varieties have been bred, and it is significant that in 1916 the carp record was held by Mr J Andrews with a magnificent 20lb 3oz 'wildie'. The varieties which were to grow so huge in comparison with the wildies, were not widely established in this country at that time.

It was the Continental fish farmers who, by selective breeding from the original, produced a fast growing strain for the table. Several varieties were produced and are known under the collective name of 'King Carp'. Not only did these King carp have a fast growth rate, often putting on as much as 4lb per year, but they achieve a greater ultimate weight as well.

Other characteristics are a deeper and thicker body shape, often with a pronounced humping of the shoulders.

Limited numbers of King carp had been handled by the Surrey Trout Farm between 1910 and 1914, but then the Great War was to

Chris with a magnificent trio of Leney mirrors.

Chris returning a lovely linear mirror to Burton.

amples were, of course, Redmire and Billing Aquadrome, both originally stocked in the early 1930s and both eventually producing fish in excess of 40lb.

The catalogue, although small, was a success with angling clubs, individuals and the like throughout Britain who originally 'took a chance' and purchased these then quite 'rare' carp up to the Second World War, and produced a real foothold for the 'Galician' strain in this country.

But size is not everything. Amongst the special attributes of the 'Leney' fish was their beautiful scaling; the mirrors would often be 'linears', one single row of scales along the lateral line, or the rarer 'double row linears' as

put a halt to supplies. Don resumed his business in carp in 1925. His supply from Holland came from a large fish farm in the Northern area at a place called Vaassen. The carp they supplied were from 'Galicia' and had been cultivated for many years. These fish were not like the deep bodied Italian carp grown in warmer conditions, but were long, sleek and powerful. Don preferred this handsome fish, their shape offering finer sporting qualities in his eyes. How true!

Don Leney's annual pilgrimage to the Dutch fish farm, in autumn each year, enabled him to virtually hand pick the best grown of the crop, usually around 4–5 inches long. Some he bought were two year olds, 5½–8 inches long, as were the Redmire fish. This Galician breed of carp provided the foundation for all our big carp fishing in this country. These fish grew so large in so short a space of time (some examples could reach 20lb in less than six years), that suddenly, in a limited number of waters, some grew to enormous proportions. The best ex-

The Surrey Trout Farm and United Fisheries, Ltd.

NOTES ON COARSE FISH.

A FINE KING CARP.

The King Carp.—This is a quick-growing variety of the Common Carp, also known as the Mirror Carp, its skin is for the most part bare of scales, where it is not bare scales are of large size and iridescent giving

A page from the catalogue of the Surrey Trout Farm.

19

well as the most dazzling fully scaled mirrors ever seen. The commons, although very much in the minority, were of a perfect asymmetrical shape and looked like carved wood.

After the Second World War, England was returning slowly back to normality and angling was high on the list of recreational activities. Clubs and Angling Associations, either already with waters or with fishing rights on newly flooded gravel pits, were encouraged to stock carp by Richard Walker. His unparalleled success in angling and writing about carp provided that trigger, for here was a fish that could test the steel of any angler; it grew big and Richard and his friends showed they could be caught. So it was to the Surrey Trout Farm that people went. King carp were indeed difficult to get from any other source.

Of the extensive records that Don Leney kept, including receipt books of every transaction he made, we learn that everyone from the London Zoo Aquarium at Regents Park, to an individual buying just two King carp, benefited from Don Leney's 'soft spot' for carp.

Reproduced here is an advert which appeared in the 'Fishing Gazette' on 5 January 1952. Don was advertising the fact that a newly discovered big carp water near Ross-on-Wye had broken the long-standing record. When news came through that it was Bernithan Court, Don was surprised and interested in the reports of even larger fish having been seen. He kept a close eye on many of the clubs and associations that had purchased these fish and was delighted whenever a good one was reported.

I just wonder if the advertisement caught the eye of a member of the Farnham Angling Club committee, for in November of the same year (1952), they purchased 100 'Kings' and stocked them into Frensham Minor (Burton). The water had only been reflooded some four years before – it had been drained during the war – and so it came to pass that these fish remained unnoticed and uncaught until the middle to late sixties, when double figure fish were reported: much larger fish were landed at the end of the seventies.

We now come to the time in the Burton story, when my constant fishing companion, Jan, takes up the story and tells in fine style, the

---

This advert appeared in the Fishing Gazette *of 5 January 1952.*

RECORD KING CARP

31¼ lb., 18 years old, recently caught
Ross-on-Wye

We supplied this monster as a yearling in 1934. It is from the same strain as the stock we now distribute. TRY SOME.

The Surrey Trout Farm, HASLEMERE

Jan Wenczka and Chris Ball ganging up on a Burton 33lb mirror.

anticipation, excitement and sheer spectacle of seeing one of these fabulous carp, either leaping in the early morning light or that heart-stopping moment when you parted the net and revealed what could be three feet of unbeliev-able beauty.

We, the anglers who fished there for those few precious years, can never forget this water and its carp.

Thirty-one years on from the original stock-ing, Jan, Terry and myself found ourselves on the receiving end of *The Leney Legacy*.

3 'I'll let you be in my dreams . . .'

Jan Wenczka

Burton-on-Sea, a place for all the family, where children, dogs and courting couples can happily play on the large expanses of sand, then dip into the not too deep and gently sloping water. Ice creams and hot dogs can be bought and consumed in the spacious car park; in fact, the ideal place for a picnic and amusement. Sounds a bit like a carp water really.

Well, actually, Burton was a name attributed to Frensham by someone as a blind, and the above description is accurate if a bit reserved. Come ten o'clock the place would be a complete asylum with every variant of aquatic hedonist one could imagine (and quite a few beyond the imagination of even the most broad minded amongst us) crammed into thirty acres

'Burton-on-Sea'.

of water. But that was at ten o'clock, which was many hours away. At this hour all that stood on that expanse we named the beach, were three piscatorial desperados, Terry Glebioska, Chris Ball and myself, loosely known as 'The Firm'.

Chris and Terry had set up together, close to the point and I was installed bang in the middle of the beach. It was with great anticipation that we found ourselves on this early July morning. The hard graft of baiting the lake had been done, mainly by Chris, most mornings before he went to work, and a great deal of which was in and around the beach area. The bait was:

6oz	casein	1oz	wheatgerm
1oz	Equivite	5ml	sweetener
2oz	soya flour	5ml	dye (red)
2oz	ground rice	7½ml	flavour (Richworth cheese)

This was made into a paste with eggs then rolled very small – about 250 baits to the mix.

I was chatting to Chris, when high above on the bank and framed by the forest, loomed a Gothic monstrosity on an iron steed, who beckoned to me to be quiet. It was Yatesy on his push bike with an air of mischief about him. Without further ado, he launched himself, legs akimbo, down the bank and hurled himself, bike, rods and accompanying paraphernalia into Terry's brolly, laughing loudly. He quickly recovered and peered around the umbrella, only to find it empty. 'Where's Terry then?', his voice tinged with disappointment. We explained that Terry was doing what a man had to do and though the prank had failed, Yatesy was in a jovial mood and the reason lay sprawled on the sand. 'What do you think of the bike?' he blurted out, 'I swopped it for the other one,' mentioning something about 1930s if I recall rightly. I began to tut, pointing to a brand new plastic front light; his hands shot behind his back and he started pushing sand with his boot. 'I know,' he said weakly, yet with hardly time to catch one's breath, he

shoved a bag under my nose. 'Red shift 2, Clare made it for me, what do you think?' It smelt pleasant and culinary and I expressed an opinion that it could catch and so shortly after an animated and enjoyable chat, Yatesy was off to fish the entrance to the bird sanctuary on the other side of the lake.

As he trundled off down the path with his hold-all on his back and landing net already made up, just as a schoolboy would, my overwhelming thought was 'how the hell was he going to get one of those long and large fish in that little thing'. It was about the size I would use for trout fishing. He was later to outdo this feat of unpracticability by swopping the inadequate landing net for a perch which looked like a bird table, which had an inscription that it was only to be used by Kingfishers and Golden Scale Club members. It eventually became a permanent feature in one of the swims which became known as the 'perch swim'.

As his distinctive figure melted into the heath and pine landscape I mulled over how 'The Firm' had ended up fishing here, and like all voyages of destiny it was a complex labyrinth of hard facts and emotions.

Back in 1980, Chris Yates did a Bob Beaman on the carp record (putting it out of sight). One of the consequences of this was that he became friendly with Mr Leney, the man who stocked Redmire, plus innumerable waters elsewhere. Through his friendship, Yatesy managed to borrow his stocking book, so, accompanied by Chris Ball, they sallied forth to investigate as many of these waters as possible.

I had stalked the Yateley North Lake fish in 1981. I didn't know it at the time, but I was going through a phase which was to last four years, where I only wanted to catch carp sitting behind rods. This wasn't a conscious decision, nor did I strictly adhere to it, but on reflection I think I felt that having stalked the largest fish in the country at the time, anything I did on the stalking front would be an anticlimax. I must

Part of the Firm at Burton. Here Jan, Terry Glebioska and Dennis Smales help Chris Ball with his three fish catch.

stress that this wasn't a conscious approach, but merely a reflective analysis of what I was doing sub-consciously.

When Chris gave me a short list of three waters to look at, Frensham Major, Minor and the Army lake, it was Frensham Minor which seemed to hold the fish of my dreams, plus the opportunity of fishing the blunt end of rods, so come the close season, we duly went out in the inflatable to investigate. We found an even depth of 5–6ft, and nothing but silt and uniform bottom, which seems quite amazing, with hindsight, because we were later to find out that, during the war, the lake was drained and a

forest planted in its place to help camouflage the nearby army camp from air raids. After the war, the trees were chain sawn down leaving 18in stumps and the lake reflooded, which produced the most horrendous snags I had ever come across; but at that time, we were innocent of such things.

We did have an ace up our sleeve, which was to prove the bedrock of our initial success. We were going to use buoyant baits, a relatively unused method at the time, though the following year they were to be known generally as pop-ups. I won't go into the various rigs for pop-ups as quite a lot has been written about them lately: just a couple of observations. One was how quickly we had to change, and keep changing the rigs, just to keep catching the fish. The other observation is to do with most people's attitude to them. It seems the vertical thinkers have taken the higher ground and are beginning to blind themselves mainly with critically balanced baits. Because this was one of the final stages in the pop-ups syndrome it is seen as a panacea of the method. In fact, it is only relevant when fish are feeding in a certain way (that is when the fish are slow moving, generally in winter time – though not necessarily). In high summer when fish are very active, it is very difficult for them to get the hook bait into their mouths, the pecs keep pushing it away and in frustration it is finally left. I wouldn't mind betting that keen advocates of critically balanced hook baits have a disproportionate amount of success in the winter.

Back to the lake. The first fish I caught was a bit of a disappointment; not the size (it was 25lb), but it didn't look a true Leney, though this fish was to become quite a character and grace quite a few nets and was to eventually reach thirty plus. But after that, the fish, quite frankly, took your breath away; they were long lean and beautiful, simply perfect Leneys with an average weight of around 25lb. In fact, we got so blasé that I once caught a fish under 20lb, my first below that weight, 19¾lb to be exact which Terry refused to photograph, saying he didn't want to waste any film on such a little fish! I now actually regret this as later on the water and its residents were to take Chris well and truly by the heart strings. He amassed a dossier on all the Leney fish ever caught, going back as far as he could and, of course, we don't actually know which fish the 19 was.

But on that bright and windless morning, none of this was relevant. Yatesy was installed close to the bird sanctuary, Chris and Terry were chatting merrily and I suddenly got *that* feeling. I went and sat close to my rods. One of

my optonics had gone flat, so I sat transfixed watching my bobbins, which just happen to be the most grotesque monstrosities you could imagine, bright blue, made out of an old white spirit bottle. They were so bizarre, Terry would collar complete strangers and frog march them down to the lakeside just to look at them. 'I mean,' he would say, 'Have you seen anything like them?' and, of course, these poor bewildered souls would nod their heads in agreement. The trouble was, that I felt they were lucky so they had to stay.

As I stared at the gargantuan bobbins, one flew up and before it hit the rod, I struck high and hard into a good fish. Before long, Chris and Terry were at my side and the now familiar routine took place. Because of the shallowness of the water close in, waders were always worn, so I would go out as far as I could to meet the fish and either Chris or Terry would come out with a landing net. This time it was Chris, but he brought with him his own landing net, which is brown with a reversed taper on the handle and I don't like it, so I sent him back for mine. This he did, muttering something about hanging being too good for artistically temperamental paranoids, but eventually returned with a proper landing net, just in time to see a big old carp come chugging into view, cruise past us and chug along out into the lake again. I tried to play it down but it was all in vain. Chris was already hyper-ventilating.

The problem with Frensham was that you could get snagged at any point in the fight and if it happened close in, it was usually a tree or large branch which some helpful holiday maker had kindly pushed in for fun, and a break off was sharp and not so sweet. That, coupled with the fact that we had both seen the fish and knew that it was over 30lb, made for some anxious moments, but eventually I steered the old girl into the net and Chris made no mistake. She wasn't pretty but at 33lb 4oz, it's difficult not to be pleased. Then a lone,

Andy Little joined 'The Firm' on Burton and here he poses with a magnificent Leney common.

disembodied, cultured voice emanating from the bird sanctuary area, pierced the silence, 'Not bad for a Pole; not bad indeed.'

On all waters you need a turning point which puts the edge on your side, and this was it, the merry band of xenophobic zealots which had plagued us from the off would now dissolve into the lacklustre obscurity to which they belonged, though the repercussions of their propaganda machine would haunt me in years to come. But more importantly, our enthusiasm would be honed to an effective sharpness, so much so that two days later, Chris, on a very foggy morning (I hear tell that you can't catch fish in foggy conditions), and nursing a monumental hangover, clonked out three fish, one of which was his first thirty. I can still picture his face when I pointed to the fish, still lying in the landing net and said 'That's it, there's your thirty.' His eyes went

like saucers, magnified even larger by his glasses, his mouth dropped open and the blood just drained from his face – but more poignantly, he was speechless, which must have been the first time his vocal chords had had a rest since birth. Terry found it a struggle but managed to get a couple of good fish, the two best looking fish in the lake, according to him (how modest!). As for me, I managed to keep one step ahead of the fish all the time and so reaped a bountiful harvest, which continued the following summer, but with a different bait:

4oz	Casein	1oz	Sucron
2oz	Calcium Casenate	½oz	Carpvit
2oz	Lactalbumin	1oz	Soya Isolate
1½oz	Ultraspice	1oz	Gluten
	in powder form	7ml	Maltrex and Red
	from Hutchinson)		Dye

More and more I became preoccupied with catching some of those dream quenchers with their scales burnished gold and copper by their winter hues; I felt I had solved part of the problem already, that of presentation. As stated, we had been using pop-ups extensively, so it followed on that everybody else started using them, so much so that from being a tremendous advantage, it turned out to be a positive liability.

Presenting a bottom bait was difficult due to the silt, which was anything up to 12in deep, so what I decided to do was put a piece of pop-up on the hook, enough to counter balance the hook plus link and tied a bottom bait on a 1in hair off the bend of the hook, which resulted in a beautiful 28lb 12oz mirror. Whether this terminal arrangement was instrumental in the fish's downfall was irrelevant, what was relevant was that it got me thinking on a new track. This change in thinking eventually resulted in a rig called the over-rig in which the hook is over the bait. If balanced right it held the bait on top of the silt, the idea being that the hook entered the fish's mouth first so allowing me to strike at the slightest movement of the bobbin.

A small amount of foam can be used on the bend of the hook if it doesn't sit on the bait properly.

The other part of the problem was a gift laid at my door from Andy Little, who, on moving into the area, had joined 'The Firm'. He had found a blood worm bed and had constructed a bait:

1½oz	Codlivine	2½oz	Sweet Casein
2oz	PTX	1½oz	Gluten
2½oz	Protex		

From its very inception, I knew it was right. Up to that point only three carp had ever been caught in the winter time there and I had caught one of these: winter fishing was really virgin territory, but I think we were both taken by surprise at just how right we got it.

The very first evening session we fished together, we caught three and lost one and carried on to plunder a glorious winter treasure trove, culminating in a brace of 23lb 8oz and 31lb 8oz for me one evening, which kept a glow in my heart for the rest of the cold and ice-laden winter. Needless to say, the fish never looked better.

From a presentation point of view Andy had completely different ideas to mine. His main one consisted of a very long tail of between 2–3ft of the 6lb line with a tiny hook, 10, 12 and even 14, I think. To this day I don't know why he didn't lose more fish than he did. With such fine line and a weight 2–3ft back, it's just begging to get snagged and snapped off, but it worked.

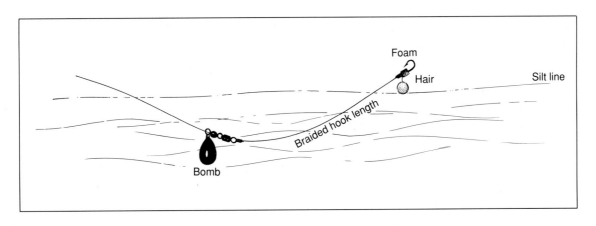

Jan looks understandably pleased with this brace of Burton beauties.

Once when netting a fish for me, he was up to his chest in water waders. I was behind, up to the tops of my waders, when one of his rods screamed off. If you can imagine someone trying to run, up to their chest in water, some thirty yards to where his rods were, it was as though the slow-motion button had been pressed on the world, which wasn't made any easier by me because I almost had a hernia laughing. Anyway, by the time he reached his rod he was down to the stop knot and when he struck I saw a fish boil, well in excess of 200 yards from where he was. When you consider that every couple of yards was a snag, the chances of getting the fish back were negligible, but back it came, without even touching a snag. I was so intrigued by this terminal arrangement I even tried it myself, and caught a fish on it, but even after that, I still didn't care for it – but there again, he didn't much care for my rig.

Screamers apart, of which there were very few – perhaps a couple each – the one thing we had in common in our fishing was the striking at very small movements. A two or three inch lift was usually all the indication we had. I'm convinced the fish were just picking up the bait, righting themselves and a few seconds later, feeling something wrong, would spit the bait out again, but by hitting these tiny movements we were successful. With this final hurdle crossed on the water, my appetite was sated, plus the financial recession which was taking a hold, was particularly severe on the art world - which meant less fishing and more graft until fishing was conspicuous by its absence. However, Andy had now become smitten by the place and he and Chris were to fish it the following year. I don't know how well they did, and it's possibly not for me to say, but I do remember the first phone call I got that following winter about a fish that had been found dead in the lilies. Chris was quite upset because it was a fish that he had caught earlier in the year, but the subsequent calls were to illuminate the full horror of what was happening.

The whole stock of heavy fish was dying. Some days they were finding anything up to six dead fish. The Thames Water Authority (TWA) were called in and one day they took away four fish; the 28.12 mentioned earlier, which was now 30.8 and another mid-twenty, both dead, plus a fully scaled mirror of 28.2 and another mid-twenty, both of which were in a very bad way. The following day the mid-twenty died and five days later the fully scaled fish died: the Authority could not find any cause of death, so there are no hard facts as to their demise.

The total of Leney fish caught and documented was fifty. Prior to us fishing there, the TWA put in another fifty seven or eight pounders, another half dozen or so double figure fish were added, then just prior to the fish dying, another stocking was undertaken. The exact number is vague but around 100 fish of

Andy Little again. It's hard to imagine a better looking big carp than this heavily scaled cracker. The fish were soon to be virtually wiped out by a mystery rare carp virus.

1½lb to 2½lb is the best consensus, these fish being shared between Frensham, Badshot Lea and Mill Lane. (Mill Lane didn't have any resident carp). At the same time as the Frensham fish died, so did the resident fish at Badshot Lea.

Chris was to personally witness 16 twenties and 2 thirties plus 3 others of the TWA stocking dead. The last fish he saw was his own first thirty at 35lb which was the last straw for him and he bade the water, that had possessed him for the past three years, farewell.

I know we shouldn't be selfish with our dreams but personally I was only there to catch that one strain that had an umbilical cord directly to Redmire, where men, fish and legend are woven into the fine tapestry which is at the very core of our sport. So for me, any introduction of fish was an anathema. Others with different dreams wanted to turn it into a more all round carp fishery, where children could learn to fish, but my point is that unless you give them waters to aspire to, you give them nothing.

I never did go back, not even to look at that butterfly of a water which emerged from a cocoon and had a glorious summer, only to die when the cold winds of cruel circumstance blew; a water that only knew salad days. On reflection it was a pleasure and a privilege to have shared that glorious summer and with many others, mourn its passing.

It's more with sorrow than with anger I pen these final lines and I hope that lessons have been learnt, though sadly too late for this water. It had the potential to stun the carp world but in the end only stands as a subject lesson, that unless you are sure of what you are doing, you should leave well alone. As I said before, we shouldn't be selfish with our dreams. It's also true that nobody has the right to impose their dreams on others. 'I'll let you be in my dreams if I can be in yours.'

4 Big Carp Waters: A Realistic View

Julian Peter Cundiff

The first question we have to ask ourselves is 'what is a big carp today?' Fifteen pounds? Possibly a twenty, or even a thirty for the more successful amongst us! If the truth be known, and that's a big IF for some carp anglers, the word big is subjective and depends on each individual's hopes, aspirations and previous successes.

Think back five years; what made the press then hardly merits a mention nowadays. Twenties galore, thirties by the score, and forties for those prepared to travel, have all upped what the press regard as big. However, the press at times tend to follow the maxim 'biggest is best and gets most press' so we will have to be more realistic as regards our target weight. For sake of argument, let's set anything twenty-five plus as big; that is big in most people's books and gives us all a realistic chance of fishing waters with fish of that pedigree in them.

No matter how good your bait is, no matter how original your thinking on presentation may be or your sixth sense as to swim choice may be, you will never catch a twenty-five plus from a water that doesn't contain one. Your water may be the prettiest in the country, it may be totally fulfilling in many other ways, but if it doesn't contain big carp, and you really want a big carp, you will be wasting your time fishing for them. It's been said so many times, by those far more qualified to say it than I am, but don't even wet a line or boil a bait until you are sure they really exist.

When I first started to compile this list, I knew it would be hard work; no doubt I will have stepped on people's toes, but all the waters I am about to write about, contain definite twenty-five pluses and although you may not be able to fish some you certainly can fish others. Some of the waters are strictly private and are by invitation only, a few are under disguise (name-wise) to protect the water. Many require you just to write a letter to the controlling angling body for a permit and some you can just turn up and buy a ticket on the bank. If you really want a big carp, there is no excuse; it won't be handed to you on a plate but if it matters that much, go out and do it.

Bedfordshire

Our first county Bedfordshire, home of catfish and carp, has many waters with fish hovering around the low twenties mark but also has at least three definite waters with twenty-five pluses in them.

Arlesey Lake, Church End, Arlesey, Hitchin

Originally more famous for its perch fishing, via Richard Walker's writings, this is an old brick pit situated on the A600 Hitchin to Bedford road. Size wise it's about twelve acres, but is very deep, with depths of 15ft in the margins and 45ft in the middle. The water is controlled by the Hitchin Angling Club on a syndicate basis. A nice looking tree-flanked lake, the water contains a few fish over 25lb, including a fish known as the 'Arlesey Beast' which hovers around the 27–29lb mark. Top weight for the water seems to be hovering around the 30lb mark, and for those of you contemplating fishing the water, there is a marvellous piece by Rob Maylin in his book 'Tiger Bay' on his efforts at the water.

Blunham Pits, Sandy, Dunstable

These are two pits both around the seven acre size situated at Sandy, near Dunstable. A lake commonly known as the 'muddy lake' to locals, contains fish to around 30lb with a few twenties hovering around the 25lb mark. Like many of the county's waters, it is fishable via a syndicate place and for details write to 224, Bedford Road, Rushden, Northants.

Withy Pool, Bedford Road, Hitchin

Now extremely well known as Kevin Maddocks' water, this pool used to be known by the names of 'Maylins', 'Junelins' and 'Cafe Pool'. Quite famous throughout the years, it has been fished by Dick Walker, and Jack Hilton wrote about it in his 'Quest for Carp' book. Small in size, about 2½ acres, the brick pit definitely contains big carp up to a ceiling weight of around 34lb or so. There seems to be around a dozen fish over 25lb but due to its clear water, and pressure from anglers over the years, it must be regarded as a hard water to catch from. Sensibly, there are very few rules to restrict your fishing and details of the fishery can be obtained by writing to Kevin Maddocks, at Withy Pool, Bedford Road, Henlow Camp, Bedfordshire, SG16 6EA. Again, articles in both Rob Maylin's 'Tiger Bay' book and later 'Carp Catcher' (Carp Angler's Association (CAA) magazine) will give you a better insight into the water.

Berkshire

Aldermaston Pits, Paices Hill, Aldermaston, Reading

This comprises a series of pits, seven in all, which are controlled and run by Leisure Sport. All the waters contain carp but carp to 25lb plus have been caught from lake 6; this is the largest lake on the complex, at four acres. A very pretty water, surrounded by woodland and grassy areas, it can be fished on a Leisure Sport 'Special Venue' permit. Write to them at Thorpe Park, Staines Road, Chertsey, Surrey. Two rods only, due to it being under a Thames licence and night fishing is allowed.

Burghfield Lake, Pinewood Road, Pinewood, Burfield

Not recommended for anybody who doesn't relish a challenge, this is a 100-acre gravel pit controlled by Leisure Sport. Both a fishery and a sailing club, the water is full of bays, islands, peninsulas and other such features. Plenty of tasty looking swims but the sheer size of the place and low stocking density make location your prime problem. Approaching the water like Chris Ball approaches Wraysbury (stalking visible fish) would seem the best bet, and the challenge is there for all to take up. Certainly carp are present over 25lb and I believe a fish of 39lb was caught two years ago. Night fishing is allowed, two rods only and plenty of good access points. Write to Leisure Sport for details.

Buckinghamshire

Linford Lakes, Little Linford Lane, Milton Keynes

A fairly new fishery this one, three lakes all containing carp but with one lake of particular interest to the big fish angler. This is the Arboretum Lake, which has been stocked with carp to 30lb; certainly fish have appeared in the weekly papers up to around the 28lb mark. I don't believe there are many fish over 25lb in the lake but at six acres it may mean you are in with a good chance. A very picturesque water, season ticket only, night fishing is allowed and unlike many waters it does seem to fish well in winter. For details write to Linear Fisheries, Secretary Len Gurd, at 23 Cemetery Road, Houghton, Dunstable.

Cambridgeshire

Woolpack Fishery, Hilton, St Ives

Again, another famous water run by the well-known pike angler Bill Chillingsworth. When it was first opened up as a carp fishery, it was claimed that 46 twenty pluses were stocked; for a four acre pit that's quite some stock. Quite a few carp over 25lb with the best hovering just under 30lb. An extremely nice looking lake with variable depths and an underwater topography that resembles an egg box. Fish have been caught on a variety of methods and baits. Few rules and it's fishable on an Anglian Water licence. For details of obtaining a syndicate place, write to Bill Chillingsworth, at The Cottage, St Peters Street, Caxton, Cambridge. Be warned, it isn't cheap!

Cheshire

Even more of a closed shop than Kent or Surrey. Plenty of waters, lots of local carp anglers and sensibly nobody giving much away. Many of the waters seem to have fish stocks which level out just below 25lb so if we are looking for the larger fish, our choices are somewhat limited.

Redesmere, Capesthorne Estate, Siddington, Macclesfield

This is a large estate mere of around sixty acres and is season ticket only from Stoke on Trent Angling Club, Linton, S Kingsfield Oval, Basford, Stoke on Trent. Used to contain two thirties. Firstly the huge common which Bernie Loftus had at 33lb; it in fact went on to make 36lbs but perished due to being spawnbound. There's certainly a mirror in the water which is hovering around 31 to 34lb and quite a number of fish 25lb plus. Receives a lot of pressure and must be classed as a difficult water. Night fishing is allowed and carp have been caught from a variety of swims on a variety of baits and presentations.

Capesthorne Hall Pool, Siddington, Macclesfield

Again on the same estate as Redesmere and also tickets are available from Stoke on Trent Angling Club. Not so many fish over 25lb but definitely one fish which hovers around 28lb or so. A lot smaller than Redesmere at seven acres, it is heavily fished and the carp have seen everything over the years. Fish are still caught on surface baits and it has been known to fish well in winter. Very few rules but a hard water to catch a twenty-five plus from.

Crabmill Flash, Moston, Sandbach

Another famous fishery which has produced fish over the years to the 30lb mark. Word on the local grapevine is that the larger fish haven't been out for some time; reasons are plentiful as can be expected. Quite a nice looking canal type water; an estate lake of around ten acres and season tickets are available from Wheelock Angling Society, Overland House, Moss Lane, Elsworth, Sandbach, Cheshire. Quite a difficult water, and again it can be very heavily fished at

Redesmere, Stoke Angling Club's big fish north west water.

The Mangrove, another little known big fish water which has produced many carp of 25lb plus.

weekends. This water was flooded two years ago and there are rumours that many of the fish were lost down the river in the floods.

Thorneycroft Hall Lakes, Henbury, Macclesfield

Two lakes of six and twelve acres. Certainly fish have been caught over 25lb but it isn't clear just which lake has produced the bigger fish. I hear it is the top lake, but check with local anglers as to this. Season ticket only, available from Prince Albert Angling Society, 2 Avon Close, Macclesfield, Cheshire. Must be rated as a hard water and expect a lot of local pressure during the summer months.

Cornwall

College Fishery, College Reservoir, Falmouth, Cornwall

Probably one of the most famous close season venues, this forty acre reservoir contains a large stocking of carp but few over the target weight we have set ourselves. Certainly contains one fish which ups and downs between 29 and 31lb dependent on time of year and bait saturation of the water. Probably a couple of fish over 25lb but the problem, if it is a problem, is the way round the 250 plus other carp that inhabit the water. Ken Townley of Nutrabaits/Carp Society infamy wrote two marvellous articles on the water in March and April 1989's *Coarse Angler* which give a comprehensive insight into the water, its inhabitants and its history. Ken has also written many other bait articles which relate directly to his fishing at College. Not a bad looking lake, plenty of swims but it can be subjected to horrendous close season pressure. Season tickets are available from South West Water Authority. Day tickets are available on the bank.

Salamander Lake, Cornwall

Another good looking two acre lake that contains a good head of carp to around 27lb. The biggest in the lake named 'Big Daddy' seems to hover between 25 and 27lb; the major problem again being the number of carp in the water under 25lb. Ken has written a chapter on Salamander Lake, and more particularly 'Big Daddy,' in Tim's first book, '*Carp Fishing*' which will give you an insight into the water. Quite a clear water, not as heavily fished as College and responds to close in fishing. Still fairly difficult as the carp have seen many anglers over the years.

Essex

Now we are moving into the home of carp catching; many waters and similar quantities of anglers. Loads of fisheries with fish to below 25lb, quite a few with even bigger fish.

Layer Pits, Colchester

An extremely famous water which first came to national prominence due to Mick Lindsell and Zenon Bojko's amazing catches in the late seventies and early eighties. Connected to a reservoir by a series of pipes Layer Pits are extremely rich in water life and have the ability to, and have, produced extremely large carp. At one stage it certainly contained both common and mirror carp over 30lb, with a best hovering at around 35–36lb. At that stage there were probably half a dozen thirty pluses in the water. An amazing head of carp in the water; today there must be a good head of carp over 25lb, even taking into account some of the malpractices the fishery has suffered over the years. Fish weights are on the up and up in this rich water and a big thirty is not to be ruled out. No night fishing allowed at the venue and the water is under the control of Colchester Angling Preservation Society. For a marvellous insight into the water, read Mick and Zenon's chapter which appeared in the fourth British Carp Study Group (BCSG) book 'A day in the life of . . .'

Chesterford Fisheries, Great Chesterford, Saffron Walden

Three gravel pits under the control of Paul Elsegood, 2 Wentfords Cottage, Clare Road, Polingsford, Sudbury, Suffolk. Extremely picturesque waters which have produced fish to over 30lb. Not a great deal has been published about the water so enquire with the fishery owner.

South Weald Pit, South Weald Park, Brentwood

Subject of an extensive series of articles by Bill Lovette in David Hall's 'Coarse Fishing' a couple of years ago, this series of lakes contains quite a number of carp over 20lb. Ceiling weight seems to be around 28–29lb, and tickets can be obtained on the bank for one lake and for the other from Hornchurch and District Angling Society. The waters have seen a great deal of pressure over the years and with anglers of the quality of Kevin Nash, Geoff Kemp etc, fishing there the carp will have become somewhat educated. Certainly a difficult water with not that many fish over 25lb in it.

Silver End Pit, Essex

Home of Kevin Nash's famous forty (41.08), this water belongs to Kelvedon and District Angling Club, 1 Francis Road, Braintree Essex. A very pretty lake, but bearing in mind you are effectively fishing for only two fish over 25lb it must be considered ultra difficult. Has seen lots of anglers over the last couple of years, the big one (now dead) had been out between 36 and

41lb and also to a variety of methods and baits. A hard water, but if you have your sights set on a twenty-five plus fish it is worth a look at.

Snake Pit, Essex

A pseudonym of course: only the names have been changed to protect the innocent! This water came to prominence due to its monster common carp. Both David Westerman and Zenon Bojko have taken the fish at 40lb plus. David's was the first capture which set the angling papers alight; Zenon's was the second due to the hard graft he put into baiting a swim and tempting the fish. A lot of the country's best anglers have tried and failed here; many more will be trying over the next few years. Lots of snags, not the most picturesque of waters and word has it on the grapevine, and lately in the angling papers, that part of the water has been filled in. An extremely difficult water. (The big common was also caught by Phil Harper in September 1989.)

Jim Eggets, Huntingdon

Not well known, due to the various names under which the water has appeared. However, it does have carp to over 30lb, both commons and mirrors. The water is an eight acre syndicate lake which is thought to contain no more than twenty fish. Most are twenty-five plus but only half a dozen or so are caught each year. A very rich water, probably harder than Ashlea and extremely well looked after.

Fishing is by invitation only and only a small syndicate exists on the water. For two detailed accounts of the water see Kevin Maddocks' book, 'In Pursuit of Carp and Catfish' (Chapter entitled 'Meadow Magic') and also an article he wrote in Coarse Fisherman's 'Big Fish' magazine entitled 'Reprieve at Heartbreak Lake.'

Gloucestershire

Ashlea Pool, Gloucestershire

Next to Redmire and Savay, Ashlea Pool is probably one of the most famous carp fisheries in the country. The lake is a dammed gravel pit of 1¼ acres and is said to be so small that if a cow urinates in the lake, it floods. Very, very weedy and extremely rich. Contains about twenty fish. Probably ten–fifteen fish over 25lb including a common of 26lb. Lake record is held by Kevin Maddocks for his big leather which he caught at 38¼lb. Biggest fish recently has hovered around 36lb or so though there may be as many as four different thirties in the water. Many anglers claim to have seen larger fish but anglers of the calibre of MacDonald, Maddocks, Kemp, Hilton etc, have failed to prove that claim. Not impossible to catch fish from as Alec Welland showed in 1988 with seven fish to 34.08 ('Lucky'). The water is, of course, a very private syndicate lake run by Peter Mohan of CAA fame; a long waiting list puts off all but the keenest. You can read about the water in Kevin Maddocks' *'Carp Fever'* book, his *'Pursuit of Carp and Catfish'* book, various articles in the BCSG books, Jack Hilton's *'Quest for Carp'* book and also many back issues of *'Carp Catcher'* and *'Carp Fisher.'* Don't hold your breath waiting to get in though!

Hampshire

Broadlands Lake, Romsey, Southampton

Up until 1988 this water would not have been included in this chapter but due to the stocking of 'Penny', the 35lb carp, this has all now changed. Whilst the lake is extremely well stocked, it contains only one large fish at 35lb, and obviously to catch this fish whilst avoiding all the others can be difficult. Penny has been caught at varying weights between 32 and 35lb, and all the signs are that she may well increase in weight each season. Varying in depths between 4–10ft and at twenty-six acres this water was formed in 1977 by the construction of the M27 Motorway. Both day and season tickets are available and in marvellous surroundings you are always in with a chance of a thirty plus carp. Catching carp at the water is quite easy; to locate Penny has proved to be more of a problem.

Kingfisher Lake – No 1 Teswood Lane, Southampton

A small gravel pit of around five acres which has produced a few carp up to 31lb. Probably half a dozen carp of twenty-five plus but is regarded as a difficult fishery. Season tickets from Mr Hoskins, 40 Aldemoor Avenue, Aldemoor, Southampton. Beautiful lake and well looked after.

Kingfisher Lake – No 2 Ringwood

Famous fishery in that it was offered for sale on a share basis of £2,000 a share. A large water of forty acres, beautiful surroundings and available as both day and season ticket membership. Carp have been caught to the low thirties and there are quite a few twenty-five plus including some large commons. Quite a hard water, fairly popular but very expensive.

Somerley Lakes, Ringwood

A well stocked carp lake which contains fish to just under 30lb. The lake is around twenty acres in size, set in beautiful countryside and can be fished on day ticket. Also available are season tickets via Ringwood and District Angling Club. Well educated fish, averagely popular but responds well to stalking and surface baits.

Minley Water, Fleet

An unattractive water of around sixty acres but has produced carp to around 30lb. The carp population is very sparse but fish have been caught by those willing to put the time and effort in. Season tickets are available and the water is on Army Property land. Related as a hard water because fish stocks are low.

Pit 4, Farnborough

A Redlands water which is available via a syndicate place. A small water, very quiet and extremely beautiful set in a woodland area. Quite a number of fish between 25 and 30lb, and does fish well in winter. A hard water, difficult to get a place on the syndicate but well worth putting your name down for.

Hertfordshire

Broxbourne, Meadgate Lane, Broxbourne, Hoddesdon

Three large gravel pits of twenty-four, thirty and sixty-eight acres belonging to Leisure Sport. Very well looked after lakes, night fishing is allowed and, unfortunately, so is sailing. Carp up to around 30lb have been caught; again it is not clear which lake this is from, so enquire locally. Due to the size of the water and number of fish over 25lb (low) it must be described as hard. Does not receive a lot of pressure and the carp do seem to be upping their weights. Write to Leisure Sports for ticket details.

Stanstead Abbots, Marsh Lane, Stanstead Abbots

Another Leisure Sport water which contains carp to at least 32lb. A total of five lakes, the largest being Lake 5 at thirty-three acres. It is said to contain larger carp but details are sketchy. Apart from work still continuing on the bypass this is a nice looking water and night fishing is allowed. Write to Leisure Sport for details.

Stanborough Lake, Welwyn Garden City

A very well stocked and very heavily fished gravel pit of twenty acres. Commonly known to locals as the 'cracker factory'. Loads of fish up to a maximum of 27lb. Very difficult to avoid the smaller fish, however there are definitely at least three fish over 25lb. One rod only to November, available on day ticket or season ticket and home of many boats!

Rickmansworth, Tolpits Lane, Rickmansworth

Quite a popular Leisure Sport Water (waters of two and six acres) sandwiched between the River Colne and the Grand Union Canal. Carp to 30lb, but fish over 25lb are few and far between. Extremely nice looking water which does allow night fishing. Has produced fish to 25lb plus in winter. Write to Leisure Sport for details.

Humberside

Tilery lake, Newport

A twenty-seven acre clay pit which opened for carp anglers in 1984. Stocked with fish from all over the country and best fish in the lake now nearly 28lb. Certainly at least four other fish over 25lb; a mirror at 26lb, a leather at 26lb and two other mirrors hovering around 25lbs. Lots of twenties and the best Yorkshire bet for a twenty-five plus. Not a good looking water;

plenty of clay, mud, swamps and mosquitoes. Has produced fish to 26lb plus in winter and offers plenty of scope. A Hull season ticket allows you to fish it in the day only; doing three work parties each close season makes you eligible for a night permit as well. For details write to Dave Littleproud, 13 Sawston Avenue, Hull, HU5 5RP.

Motorway Pond, Newport

Another Hull and District water which was, in fact, three pits, now all joined together. Very snaggy, lots of sunken trees and bushes. Loads of features such as bays, bars, plateaux, islands and shelves. After the initial start of season rush it sees very little pressure and at twenty acres or so there is always a good swim to be had. Quite deep in places with a fair amount of bottom weed, this place has yet to really be taken apart by anybody. Best fish in the lake between 28 and 29lb, certainly two other fish over 25lb and judging on weight gains found, probably one or two more fish will be pushing this size. Again fishing is available via Tilery work parties and for details write to Dave Littleproud.

Bill Bakers, Newport

A small featureless water (apart from one island) that is absolutely stuffed with carp. Possibly one or two are twenty-five plus, and one of those is a common. Not a difficult water: your main problem being trying to get a swim during early season and the problem of trying to locate the bigger fish from the smaller ones. Day ticket only and as far as I know, no night fishing. Fish to all methods especially surface baits.

Kent

To many carp anglers, the promised land, but to many others the home of competitive carp fishing. Lots of waters, many now on limited club tickets, so don't expect to get into them all.

Brooklands, A225 Princes Road, Dartford

Brooklands is split into four lakes totalling nearly thirteen acres. The lakes A2, Slaughter House, Baldwins and Powder Mill are all linked together and access to all banks is very good. Jack Hilton fished here in the sixties, it appears in his 'Quest for Carp' as Goodwood and over the years anglers of the calibre of Gerry Savage, Fred Wilton etc, have fished it. Best fish in the lake will go around 30lb or so with quite a few twenty-five pluses also present. Fishes very well in winter. Due to pressure and the age of the fish is certainly rated a moderate to hard water. Day tickets are available on the bank but be prepared for huge early season crowds. For those of you with a copy of 'Carp Fisher 4', Mike 'Curly' Hatchman wrote an in-depth piece about the water which is essential reading for those considering fishing there.

Darenth, Parsonage Lane, Darenth, Dartford

A very famous fishery with an incredible reputation for producing big fish over the years. Fishable as a special venue on a Leisure Sport ticket you will probably need to get your name on the waiting list to be able to fish it. Consists of a total of four lakes, Big Lake (thirteen acres), Long Lake (four acres), Tree Lake (three acres) and Tip Lake (nine acres). Big Lake has fish to 30lb plus, Long Lake fish to 28lb, Tree Lake possibly one or two up to 25lb and the Tip Lake fish to the upper thirties. Despite being a very popular series of lakes, it remains one of the country's most beautiful fisheries. Trees, islands, weedbeds. Character and big

The Gap Swim on Leisure Sport's Darenth Tip Lake, a water fished by many big fish men over the years and now the home of a number of fish over 30lb, and many over 25.

fish, it has them all. Home of many well known big fish 'The Pilgrim', 'Big Bollocks' etc, and over the years the country's best anglers have fished here. Ian Booker, Pete Springate, Alan Smith, Lee Jackson, Fred Wilton, Lenny Middleton, Kevin Maddocks, etc. On all the lakes you are in with a chance of a genuine 25lb plus and it does usually fish well in winter with fish to 32lb being caught in even the most extreme conditions. Lots of articles have appeared about this venue; try back issues of '*Carp Fisher*' and '*Carp Catcher*', Kevin Maddocks' '*Carp Fever*', Tim Paisley's '*Carp Season*' etc. Has to be rated as hard but an excellent choice to try for a 25lb plus.

Horton Kirby, Dartford

Another well known water consisting of three gravel pits of a total area just under fifteen acres.

Plenty of good carp but few over 25lb. Best carp will go between 28 and 30lb dependent on time of year. Day tickets are available on the bank but no night fishing is allowed. Not an overly pretty water but a water which does contain good carp.

Johnson Pits, Larkfield, Maidstone

A series of three lakes and very underrated as a carp fishery due to its popularity as a tench water (10lb plus!). First lake is the Road Lake (nine acres) and has carp in it over 25lb. Second lake is Island Lake and has at least one 30lb mirror and a mid-twenty common. Lots of features in this lake; snags, bars, plateaux, islands etc. Last lake, the Railway Lake is undoubtedly the best carp lake on the complex. Size wise it's about sixteen acres and is said to contain up to a dozen thirties. Is reputed to have an upper thirty common, certainly has a leather at 36lb and quite a number of fish between 31 and 35lb. Also a few 25lb pluses to supplement the larger fish as well. Surrounded by trees and with lots of underwater features, the water can be very hard and has been known to be very popular in the first few months. Night fishing and boats (with discretion) are allowed; season tickets from the owner on the bank. Does receive a lot of pressure and despite its quite horrendous litter problem is well worth a try.

School Pool, Faversham

Well known water due to its famous fish 'She'. She is a beautiful scaled carp which is 'apparently' caught quite a lot between 33 and 36lb. The water contains a common which tops 30lb plus and some upper twenties. Size wise the water is around twenty acres (a gravel pit) but is pretty open and featureless. Day tickets are available on the bank but no night fishing is allowed. Not a pretty water, it's surrounded by a school, houses, a road and a factory; does receive a hell of a lot of pressure but can produce the goods.

Linton, Maidstone

A small 1½ acre, weedy and extremely rich water. Contains carp to 35lb plus including two or three thirties. Very hard, fish can be seen but hard to catch. Fishing is via a season ticket from a local club; membership very hard to obtain. Because of its size it can be overcrowded but if you do have a ticket it's well worth a try.

Larkfield, Maidstone

A large 'sea' type water behind the Johnsons Lake. A total of three lakes of around 100 acres. Available on a Leisure Sport ticket and definitely contains carp to 30lb plus. Main problem is size of water and fish location. Very deep and very open. Receives very little serious carp angler pressure and could always produce a surprise large fish for those willing to put the time in. Night fishing is allowed but no boats.

Lincolnshire

Home of many carp waters but few places where a genuine 25lb plus can be caught. Lots of waters like the Lido etc, contain low twenties but the only genuine big fish water is Rod's place. This is syndicate only and by invitation. Largest fish now in mid-thirties and often features in the press.

London Area

Staines, Wraysbury, Middlesex

Also known as 'Longfield' and 'Fox Pool'. A four acre pit which contains some of the big-gest fish in the country; however, is probably one of the hardest lakes in the country as well. A truly beautiful tree-surrounded water, very rich and very weedy. Contains at least one forty (possibly two), probably 6 or 7 thirties including the famous 'Big Scale' at 37lb plus. Also various other carp at 25lb plus. Some big fish perished due to being spawnbound, or from gill fluke, others still gain weight. Heavily fished by the country's leading carp anglers, long stay anglers even install carpet in 'their' swims. Fish are very, very hard to catch, one a season can be good going. Odd fish have been caught by anglers stalking fish. Not recommended for anybody who hasn't done-it-all. Available as a special venue only via Leisure Sport. Has appeared in various publications but try back issues of 'Carp Fisher', Kevin Maddocks' 'Carp Fever' and Rob Maylin's new book 'Fox Pool'. (Sadly, Longfield closed as a carp fishery in January 1990.)

Savay Lake, Denham, Middlesex

Along with Redmire probably the most famous water in the country. You will find it at Moorhall Road, Harefield, Denham just behind the Harefield lake. An absolutely gorgeous water of around seventy acres with every possible feature you could imagine: islands, snags, bars, gulleys, the lot. You can fish it on two schemes. Firstly day tickets are available at local newsagents and secondly, season tickets from Peter Broxup, 309 Shirland Road, London, W9. Both of these do not allow you to night fish. However, a syndicate does exist whereby certain members of two rotas ('Toad Rota' and 'Loony Rota') can night fish. Membership of this night fishing syndicate is very hard to come by and you may well have to wait a long time for it. Contains fish to 39lb and probably more thirties than any other water in the country. I have been told it does contain as many as 30 different thirties and lots of twenty-five pluses.

Action for Roger Smith at big fish water Savay Lake.

Home of many famous fish, 'Sally', 'Popeye', 'Sally's Mate', 'D A M Advert', 'Beast' etc, it is fished by the country's leading carp anglers. Has got to be rated as hard but also has to be rated as probably the country's best carp lake. Has been written about by many, many anglers. Rod Hutchinson covered it in detail in his '*Carp Strikes Back*' book, both '*Carp Fisher*' and '*Carp Catcher*' have long interviews with successful Savay anglers and an in-depth article with Andy Little appears in the Carp Society's first book, '*For the Love of Carp*'. Rob Maylin covered it in his '*Tiger Bay*' book and no doubt it will continue to be written about for years to come.

Wraysbury

Two lakes. Lake 1 (sixty-two acres) at Douglas Lane, Wraysbury and Lake 2 (seventy-seven

The ultimate big fish challenge. Pete Springate returns a good mirror to Wraysbury, a huge, lightly stocked and very hard carp water.

41

acres) at High Street, Staines Road, Wraysbury. Two huge waters which contain carp to upper thirties; most carp caught will be 25lb plus. Picturesque lakes, lots of hidden bays, trees, islands etc, but huge and windswept. Carp are very hard to find, hard to tempt and very hard fighting. Consequently, it is a very difficult venue. Could produce a fish over 50lb. Successful Wraysbury anglers, Peter Springate and Chris Ball have both written about the water; and an in depth feature appears in 'Carp Fisher 12' by Pete, which is absolutely essential reading for those of you interested in fishing it. Said by many to be a 'water to retire onto'. Both Leisure Sport waters.

Walthamstow Reservoirs, Ferry Lane, Tottenham N17

Has produced carp to over 30lbs. Available as day and season ticket on the bank, but no night fishing. The reservoirs are controlled by TWA. Walthamstow 1 is nineteen acres, 2 is thirteen acres and 3 is twelve acres. They do seem to fish well in winter and hardly ever freeze.

Lockwood Reservoir, Lee Bridge Road, Walthamstow

A huge open reservoir of eighty acres. A bit like an inland sea. Very open, very weedy in places. Very strict rules such as no groundbaiting, no wading and no night fishing only go to make it even harder still. Contains a lot of carp, certainly into the low thirties with plenty of twenty-five pluses. Private membership only but one day it will produce a whopper for a lucky angler.

Rodney Meadow, West Drayton, Middlesex

A William Boyer fishery available as a special venue providing you get past the huge waiting list. Contains carp up to 36lb and plenty of upper twenties. Ten acres in size, a nice looking lake fished by many of the country's leading anglers. A water of the future and at ten acres everybody is in with a chance of a good fish. Write for details to William Boyer, Trout Road, West Drayton, Middlesex. (This is another water that was closed down in the spring of 1990. The fish are being moved to Harefield and Farlows.)

Harefield Carp Lake, Moorhall Road, Harefield, Middlesex

A large Savay type water controlled by William Boyer. Contains fish to 35lb and lots of upper twenties. Again, to get a place you will need to get on the waiting list. A 100-member syndicate, and very popular with leading carp anglers. Best mirror goes around 36lb and also we hear reports of 35lb plus commons. Contains around 200 plus twenties!! Write to William Boyer for details.

Midlands

Cuttle Mill, Wishaw, Sutton Colfield, Birmingham

A very famous fishery, once owned by the equally famous Albert Brewer and now under the comparatively new ownership of Tony Higgins. Cuttle Mill is a very heavily stocked five acre lake which has produced carp to around 30lb. Best is probably now about 28–30lb, and a few over 25lb. Local knowledge says you can expect to find maybe half a dozen 25lb pluses there. Two rods only, no night fishing and day tickets are available by booking in advance. (Ring on 2 January if you want a summer date). Less heavily booked through the winter months. A good water to get to grips with carp fishing and always a chance of a 25lb plus. Well recommended. Phone 0827 872253.

Cuttle Mill, the Midlands water which has been the venue of many 'first twenty' captures.

Pool Hall, Lower Penn, Wolverhampton

This is a twenty-five acre lake which is unusual in that it is one of few waters to contain genuine 25lb plus commons. A very picturesque water set in woodland but has a litter problem not unlike that of Johnsons, Kent. Known to contain a mirror around 30–31lb and is available on a day ticket basis. Quite an easy water but very popular with picnickers etc.

Blackroot Pool, Sutton Park, Birmingham

A twelve acre estate lake which is a very difficult water. Contains mirrors to at least 25lb plus and possibly one or two nudging the 30lb mark. Not heavily fished, day tickets are available on the banks and night fishing available for those who enquire and use common sense and discretion. Fish do respond to those prepared to look for them; stalking is a good bet, we are told.

Patshull Park, Wolverhampton

Probably your best venue for chance of a 20lb plus common. Unusually most of the bigger fish are commons. Plenty of 25lb pluses to just under 30lb, has received a lot of specialist angler pressure and the fishing is very difficult. Lots of problems with eels and shy feeding fish. Around fifteen acres in size, very attractive water with trees, weeds and lilies. Quite a deep water in places but fish do seem to respond to surface baits. Membership very difficult to obtain; photos of good commons from the water often appear in the national papers.

43

Norfolk

Again a county of many fisheries but many on a closed-shop basis. Plenty of waters containing fish to low twenties; one or two waters with fish now nudging 30lb plus.

Waveney Valley Fisheries, Wortwell, Harleston

Again, another famous fishery which like Cuttle Mill, changed hands quite recently. Contains eight waters from two to six acres but of interest to the big fish angler are lakes C, D/E, F, G, Yew Tree. All are available on a day ticket basis, cost depending on number of rods and hours to be fished. Lakes C, D/E, and G all contain definite 25lb pluses. In lake D/E you will find at least two definite thirties, 'Big Scale' and the 'Leather'. Both seem to have peaked around 30lb. C lake contains a definite thirty as well which has been up to 35lb in weight. Unfortunately, odd fish are moved from lake to lake so definite fish stocks are hard to estimate. All lakes are quite hard,

doubles not so hard to catch but the bigger fish seem to fall to those who are prepared to make the effort. For details, write to the fishery owners at Lakeland Bungalow or enquire at the site. Many articles have been written about Waveney; try back issues of '*Carp Fisher*' and '*Coarse Angler*'. Also Rod wrote about them in his '*Carp Strikes Back*', including a map of G Lake.

Homersfield Lakes, Homersfield

Not too far from Waveney Valley Fisheries is a beautiful thirty acre lake called Homersfield. Probably one of the country's best looking lakes it contains just about everything you could ever want. Trees, bays, islands and lots of good sized fish. Best fish in the water could be up around 35lb; you've got 'Spike' at 31lb plus, 'Long Fish' at 25lb plus and a number of other 25lb pluses. Possibly one or two commons are around 25lb as well. This is a syndicate water and in effect it's by invitation only. Very few rules and a place that you could happily fish for life.

The join of the lakes of Waveney's D and E lakes. This is actually one water connected by a channel which runs between the bivvy and the bushes beyond it. The big oak is in the background beyond the corner of E lake.

Homersfield Lake in Suffolk, home of a good head of twenty plus carp.

Greens Pit, Shropham, Snetterton

A shallow, one acre pit which produced a 30lb plus in 1984. Having seen the newspaper clipping, the fish looks the size and if the location is correct then it's worth trying the venue. Quite a nice wooded water, not heavily fished but details of 25lb pluses are patchy. Day tickets can be booked in advance by ringing the fishery owner on Caston 735.

Taverham Pits, Norwich

Not much known about big fish from this water but we have a report of a genuine 28-pounder being caught. Quite popular and very picturesque, you can fish it via a Norwich & District Angling Club book. (The fishing is now controlled by Dave Plummer of Norwich Angling Centre.)

Northamptonshire

Billing Aquadrome, Northampton

A very famous fishery made known by Bob Reynold's captures and Ron Clay's 42-pounder in 1966. Very little is known about the water of recent note but last year produced a 25lb plus to a local lad fishing with a worm. Due to its size, scarcity and age of fish it has to be classed as very difficult. Fish at your peril! There is a detailed article about the history of the water in 'Carpworld 7'.

Oxfordshire

Dorchester Lagoon, Oxford

A very hard Amey Anglers Association water which is in fact three lakes. The one of most interest is Lagoon Lake at forty acres, a lake also used for sailing. This contains one definite low thirty and a few 25lb pluses. We also hear reports of much larger fish but few people can verify this. At forty acres, the lake is very hard but at £10 a season from Amey Anglers Association it is very good value. Write to Amey Anglers at Fisheries Office, Besselsleigh Road, Wootton, Abingdon, Oxon.

Shropshire

Hawkstone Park, Hodnet, Wem

A very narrow but long lake; in fact it is over a mile long. A totally private lake, no day tickets and syndicate place by invitation only. Contains both mirrors and commons to over 28lb. Alleged top weight of fish is just under 30lb. Reputed to contain 25lb pluses and 30lb pluses. Fishing from one side only, very hard but does produce in the winter months for those keen enough. Brian Garner wrote a detailed article about the water for the Nutrabaits' 1989 publication 'BAIT'. Home of big Crucian carp.

Surrey

A carp angler's dream. Lots of very pretty waters containing fish up to 25lb; most very pretty and very crowded. Quite a few waters have fish 'well over' 25lb but many are closed shops, syndicates or locals only.

Cut Mill, Elstead, Farnham

A beautiful looking estate lake of under ten acres. Lots of good fish; best fish going just under 30lb. Quite a few 25lb pluses and responds well to a variety of techniques, baits and presentations. Plenty of linears, commons and scattered scale carp. Very few swims and extremely popular. Due to this and the age of the fish it's got to be classed as a difficult water. The water did feature in the Richworth videos and various anglers over the years have written about the lake. To obtain a ticket write to Farnham Angling Society at 49 Cambridge Road, Farnborough, Hampshire.

Tri-Lakes Fishery, Yateley Road, Sandhurst

Two immaculate gravel pits of twelve acres; very nice looking lakes with lily pads, islands etc. The water isn't heavily stocked with carp but does contain some lunkers. There certainly are two fish which vary between 34 and 37lb, one of which came out at 43lb some years ago. Not over fished by carp anglers during the season but does receive lots of attention in the close season. Just turn up and purchase your tickets before fishing. Day ticket only, and rated difficult. No night fishing.

Burton Lakes, Farnham

A big lake which used to, and may still, contain some of the huge original Leney fish. It was stocked with these original fish in the early fifties and at one time there were around twenty-five fish over 25lb up to a maximum of 35–36lb. All were gorgeous linears with the odd good common or mirror. Unfortunately only a few years ago, many perished due to an outbreak of a rare carp disease and now fish are even fewer and further apart. It's over sixty acres in size, surrounded by trees and rushes and very shallow. In summer the whole water is covered in picnickers and water sailers. Chris Ball and Andy Little do a marvellous slide show about the water and various in-depth articles have appeared in 'Carp Catcher' about the water. Very hard but could produce a surprise. (See Chapters 2 and 3 by Chris Ball and Jan Wenczka.)

Send Pits, Woking

A very nice looking water with genuine fish to 30lb plus in it. Quite a few 25lb pluses as well, but restricted to local anglers only. Andy Little and Ron Buss have had some very large fish from this water. Enquire locally.

Yateley, Sandhurst Road, Yateley, Camberley

A series of fourteen lakes with many of these producing huge carp to specialist anglers over the years. Available on a Leisure Sport special venue ticket, these waters are hard and do not receive the pressure many of us expect them to. All very good looking lakes, surrounded by trees and with plenty of islands and other such features. The only problem is the mud, tackle thieves during the summer, and litter.

Lake 11 – Match Lake (twelve acres). Dotted with islands this lake contains lots of twenties up to a maximum weight of say 27lb. Always a chance of a good fish, hard but still popular.
Lake 12 – Copse Lake (five acres). A very famous lake which definitely contains fish up to, and possibly over 40lb. There's the 'Parrot' at around 36–38lb, and also a fish known to the locals as the 'Pig Fish', or 'Pineapple'. This apparently dwarfs the 'Parrot'. Very, very hard. All season for one fish is a good result. You can see them – catching them is a lot harder!
Lake 9 – Car Park Lake (ten acres). Produced a fish of 42lb to Ken Hodden but this died, due to being spawnbound. Also it's the home of 'Heather the Leather'; she's been out at weights between 34lb and 41lb over the years. At the moment she appears to be on the up. Certainly contains three other fish 25lb plus and despite its mud problem, and rating of very difficult, it's well worth a try.
Lake 4 – North Lake (thirteen acres). Produced a famous 45.12 carp to Ritchie MacDonald in 1984. This fish has been out quite a few times over the years to anglers at varying weights. Kevin Clifford had it in 1976 at 30lb (a Midlands water indeed, Kevin!) and this year it came out at just over 44lb again. Contains a few other 25lb pluses; if you get a chance it will probably be a big fish.

Those are the more famous waters in that fishery; most on the complex contain large carp so it's well worth obtaining a ticket. Various articles have appeared in the papers about the water and in his book '*Ritchie on Carp*', Ritchie MacDonald provides an insight into the Yateley complex.

Yorkshire

Not widely known for its carp fishing but looking at the whole region there certainly are a couple of waters which contain genuine 25lb pluses in them. Many more contain fish to low twenties; as the seasons progress I'm sure many more will.

Hardwick Hall, Hardwick (off M1)

Two lakes; the biggy is located in the smaller of the two. This fish hovers around the 30lb mark but as well as this there are at least two other 25lb pluses. The big one hasn't been out for a while; however, many local anglers still believe it's there. The venue is day ticket only, no night fishing and two rods only on a Yorkshire licence. Day ticket from the bailiff on the bank and always a chance of a 30lb plus!

A1 Pit, A1, Newark

Visible from the A1 and a huge water of sixty acres plus. Very open and adjacent to the Trent. Not a good looking water, does receive quite a lot of pressure but definitely contains at least three 25lb plus fish. All you need to do is turn up and pay on the day; night fishing is allowed. Lots of snags, bars, shelves and very deep in places. A prolific water and an ideal starting point for big fish if you live up north.

Ryehill, Winterset Reservoir, Wakefield

A huge ninety acre reservoir where you can obtain tickets on the bank. Contains a few fish between 25 and 27lb; however, it does contain a lot of smaller ones. Location is your big problem; once located they aren't that hard to catch. Usual tactics should produce. A daunting fishery which has broken many a local expert.

Dringhouses Lake, Moor Lane, York

Also more popularly known as 'Hoggys'. Contains a reputed common carp of 30lb plus and at least two mirrors over 25lb. Best carp recently has been around 27–28lb. A nice looking lake, but large and very hard. Day tickets and night permits used to be easy to obtain but a change of fishery ownership has put this in doubt. Geoff Crawford has written an article in 'Carp Fisher' about this water, and fish caught from it do appear quite regularly in the papers.

Knotford Lagoon, Otley

A Leeds & District water which has quite some potential according to local anglers. A large venue, very picturesque and has reputedly produced a 30lb carp (very doubtful). Certainly carp to 25lb plus have been taken and its potential has yet to be realised. Available as day ticket; for membership, enquire locally or in Leeds.

Bacon Factory Pond, Sherburn

Again an unknown quantity this one but we can verify one 25lb plus being caught and an unconfirmed thirty. Carp anglers are discouraged, litter is horrendous. Day tickets on the bank to those willing to give it a try. Very weedy and very hard.

Wales

Redmire Pool

What can be said about this water that hasn't been said a thousand times before. Home of the record carp, produced a 51.08 for Chris Yates and considered the birthplace of carp fishing.

A pleasing Marc Ridgway study of Redmire Pool, the original big carp water.

Now a Carp Society water so to fish it you have to be a member of the Society. Details from Vic Cranfield, 33 Covert Road, Hainault, Ilford, Essex. Available to all nowadays on a specified week basis. Has recently produced carp (common) to 28lb plus and has the ability to produce even bigger fish. '*Redmire Pool*', '*Pursuit of Carp and Catfish*', '*Stillwater Angling*' – all contain marvellous descriptions of the water, its inhabitants and its history. Well recommended, a beautiful water.

Other Waters

As well as still waters, many rivers and canals have the ability to produce 25lb carp. Of particular note is the Trent which has produced commons and mirrors to 30lb, the Thames which has produced fish to mid-thirties, the Nene which has produced 30lb carp and the Royal Military Canal which produced a 32-pounder to Bill Phillips. Location will obviously be more difficult on the big rivers and the potential has yet to be realised.

Hopefully, that's given you all an insight to just how many waters there are available if you want that twenty-five plus. There are many, many more if you are prepared to go and look for them. All you need is an Ordnance Survey map, your eyes and plenty of common sense. Look through the angling papers, have a talk to your local fishing shop owner, keep your ears peeled at meetings. Most of the secrets in carp fishing have already been put into print and waters are no different. Do try to remember that your new water may be somebody's local water and treat it like you would expect your local water to be treated by a visitor to it.

Most of all, enjoy yourself and if you need to set targets, base them on your levels and not anybody else's. Good fishing!

5 Rod on Big Fish

Rod Hutchinson talking to Tim Paisley

There is no one with more to say about carp and carp fishing than Rod Hutchinson. Those who see him from a distance and know of him only as a prolific catcher of big fish from the hardest waters in the land – and beyond – over a quarter of a century can have no concept of the vast storehouse of knowledge that Rod's extraordinary mind has accumulated during his carp fishing years. We talk a great deal and almost without fail Rod surprises me afresh with his comprehensive grasp and understanding of all things carpy. In the conversation that follows, which was taped at the side of Rod's big fish syndicate water in Lincolnshire during the summer of 1989, he talks some authoritative and illuminating good sense about what makes big carp big.

You're no stranger to big fish Rod, and we're here on your own water in Lincolnshire which contains some very big fish. How did you set about getting your own water and making it into a big fish lake?

I believe that a carp will grow to 50–60lb maybe; I think that's possible in this country. It's only possible if the individual carp has got as much food to eat as it wants. I do think carp will grow big in an unfished atmosphere. I think it's very much a biological factor that every time a fish is damaged in any way, it can't grow until the healing has taken place. Now I think, however much we try, when we catch carp, they are damaged, even if it's a cut in the mouth, a cut in anything. We had a couple of fish growing nice and fast, they've got in the mid-twenties; they're getting really greedy, they're feeding all the time but they're getting caught more and more and their weight stays the same – maybe even goes down a bit. Then, for some reason, I say for some reason but the main reason, we had two very prolific years with the food growth very high; the weed came; the snails came. The basic diet of the carp in this lake is water snails. Any water with lots and lots of water snails, to me, is a big fish water.

Tim and Rod talking big fish (and dogs) on Rod's syndicate water.

I got this idea originally, going back to '71/'72, and Roy Johnson was in business. He at that time controlled a few waters in Kent and he had his own water. Anyway he managed to get some Redmire fish. He bought them off Jack Hilton the same as Kevin Clifford did. There were lots of small Redmire carp went in Kevin's lake, none of them did anything, but Roy Johnson had a few snails and the trout ate these snails to a certain degree; they put the carp in and they went crazy; in two years, a couple of these doubles from Redmire went to about 28lb, another to about 24lb. Absolutely incredible, not seen anything like it. I kept in touch with Roy Johnson a bit and they very quickly ate these snails up and he started supplementing the water, buying water snails in from Holland, putting in half a ton, a ton of snails. These fish did incredibly well until the snails ran out and all of a sudden there wasn't enough food for them and the growth stopped. I think, to keep control of the water, as the fish breed, I've got to take fish out. The best day ticket waters you hear about have worked well and waters you hear about have worked well and you'll get a very good growth rate at 400lb per acre of fish: I thought, 'Well, if that's any good, 200lb would be a lot better' and that's why I stocked my water on the basis of 200lb per acre and no more.

Was that your starting level?

Yes, that was my starting level. I think what happens is, when they do breed you think you've got 200lb of carp (per acre); the fish get bigger and bigger and bigger; even without breeding the original 200lb within three years should be past the 500lb level because of the growing and very soon you run out. Then you've got choices; for instance you can supplement feed. Now to a fair degree the anglers on the lake are supplementing the feed with the baits and everything they are putting in, and I think they all eventually get eaten. They might

not get eaten on the session, but I think they all get eaten; even if the carp don't get them the coots get them or something like that. You are supplementing to a degree there but the more you get them dependent on your food, the more they'll get caught, the more they'll get damaged, the more it will slow down the growth rate. I don't like to see carp come out more than once a year because I think repeat captures are going to damage its growth.

Even if you go somewhere like Lake Cassien, the first two years the fish had phenomenal growth, absolutely phenomenal. The first session I went, on the very last day Jim Hepper caught – it's in 'Carp Now and Then' – three all at the same time but one of them was very distinctive, I think it was 37lb 12oz; this was in June; come October, the end of October, Ritchie caught it and it was 43lb 12oz. It's grown something like 6lb in six months and I thought 'Grief, it can't be true'. Two years later, me, Annie and the kids took our tour of Europe. It wasn't really a fishing tour, we looked everywhere, looked at some lakes, we had a dabble everywhere and we stopped on Cassien for two days. Terry and Karen had been on Cassien for about three months and we were talking about the identification of fish and all that and Terry came up and said, 'Well, I've got one sacked that nobody else has caught.' It was just short of 50lb, I think 49lb 8oz. He pulls it out; it was Ritchie's fish, Jim Hepper's fish . . . It had somehow gone a couple of years without getting caught and it was nearly fifty. I get all the pictures, the fish I caught at Cassien, the forties and fifties. The lads who've read my book, they catch a fish and they send me the pictures and I see how the growth rate's going. If a year went between captures, there would be a 6lb growth rate. The food in there is incredible; they've got the food. If Cassien had been 'revealed' three years later, I'm convinced the world record would have been broken several times. I probably shouldn't say this, but Cassien was only given away for commercial reasons wasn't it? I think Cassien would have produced world records within three years; that's how fast the fish were growing. Now they've nearly stopped, the big ones.

Do you think they've become acclimatised to this being caught eventually?

I think they've become acclimatised; all you've done is slow down; like slowing down the metabolic rate because they're getting caught. I don't think that *bothers* them but it's like, they've not got the rush of youth, where they've got to feed, feed, feed, go in for everything. If they do slow down . . . I mean in a lake like ours, I come up here almost every week and there's not many times I don't see those big fish and that's on a two day trip, I generally have two days to myself, where I can walk round. We see these big fish, but they don't get caught and the reason they don't get caught is the ones in here don't feed as much; the big ones don't feed as much as the smaller ones. We see them time and time again, hang back, go in there and have a little feed and come out of it. They went through that period where they ate everything and got caught a number of times when they were younger, and now they seem to be a lot more selective; we've seen them on the baits, the young ones take it first and they're away, no ifs and buts, no messing about with the baits, then the big 'un comes in and he'll blow it out three or four times. He's still feeding; he's there but he's a lot craftier. Those two big fish of ours, for some reason, that year there was prolific natural food growth, they didn't get caught. When the snails have been back for two years, I don't know why, the water might . . . I didn't check anything but . . . it was pure water, very high in alkaline – it might have been because we had two rainy years, a lot more calcium got into the

Rod's wife Annie with one of the big leathers in Rod's water.

water and when the snails are back in it, this lake's at its most prolific, that's what it is. I think it's just the calcium. Waters I know in England, for example, Johnson's water – I don't include Redmire because that was a whole different ball game to what we're talking about now; Redmire's stock put into other waters all did well. Redmire was probably the richest of the waters that were stocked and those fish were really growing, growing and growing until all of us went on the water. I don't think we've seen the peak of what our islands could do in terms of carp weights because I don't think there's any carp in this country left in a rich water that's unfished. I don't think any of the known fish of today will grow much bigger because they're fished for so much; no matter how hard we try, they get damaged in some way when we catch them. I don't think we'll ever see the full potential of the English carp.

You mention one or two waters there and even within those big fish waters there have been one or two outstanding fish. What produces outstanding fish? Why is the odd big carp bigger than the other fish in a water?

Pure genetics. Dick Walker comes into this again, but let's face it, he was probably the first one to argue against things and point out the right reasons – going back quite a few years with Abingdon trout fishery and Walker's fish was, I think, the biggest at the time. People arguing and saying 'Oh, they're all stew pond fish', and Walker was saying, 'No, these are the fastest growers, bred with the fastest growing ones which produce these Abingdon trout'. I know loads of people in the trout game and to grow regular 14-, 15-, 16-pounders, that's fluke; you don't grow them that size regularly: one or two of those fish come out. You can do genetic breeding in fish. I mean, the Japanese have been doing it for donkey's years with the koi: that's genetic breeding. You put in your best strains together and I think there is a few that make it, the offspring of a few that have been exceptional fish before. I think in this country, I don't think there's any professional stocking done. What I love to do is be involved with fish – and with fishing – and there's so much can be done with carp. I mean in Holland they've always had their water board that's bred their carp for them, put them in the canals and so on. We've got nothing in England; we haven't got a national fish breeding centre; we've got nobody trying anything, have we? We've got a few little water boards, we've got a few stock ponds, but we haven't got a national plan.

It's down to a few individuals and a few water boards.

It's entirely down to a few individuals, who've got a water and think 'Well, how do I make the best of it?' They buy carp from whatever source they can; it's such a hotch potch when people try to create a fishery nowadays because you've got a choice; you can buy a load of fish from one water of a certain size, which are small, or you can go to the fisheries and you can get the odd big fish of dubious background.

What do you mean by dubious background?

Well, what I mean is, you can go along to a lot of these places and say 'Where's this fish come from?' – they don't even know; they've bought it in. A lot of fish farms buy fish in. There's a hell of a lot of waters get filled in, through the motorways. We can never keep control or see what could really happen until we have a controlled exercise in it. England is the centre of the world as far as carp fishing goes and we're never going to see what could have been. As far as I am concerned there is no reason whatsoever why England can't produce 60lb carp.

Let's just have a look at the history of the big fish because it's a fact that weights that were mythical fifteen years ago are now commonplace. For all that, Walker's 1952 fish is still a sort of target weight. Apart from Yatesy's fish which, for whatever reason, made 50lb plus, 44lb is still a very exceptional fish. How come that we've got so many fish coming through into mid-thirties, big thirties and forties; but still we've got fish struggling to make it to the 45–50lb range.

Because they're getting caught.

That's the main reason?

The very main reason, yes. Walker's fish grew to that size without ever having been caught before and Walker said, at that time, to his knowledge and everybody believed, there were fish in excess of 50lb; I believe somebody netted one. Those fish had been left to grow unhindered . . .

But now, we've got so many fish coming through, mid thirties and big thirties but for all the bait and all the numbers of the fish we still can't get anything . . .

I don't think we will do now. Most waters are overstocked, not only with carp but with other fish. We have to supplement it; we produce big tench, we produce big bream . . . There's all this fragmentation; too many societies, too many groups run, it should all be one united front.

That's people, isn't it?

You know, people get control of waters – and there's a hell of a lot of people who put a lot of work into the waters – but when it comes to the fish they can't go to a national carp farm where you *know* the pedigree of the stockings, where this came from. It happens in other countries, Tim.

It's too fragmented. A big fish comes up now and someone's going to sell it and someone's going to buy it. It's like here, you can't say, 'Right, I'm going to have six fish in this water.'

No, but I couldn't get the fish.

No, but I mean you could now say, 'That one's done six pounds, that one's done six pounds, I'll just have those six', but unless you were very, very rich, you couldn't do it, could you?

No, you couldn't do it. I don't mean like that. I mean, even from small fish – if you had a National fish farm and you're trying to produce

good fish, you'd produce protégés of two fast growing strains, which have done well in a good environment and you breed those two together; you don't just make it a hotch potch. You breed good fish and then you tag them; everybody knows exactly what they've got in. I wish all carp fishing was wild, like the old days, when we knew nothing about it but, having said that, I've been around so long and it grieves me when I see some people try waters – and they get fish that I know you've got no chance whatsoever with. I know they haven't got the basic ideas about water management. They generally get their advice from the people they are buying the fish from.

Coming back on to the big fish; just reverting to this theme of the size of fish. You're familiar with all the 40lb plus fish, or almost all of them, that have come out. Has there been a genuine forty in this country that was over 40lb for any other reason other than it was carrying spawn?

Yes. I will say definitely the Yateley fish, that's not carrying spawn. I mean the Yateley fish is a natural 42, 43lb fish. I'd say 41lb definitely. Nowadays, he's averaging 44; there was a time when he was jumping 42, 43 but he's generally 44 now; that's a very, very big fish. Even then, you take his life cycle – the minute he became a big fish, he's out in the paper, everybody knows about him, everybody goes to try to catch him and he's under pressure every week of the season. He's not living in a natural environment; how many times does he . . . well I know this for a fact, ('cos he told me!) there's many a time he wants to go round the Point, in behind the back bay there. It's where he likes to feed naturally but then he gets to the front of the Point and there's lines all across it and he has to go to another area of lake where there isn't as much food. He has to make second and third choices; he's not getting his full complement of food. The anglers know where the

Rod with one of the biggies from his water, Scaley at 35lb.

food is, the anglers congregate on that Point and it forces him into areas where the food stocks aren't as good. You get this on every water. Once a fish becomes known, everybody wants it. 'Where did he get caught? – oh, you get a lot of fish off there, nice bloodworm bed out there.' That area becomes under pressure. It becomes under pressure, but why do you catch them there? Because that was their favourite food hoard because that's where the food's most abundant. Anywhere else they go, they've got to work harder for it. Does that make sense, Tim?

Yes, a lot of sense – stopped me in my tracks – on that theme. But for the most part we're talking about fish carrying spawn.

No, you are! I tell you what, Tim, I'm not quite in on this so can you give me examples of fish carrying spawn? See I don't know those Shropshire fish. Are they carrying spawn?

Pinky isn't, certainly not, that is a genuine big fish but I think that's gone now. (Wrong. This was taped in the close season 1988/1989).

The er, what shall we call it, Fox Pool? Definitely a genuine forty in there.

Is it? Oh, it looked a little bit gutsy. Fair enough.

There's a few natural forties about. What do you call a gestation period?

I don't know.

No, I enquired about this, twenty years ago and I was told, 'Well, we consider the gestation period to be from the minute it drops its spawn to the next time it comes up again'. The minute it's dropped its spawn, it's then building back up to it. So at what time of the year is a carp not carrying spawn?

Never.

I've been doing this for thirty years now and right at the beginning, I'd left school where my best subject was biology and I was into things a lot more then, red hot into it, right at the beginning; I was arguing with fisheries' managers and everyody about all this spawning thing. When people talk about a spawny fish, they're no different from any others, and I've seen this. They grow up, it's a slow progression. A fish isn't full of spawn for three or four weeks, not what I call a fish spawning; that's only like at a good weight, it's up there. If a fish that's going to be 36lb when it comes to spawn, he's holding his weight good, doing well a month, two months before: if he's a couple of pounds under, he's holding it well. The full weight comes in the two day period; the minute that heat comes on and they come spawning, there's a hormone, the eggs fill up with water and *they put on a couple of pounds there, at that time.* Should you catch them then, you've got what **I** call a spawny fish. I caught a spawny fish with the Kingsmead fish. I caught it on the day – I couldn't believe it, it was so late in the year, they must have spawned before. I checked with Ritchie and Hankins who had been down before when they were spawning and I go in two months later . . . They hadn't spawned, they'd had several goes at it. It was a deep pit and everything's got to come exactly right. Walker reckoned you had to hold a 68° temperature for 24 hours around the clock. I don't agree, but he was very close; I think you've got to hold about 65–66° around the clock, not to drop below that. It's so easy to do a water temperature at one end of the lake and the other and you get entirely different readings. You couldn't get a warmer night than tonight could you? It's absolutely gorgeous but I can guarantee that on that clock thermometer now we haven't got more than 60° out here. In the shallows there, we've got somewhere around 68°. The sun's on it all day, it's shining off the sand; the small fish go up there and any fish that go down there start getting spawny unless they come out of it. But the fish up the top end, the big ones, always spawn on the top bank and because they're in a different temperature, it takes about two months longer for the temperature up there to reach the levels for them to spawn.

I agree with everything you are saying but when I first came into contact with big fish circles I was on the Con Club with Bob Davis. Bob was talking about the fish and he said, 'They're all two or three pounds up', I don't know whether it was his original idea or somebody suggested it to him, he said, 'I've seen this before, they're all going to be down next year or the year after because it strikes me that they've got to build up a store for two or three years, and then they get the right conditions to release it'. So you get like this cycle of fish generally in a water putting on weight and then, bump, they get the right conditions, after three years, because they don't spawn out every year do they? It doesn't always drop right for them in this country.

No, it doesn't always drop right but I think you'll find it drops right a lot more than people think. The main thing in this country is, when we do pretty well, there's not that many waters where the survival rate is very high; there's not many get through the first year of our winters. Like Bob may say – I'm not disagreeing with the man – what I'm saying is, I don't think every year the conditions hold out long enough for them to manage a complete ejection of spawn. I think some years the temperatures come right for some time and they go in – we see them here – going really into spawn and bump, the weather changes so quick and they've not fully ejected that spawn. What happens that year is you've a very low survival rate of what has come off; so low that people probably haven't noticed it. People only notice spawning when all of a sudden you've got a stack of new fish. If they just tick over, one by one, I think certainly there's a lot of years when they don't get rid of all their spawn. I think most years there is some spawn left.

Yes, I think what I was saying is that you've got a sort of length limit in this country and your higher weights, you know, we're getting an increasing number of big thirties, genuine big thirties but for the most part the fish that make it beyond that do so because of an accumulation of spawn or a temporary increase in weight of some sort which fluctuates a great deal.

I think what we have to take into account. Being quite serious about things, this isn't wanting to offend anybody in carp fishing, you fish for what you can fish for, that's it. But a 30lb carp is not an exceptional fish. Carp can grow to 30lb in Norway and Sweden; in Poland they grow to 40lb, well over 40, with temperatures worse than ours but because they have an unrestricted life, nobody fishing for them. That's the only major factor in this country. What we have done is – 30lb carp isn't exceptional – I mean, honestly, if you go abroad, while there's enough food for fish, I think most carp should make 40lb. I think the freaks are the bigger ones but I think most carp are capable of hitting big thirties or forties, providing they've got enough food.

Right. You're familiar with carp in this country and have been for a great many years; for a number of years now you've been familiar with carp on the Continent. We tend to look at Lake Cassien and the monsters that it has started to produce, and you immediately think that is the potential of all waters in France – but is that so?

No, certainly not. I feel funny saying this, but what people have to appreciate is that Cassien is a stocking water. Now they may go in as small carp, 8-, 9-, 10-pounders, 14-pounders; in the original stocking, just going by memory, twenty something 20lb plus fish. We saw the bloke who stocked them and they were not regarded as good fish. I can't remember if the biggest one was 24 or 28lb. Second lot in have done very well and the third lot; they were all big carp when you talk about 30 forties, fair number of fifties. Unfortunately since Chef's fish, Chefan Hovin, well, it's all the same fish; Cottis's fish, (Max Cottis) Alice's fish, you know, the big one, got caught several times and every time everybody caught it they all had to nurse it back to strength. You know it was going to cough it sooner or later, that was at the end of its life, you know it wasn't going to do anything. The second generation of those carp, the second stocking, I think, were the

best fish in there; the ones growing the fastest, but nowadays they've been slowed down by angling pressure. It's not just being caught; the pressure from anglers is stopping fish from going in where they naturally want to feed. You walked up to Lake Cassien in the first year, Tim, and you knew where those carp were, you could read them like a book, but now angling pressure has pushed them out of those areas into areas where they never used to feed before. Can't feed 'em in 16ft of water. To break the real record now, I don't think would be very easy. People can look around France, actually Spain – I'm only giving an opinion – just my opinion. My opinion of Spain is that the temperatures are too high and they breed far too prolifically. Spanish fish, they grow for their length right at the beginning and then there isn't enough food to sustain the weights after that because there's so many carp in Spain; I've got a picture of a 70lb plus common from Lake Santilana near Madrid but these big fish only go in once a year to spawn and they're out, lost in a river tributary. I think that was an exceptional fish, the fact that it was caught at spawn again. That's almost like the Cassien fish; when does everybody go? They all go in May when they're in the West Arm to spawn and the big 'uns come out, so even those fish, you know, nothing special comes out after them. I mean fish come out, but no weights beat those weights that were caught in May. How many were what I class spawning – to me spawning is within two days of spawning – not within a week or a month. It's like a woman breaking water, the eggs fill up; they need the water in the body to force the eggs out. It sucks in, fills up and then the eggs go out.

The disquieting thing is that there is this trend that the exceptional fish that are making big weights, a number of them have died; is this part of some cycle?

Do you mind giving me some examples?

The Con club fish, that Clive had at 39.

The one Clive had at 37? It made 39.

I think two or three of the big Savay fish died, which again, might be age. I think the Kingsmead fish died although I've recently heard a rumour that it's turned up in a trout lake.

I'll just put this on record – I don't believe the Kingsmead fish died; I think it was lifted. I don't know anybody who fished the water at the time who thinks the Kingsmead fish died. There were four of us regulars on the water and nobody thinks it died.

Rod with the big Kingsmead fish at nearly 40lb.

I've got a feeling, and it is only a feeling, that it was all part of some cycle that the fish that are making this extra bit of weight, they become abnormal and eventually they die because of it. That might just be an unscientific gut feeling.

How about an unscientific gut feeling for the number of times they get caught? That's what does it. I sometimes wonder whether you should say what you truly believe because you're leaving yourself so wide open for the antis, but every time you hook a fish, you're leaving it open for infection. I just believe that the faster growers, they're eating, they're eating, they're eating; they're getting caught. I think some fish seem to be immune to the experience of being caught and then there are other fish which seem to be absolutely shattered by the experience.

Where are the future big fish waters, here and abroad? Are we going to see any fifty plus in this country?

Are we going to see any fifty plus in this country? I think if we do, they will be from small syndicate waters where people really know what they're doing and are into fisheries management – and really trying to produce big fish. It's the old maxim to me, there's a certain level of what you call sport in fishing and a certain level of specimen fishing. Take it like the National Association of Specimen Anglers (NASA) lads after the bream; if you want to be in with a chance of the bigger ones you go to Queensford Lagoon where you're not going to catch anything most of the time. You've got to have a low head of fish for big carp, which means going to catch less. I think that's it, really. The waters have got to be controlled for us to produce a fifty; I don't think anybody's going to produce a fifty in a pressurised water, I honestly don't, and that can include all the Home Counties gravel pits; I don't think one of these fish is going to do it because I think they get caught and I think it stops their growth rate; but the most important thing is it stops their growth rate right at the end of the growing years. The years when they are growing the fastest and they're getting caught the most is when the damage is done. They've got a couple of years left, when if left, unpressured, just to feed anywhere they wanted, this country would do fifties. If we are going to do an actual fifty, and I'd love a natural fifty, it's going to be a private syndicate water or a private water or one which hasn't been carp fished yet. I still think there might be a few big pits around which haven't seen the masses on. I don't believe there's any secrets in Wraysbury, for example. That's the funniest thing, after travelling abroad, waters we used to look at as big waters suddenly look like puddles.

So you think most of the known big fish waters have hit the ceiling?

I think the known fish waters, yes.

Are there any unknown ones?

I'd like to hope so, wouldn't you? I don't know – you can ask me, but you're probably more in the know than me on those things, with your Carp Society involvement from all the areas of the country.

No, I mean it's like you say . . . I recently heard of a big fish water that got wiped out, although I'd never heard of it. It was a small water but a lad had had a forty out of it a couple of times, and there were a number of other big fish in, and it was accidentally drained and the fish died. It won't be the only one in this country, will it? He was the only one fishing. Whether or not that's pressure or not, I don't know.

One person fishing. I say it's not just the damage, it's when you learn where they feed, that everybody fishes there. The fish become crafty and think 'hang on, this ain't right', and turn around. You've driven them away from the best feeding on the lake, that's as vitally important as getting caught. You're forcing them into areas which are pretty much barren; they survive them, they might even be a pound up next year but if they could go into any area they wanted, unrestricted, feed, feed, feed, I honestly think we'd see numbers of 50-pounders in this country.

What about here? I mean there must be waters like this. Your biggest fish at the moment, well the biggest fish you've caught are mid thirties, but you've got a lot of big twenties coming through very quickly. Are you going to get a shooter out of these that could do it?

I hope so because the fish that are coming through quickly are the progeny of our biggest fish. The mid-twenties were all fish born in the lake but it's a shame that the moment we have a nice balance – you know it isn't an easy lake although we haven't been here for long, we've been here only a few hours and we haven't had one yet – when they're all feeding at a certain time, the indicators can be rattling as they come through; but at the same time, those are good days; you do a lot of blanks. I think for my fish to go any further, the only way I can do it is to realistically take it down to the original balance, under 500lb an acre.

Now this is where you make the compromise, Tim. Me personally, I like coming here and know there's some nice 30lb fish; there's a good head of 20lb fish and there's a lot of double figure fish. They're all lovely carp. We've got fish up to mid-thirties and we've got a good spectrum of fishing. Now do I take away a third of those fish, take the doubles away, knowing in my own head that I can push a certain percentage, maybe two or three fish, up over 40lb? That's just a scientific exercise,

Rod with another of his many big fish, this time from the famous Savay Lake.

that's got nothing to do with sport, that's not got anything to do with enjoyment.

I must admit, when I took this over I was a bit of a pseudo boffin. As I say, I'd left school where my best subject was biology and I always believed I could produce a record carp because I thought I knew how to produce one, finding the right way to do it. I've got it to a level, but now we've got good fishing. Do you take good fishing away to prove something. I mean, it's no big deal if I was proved wrong. I don't believe it would be difficult to produce 40-pounders providing you control the environment but the sport's more important to me. I'd love to do the thing in a controlled exercise where it wasn't my lake, where I wasn't fishing, where you had a national policy and you looked at carp and really saw what they could do.

Do you think that the syndrome that we're now hitting, the fish aren't going to grow to the size that we want them to because we want to catch them now, do you think that's going to affect the potential size in France as well now?

Oh yes, I think the potential size in France has been affected a hell of a lot in the past two years, one hell of a lot.

But there will still be a lot of surprises over there?

Oh, there's got to be a load of surprises, Tim but at the same time, I still look . . . We have travelled a bit and the fact is, in France, they've been allowed to grow without getting caught, so in a lot of waters fish have been able to do their natural best. They seem to be able to get just into forty, just into early forties and survive; every year the spawning, every year there's a whole new lot come on. Compared to our waters – 'Oh, maybe one or two carp in there' – the well stocked waters, that is! They seem to get into forties all right and they seem

to be getting long fish; and they grow out and that's the natural thing in France but you have a higher survival rate in breeding, in spawning each year: you know, the waters get overstocked very quickly so you go into waters where there's thousands of fish but if you can sort them out, the top end of those fish are always in the forties.

Cassien, that's an entirely different thing, because that's a stocky water; the fish go through the hormone changes, like a salmon, they go back every year to spawn but what comes off is untrue. It comes quick; the high temperatures are in April, May and the fish rush up that Arm to spawn, but at the same time those high temperatures are melting the snow in the Alps, which is coming down and keeping the water cool; so in there you've got your stockies which has helped make an exceptional water. You go over the other side of France, more to the Spanish side, your San Geniez, fish in there, everything survives; there's several 40lb fish been caught. Personally, I would expect a world record to come from a water on the latitude somewhere between Cassien and Switzerland, where you've got a very long, hot period but you've also got sharp contrasts; when it's cold, it's really cold. You get ice, you get ice water, where you can't get overbreeding. You want that fine line between the most sunlight hours you can get, but severe cold to stop over-breeding.

It's almost as though, to really make a water work, you've got to go in for some form of sterilisation.

Oh yes, you've got to hold them back.

Do you think that Cassien was a one off then or will there be another Cassien in France?

I certainly don't think there's lots of Cassiens because as I say, it has got the Alps water going into it, stopping over-breeding – that's a very important thing – it's the most important thing. Say you go to Spain, you go to San Geniez, everything breeds like mad, every year; there's another couple of thousand carp to fight against. In Cassien they've only got what's stocked that year, which is a hell of a lot of difference. Cassien would have produced a world record if only it had been kept quiet another three years.

So what does it take? What have you got to have? Spell it out, for a water to produce a fifty plus fish, provided you've got the right fish to make it.

In England? A very high alkaline water, that's absolutely essential for crustaceans. Simple logic tells me that if they can eat one substantial food item, a water snail, a swan mussel – a crustacean basically – they can go whomp, whomp and eat them to their heart's content; a fish eating like that has got to grow a lot bigger than a carp that's got to sift through the mud for minute particles. They'll grow to a certain size but to me, in the old days we used to say 'Well why does this high pH produce it?' To me it's just because of calcium; all your vertebrate need calcium, I mean the highest pH, really as high pH as you can go. If you produce lots of water snails, lots of crustaceans, lots of vertebrate type animals, you're going to have big fish. You're going to get good thirties, maybe mid-thirties on a good

ground bait but the big fish, the fast growers, need lots of crustaceans. You need a rich water. I don't think you can do it on poor water.

We're on chalk stream water here, straight out of the wolds there; there's several waters like this. Take any chalk stream water – there's been a few good fish out of the old Cotswolds, hasn't there Tim? Actually, Hampshire's done one or two nice individual fish as well before everywhere got stopped. Quality water produces quality food and then a small population of carp.

Take it the other way, just the other side of the river, old Brandsburton. You take those places for granted, but over the years they've been hammered.

They haven't done bad with fish; old Jumbo made that size because he wasn't fished for, but he was in chalk stream water, out of Driffield Beck in the Yorkshire Wolds; he was in pure chalk stream water. Got very high pHs on those lakes up there; he had everything, he was unfished for, he had all the food he could eat. If he hadn't been netted at that time, if you'd taken him in three or four years' time, I bet he would have been a darn sight bigger.

That emphasises what I've been saying: one of the biggest influences on carp growth today is the angler.

Yes, fair comment. Thanks a lot.

6 Big Carp and Big Waters

Pete Springate

A lot of my fishing has been on big waters. I find them hard work purely because of their size and the problem of locating the fish but I don't find them daunting. When I was roach fishing many years ago, I used to fish for the roach in the reservoirs at Barn Elms and Knight and Besborough and they really are big, the sort of places where you fish all day for one bite whatever you are fishing for. So really I suppose in my early days of fishing I was accustomed to fishing big waters.

Once I'd caught a few big carp, at Darenth and a number of other waters the prospect of going back to Wraysbury where I used to tench fish many years ago, didn't really worry me too much. The problem with the big waters, especially Wraysbury, is knowing whether you're anywhere near fish. You tend to waste a lot of time fishing areas that you think might produce. You could be lucky and hit an area straight away or . . . I spent a lot of time walking round looking at the water, jotting down where I've seen fish, particularly in the close season, then going round, doing a bit of plumbing, trying to work out where there's any bars; climbing trees, looking to see if there's any features out there. I just can't emphasise enough the importance of finding the fish before you start fishing a really big water. You can soon discourage yourself if you keep fishing nowhere near them. You've got to get an idea in your mind of where you want to fish. That doesn't mean to say that the fish are going to be there but you work on that sort of idea; you pick an area and if there's two or three of you, you pick a couple of areas and work on those areas, pre-baiting and whatever and if they don't produce or you don't see any signs you either move to the next most promising area or you start all over again. You've got to be really determined to catch the fish to persevere with a water like Wraysbury, or any of the sparsely stocked reservoirs or gravel pits with fish big enough to be worth pursuing.

Once I've decided to fish an area, I'll fish it for three or four weeks even if I don't get anything; I'm not worried about not catching, that's part of getting to know this type of water, but I am constantly watching the water for signs of fish; it doesn't matter whether I put a fish on the bank or not, provided I know that there are fish around.

When I start fishing a big water I'm not too bothered about the baits to start off with; I'll usually use sweetcorn, or luncheon meat, until we've fished there for a little bit then we'd start putting in the boilies. Use a bait you know unpressured carp will take more or less straight away when you move onto a big water. When we first started on these big waters we found we were wasting a lot of time trying to pre-bait areas with boilies if the fish weren't there; especially with protein baits, those sort of baits could be out there for two or three weeks without a fish coming across them and you've really blown that bait before you've even started. So we used to start off with sweetcorn or luncheon meat, find the areas where the fish were, then we would start baiting up with boilies and keep baiting it and keep it going.

Pete, the most successful Wraysbury angler of all time holds a magnificent mirror of 36lb.

On those big waters, you can get the fish to where you want them, within reason. It's funny, I fish a lot with Ken (Kenny Hodder) and we always discuss it and we always have a bit of a disagreement about it! Ken likes to find an area and bait up a couple of hundred yards out in the lake by using a boat to take the boilies out; but in between the area and the bank you might have a mile of weed and sunken gravel bars that you can lose fish on. To my mind, I would sooner draw the fish closer in; it definitely works; you can do it. Heavy prebaiting – not necessarily heavy – consistent prebaiting will often get the fish moving into the area. Then you can set about trying to pin down where you might catch them within that area. It doesn't pay to prebait too tightly in this kind of situation, because even within that area carp will still have preferred feeding spots. I'll come back to that.

My first big water was Yeoveney. My prime concern is always location; I mean, for example, you could be fishing at one end of a lake and not have a fish within half a mile, or even a mile of your baits. When I start off on a big water I try to find a vantage point where I can see a lot of the water; fish off the end of a point where you've got a view of as much of the lake as you can get so that I can keep watching that lake. I make a note of where I see fish roll or leap then you can begin to build up a pattern as to where these fish are or where they regularly patrol and then I try to find out if there's any reason why they prefer that area. Like Yeoveney, we fished there and we found some nice little bars not far out, which we thought were the ideal place and, sure enough, I started there one afternoon, and next morning I had a fish out, on sweetcorn. We thought that had to be the area and we spent an awful lot of time in that area. Kenny had one or two from that area but we never had any more. It wasn't until after watching the water, I noticed a few fish sort of rolling right on the far bank. I

Wraysbury again and another big mirror, this time at 34lb.

went round to that bank, it was a long, long walk; I fished from that bank and that's when I had the brace – from that bank; it was deep water. We had spent an awful lot of time in the daytime, when nothing was doing, just wandering around the lake, walking round, looking to see if we could find anything and quite often, you never even saw a fish.

One weekend, we found a few fish in a weed bed at the very top end; I threw some floater out to them and they weren't interested at all. That week I came home and I made up some floater, chopped it up into quarter inch cubes and I took a great big bag down there with me and I thought I'd just cover the weed bed with it; they've got to know it's there and they've got to sample it. So the following weekend I went down and sure enough, they were still in this weed bed; I threw the whole lot in and covered the weed bed. Over the period of the weekend, they started taking bits and we went back in the weed bed, feeding them with more floater and they were beginning to get quite confident on it. Unfortunately, we had planned to go down to Somerset for a week. We went down there and when we came back they had completely disappeared; we never saw them again. We might have had a chance if we'd tried for them. The funny part was, looking at those fish in the weed bed, I wouldn't have put any of them over 20lb. It wasn't until October, when Ken went down to Somerset again that I decided to fish the other area on the point on the far bank; I saw the fish beginning to roll and I knew that they were big fish. I didn't get fed up with that lake at all although I wasn't catching; you had the odd very slow take, it'd take the line off, you'd wait and you'd strike and you felt nothing; whether that was carp or what, I just don't know.

Yeoveney was a water I liked sitting on very much, it was so peaceful; there were no other anglers on it. It had so many features; one end was just bars, upon bars, upon bars with willow saplings growing off them where the water had gone down in the 1975/1976 drought and these willow saplings had grown up on these bars; there was every kind of weed there; the water was just full of life, different bugs or whatever. It was just so peaceful and so in that sense, I didn't mind sitting there all season. We'd been to Longfield and Yeoveney was so completely different. It was all new, although it was very like Wraysbury, I suppose.

When we started fishing Wraysbury I found that very hard work to begin with. Kenny managed to put a couple on the bank, floater fishing, walking round, finding a couple of fish

Wraysbury at the start of the 1986 season.

Pete with a magnificent brace of 38½lb and 36½lb from Yeoveney Lake.

and putting a floater to them, but to actually try and catch them off the bottom, trying to locate them, finding feeding areas was almost impossible. I found it very hard because we spent an awful lot of time fishing areas and not seeing a sign of the fish. In fact one season we spent nearly all season just fishing the North lake without even touching the South lake – and never had a fish. You find areas that you think you should catch from and you can't understand why you're not catching – they should be there. I feel, the more you put in, the more you are likely to get out. It's just persevering – very difficult to explain really, how you can go and sit on a water and catch one fish in a season. I never got the feeling, 'Oh my God, I've got to go there again'. I say that but I must admit that after doing about five years on Wraysbury No 1 you start to feel that you've done as much as you can and you want to move on. The thought of the very big fish kept me going back for eight or nine years but I haven't seen it for two or three years now so I've got to think it might have died. You can keep telling yourself it's just keeping out of the way for a couple of seasons, but then you start to lose faith and there's not a lot to keep you there after that.

I laugh about the first time we went to Harefield. That was nowhere near as big as Wraysbury. We decided to do the first week there. We got there and there was one other guy and he was set up in the Caravan Bay I think it was. I'll always remember it because he came round to us on the morning of the 15th of June (people started arriving in the afternoon – I think there was seven other people there for the start). He started chatting and he started telling us how *hard* this water was. He said he had had one fish out in a couple of years, nobody ever catches, they might get the odd one or two in a season. I turned round to Ken and I said, 'Ere Ken, I think he's trying to put us off; he thinks we aren't used to these hard waters'. It was comical really.

I've got to like a water. I couldn't just sit on any old water for a season or two seasons. I've got to like the water first. Like now, this season, we've been looking round, trying to find a water, but it's very difficult now. Most waters that have got big fish are known about, the carp have been fished for. We're just trying to find somewhere that's quiet, not many people fish there and that's got big fish. It's very, very difficult. Once I find it, I'm willing to sit it out.

Wraysbury is as hard a carp water as I'm likely to come across. When we first started there, not the first season, but certainly the second season, we prebaited very heavily. We used to go down two or three times a week prebaiting and the results were . . . it was a complete and utter waste of time. Because there were so few fish in there, they moved about an awful lot and they will only stop in one area for a maximum of two days and then they'll be off to another area. We started prebaiting with particles. Years ago we prebaited with maple peas, and the only problem with that was that we started catching loads and loads of tench. When we switched to the tiger nuts, we found it took four days before we got a take. The baits had to be out there four days. I think that was how long it took them to come across the baits. We had three or four fish and those baits had been out there for four days exactly. I'd get one when my baits had been out there for four days, then four days after he put the tigers out, Ken would get one. That's all very well but to me that isn't fishing, knowing you're going to have to wait four days before you get a take. I mean you often have to wait longer than that, but you don't know in advance that you're going to wait a long time. You're usually fishing with the hope that it's going to fly off at any minute – not four days after you get to the water! That's a joke.

I still like to use boilies on the big waters; I've used a lot of different particles over the years as well, but I do like the boilies, but, I

Wraysbury isn't noted as a commons water, but there are a few, and here Pete holds one of 25lb.

think you have got to be sure that the fish are in that area before you start baiting up.

I've had a look at a new water, I don't know whether we're going to fish it; it's a very big lake and it's all split up into little bays, loads of islands, but we've found a couple of interesting areas, deep water, very clean gravel in the margins and there's a few bars further out. You've got bars off the islands. What would I do? I would start off in those areas and work from there, just watching the water all the time, wandering around, looking, until I build up a picture of where the fish are, or where we think they're going to be.

I do a lot of plumbing, spend an awful lot of time plumbing, getting to understand the nature of the bottom. If there's a lot of weed in the lake I try to find clear gravel bars and fish either on the gravel bars or on the slopes of the gravel bars. You're looking for promising features. The other year I was fishing an island with overhanging trees. The fish used to come in underneath the trees. There was a gravel shelf running off the island; it was twelve foot deep but its shallowest part came out about three feet away from the island, then just sloped straight down to about sixteen, eighteen feet. You had to be very accurate with your casting to get on to that shelf in between the bushes. If you were a couple of feet short, your end tackle would just slide down the shelf. I found the difficulty there was holding on to that shelf because of the current and the weeds; so I made 4oz flat leads to hold out there but when you'd got a really strong wind I found that wasn't enough, I had to go up to 6oz. I wouldn't like to use the sea leads for carp. I had some problems but I've certainly caught a lot of fish that way. By plumbing, I found a little bar on open water, it was about eighteen feet all round it and this bar was about twelve feet deep – only a little bar; I put a marker out there because it was so difficult to find and I kept baiting that area, all the time, baiting and baiting and baiting and eventually, I started catching fish. I caught some nice ones. I think if you can find areas like that and if you're fishing an area, continually putting bait out, eventually the fish will come in onto that.

I've done well at Redmire and in Kent and on those smaller waters the main problem is getting the bait and presentation right. On bigger waters location is the major problem; they haven't had the pressure. Having said that, when I was fishing the shelf that I have described, I found that I was getting little lifts and couldn't get a decent take. I had to go right down to 4in hook lengths, fixed lead and a sort of semi-hair, to get a good take. I suppose I'm contradicting myself a bit there, because there was a presentation problem on that water. But you've got to believe in what you're doing. If you catch carp from small waters, particularly pressured waters like Darenth, then you can be confident that you will catch them on the big waters – provided you can find them.

What decides me on whether to fish a new, big water is simply seeing some decent fish in there, or if I have it on good authority that the fish are there. We've looked at a lot of waters; I've just come back today from looking at a water which, I have no doubt, should have a couple of good fish in it but it just didn't appeal. It was a big water but it just didn't look as if it had any life in it at all, really. I would like to see a few more fish in there. If it's got a few decent fish in there, it would be a big challenge; I'd quite like that.

The problem with the smaller big fish waters now is that there are too many people competing for the same fish, and really there are ten, fifteen, twenty anglers on waters that should only have two or three. When it's full up you can be fishing round one area, the fish could be rolling in another area but you know that there's no way you're going to be able to get to it because there are people already there: you're snookered. At the waters I fish on I usually get a fairly good choice. Having swim choice is critical. I fished a little water this last winter and I really enjoyed that, but even on that small water there was one particular area that the fish were coming out of all the time. Again, that was a funny water because you had to fish tight to the far bank, really tight. As soon as I saw the water I thought I'd be able to catch them under the rod tip, but no, they hugged the far bank. It's like the Redmire problem.

Bait placing is a major problem and on a massive water you can't be as precise as a little water; but you're going to have the same hot spot problem – and it takes a lot longer to find it. No matter how big the water is, there's only half a dozen swims at the most that are going to produce and you need to find those swims. If you are on a small water of a couple of acres, there's only one or two swims that normally produce and you've got the same thing with big waters.

It is getting harder and harder to find places that are a pleasure to fish and a big fish challenge. I can wait for ever for the right fish provided I really want to catch it and I like being there. I can understand that it's not everyone's cup of tea, but I need the space, and the mystery of the unknown, and the challenge. Carp fishing has got to be a challenge: I can't just keep fishing for known fish and repeat captures. There is a challenge in coming to terms with big, difficult waters and that's what keeps me going back to them. I've heard Wraysbury described as a carp water to retire onto; in other words you mustn't be in a hurry to catch fish from it because it might take you the rest of your life! Well I've left Wraysbury and I'm fishing the biggest carp water in England now – the Thames. It's a terrific challenge, and I've already had a few fish from it, including a couple of twenty pluses. I don't exactly know that I've retired onto it, but it will do me for a few years until something better comes along.

7 The Sixth Sense – Dowsing for Carp

Chris Yates

*I love Yatesy's book 'Casting at the Sun' and have reread it a number of times. His use of words excites me, as does his feel for fishing. One particular passage in Chris's book made a greater impact on me than any other, and that was the one that follows, which describes the workings of **instinct**. I was able to relate so well to the paragraph that I asked Chris to enlarge on it for 'Big Carp', which he does here. The paragraph is part of the lead in to the capture of his first Redmire monster, the common of 43lb 12oz; it appears in Chris's book (page 122) and is reproduced below.*

As far as I'm concerned, one of the most interesting things about fishing is the way it provides one's instinct with a unique opportunity to express itself. This is especially so with carp fishing. As I wait through day and night for something dramatic to happen, the long periods of calm settle my mind and give it a clearer depth. The moon rises and sets; the sun climbs out of the dawn mist and sinks into a haze of hot colour. Then, in the middle of all this, I suddenly notice how much I'm being attracted by a fairly nondescript corner of the lake, where nothing seems to be happening but where everything seems to be leading, so I up and trot along with my rod and prepare for a big fish. Had I just arrived at the lake I wouldn't have immediately sensed that potential. Only my surface thoughts would have been active for it takes hours of calm before my instinct becomes acute. But when it *is* sharp, when it helps me understand the atmosphere that hangs over certain things, when it gives me an insight into something that I have only a vague feeling towards, then I'm often transformed into a successful angler.

When discussing a subject like the sixth sense sceptics will always rationalise and claim it's nothing more than coincidence and luck. I admit that it can appear that I, an intuitive rather than a rational person, have been very lucky in my life. I will also admit that there are seemingly odd coincidences going on around us all the time. In fact there is a weird 'coincidence' happening even as I write.

I am not writing at home, where I normally work, but on a train. I am making the hundred-mile journey from Tisbury to London. The trip will take two hours and I shall be using the time to write this article (sic), which is long overdue and which has tested dear Tim's patience to the limit even before I penned the first word. (It will probably test his patience beyond the limit when he finally reads the finished product!)

When I got on the train I found it crowded and was lucky to get a seat. (There is a table as well so at least I can write in comfort.) The man sitting next to me saw the sub-title for the article and stunned me by saying 'I am a dowser too, but, like you, I dowse for things other than water. I dowse for deer.'!

We then had a long and stimulating discussion about the subject, comparing similar observations and experiences. I think that's a pretty good example of 'synchronicity', or the force of destiny, fate etc – or coincidence. Here I am with an article to write. I've written the title and sub-title and I'm then thinking how best to describe my subject – a subject a lot of people dismiss as pure mumbo-jumbo. What examples should I use to illustrate my argument – that there is nothing particularly unique or fantastic about the sixth sense? Then I encounter this total stranger who happens to be the first person I've ever met who thinks exactly as I do about 'the reality of the invisible' and has now given me all the encouragement I need to finish this in one go.

Excuse this preamble, but it nicely sets the scene. As I said, there are seemingly odd coincidences going on around me at the time. The more I'm aware of them the more they seem to happen. My belief is that it all depends on how the sixth sense responds to the potential of your surroundings.

Richard Walker believed in that, too, despite his scientific, materialistic turn of mind. Here's the beginning of an article he wrote in the late fifties:

> I'm going to run the risk of being thought crazy. I'm going to talk about something that may not be believed, isn't generally understood and is hard to explain. Success in angling comes from many things and I have always said that much of it comes from logical, intelligent thinking. Skill of hand plays a part, sometimes a very important part, but sound thinking comes first, especially when you are after big fish.
>
> I have to admit, though, that although an angler can succeed by using his brains and skill in combination, there is something else that can make him a good deal more successful; something that is difficult to name. I have heard it called instinct.
>
> For many years I knew that I could sometimes tell when a big fish, especially a big carp, was approaching my bait, even when it was quite dark and nothing could be seen or heard. I have sat quietly, relaxed and then suddenly become alert and ready, knowing that a bit would come in a minute or two. I never mentioned this to anyone, because I expected to be told that I wasn't taking enough water with it.

The article, entitled *The Angler's Sixth Sense*, went on to encourage ordinary, unintuitive anglers to develop their instincts and so become better fishermen, because – I quote again –

'everyone has such instincts, deep down, to some degree'. Richard also believed he could tell where the fish were in a given stretch of water just by switching his mind **off** and letting his eyes wander aimlessly across the surface. After a while he would find himself concentrating on a precise area, and a cast to that area would invariably produce a fish.

As far as I am aware there were no other anglers before Richard who had written on this subject, and only a few since. Though I've mentioned it in one or two articles and in my book '*Casting at the Sun*', I've never given it the space it deserves. Here's where I redress the balance.

As far as I'm concerned the evidence for the existence of this extra sense is now so overwhelmingly convincing that there should be no argument about it. But until I had personally experienced its influence I had no strong views about it, one way or the other. I certainly would never have believed that a time would come when the sixth sense would guide me towards the biggest fish in England. Even now, I sometimes shudder when I remember that, were it not for my instinct, I wouldn't be here at all. More about that later.

As I said in '*Casting at the Sun*' the main reason I sometimes catch an outstanding fish is because I now have an unshakable faith in my sixth sense. It's true that I have some lovely old cane rods, far superior to anything in graphite or boron: it's also true that I have some superb pre-war reels – and even the managing director of Shimano UK admitted to me last week that he couldn't match the craftsmanship of a Hardy Altex reel. But these are merely material objects, unimportant in the larger scale of things. My knowledge of a carp's habits, likes and dislikes is an obviously important part of my carp fisher's make-up. I can cast a reasonably straight line, with reasonable accuracy – though I've never caught a fish at a distance greater than fifty yards in my life. I can creep about as quietly as the next rat. But all these things are fairly insignificant when compared to my occasional flashes of vivid intuition, when I know with a cast iron certainty that if I do such and such a thing at a certain place then I *will* catch something worthwhile.

It's curious that my most vivid experiences of the sixth sense are all connected with my biggest fish and nearly all took place at Redmire. This isn't so much because of Redmire itself, as I used to think, but more to do with the fact that the place is peaceful and remote and undisturbed. When I'm fishing I need long periods of quiet if my instinct is really going to work and so somewhere like Redmire is perfect. I like a carp pool that allows me to feel my way about as much as I see my way about, therefore I need as few distractions from the actual fishing as possible. (This is why I detest all the usual twentieth century disturbances – planes, traffic, engines, crowds, artificial light at night and, naturally, the nasty electronic bleep of an Optonic.)

It can often take a while before my sixth sense really begins to tick, and I think this is because it takes time for me to settle into the slow rhythm of the landscape. It's like coming into a darkened room from a place of bright light; for a while you can see nothing at all, then, gradually, objects begin to appear from the dark and, finally, you can see your way around reasonably clearly. However, to take the analogy a bit further, most people are too impatient to wait for their vision to become more sensitive and they just switch on the nearest light. So, too, when they're fishing, they prefer to rely on familiar techniques and obvious evidence and never give their instinctive talents a chance.

At Redmire I sometimes became confident enough in my sixth sense to actually predict to others what was going to happen and, occasionally, I could even convince arch-sceptic Rod Hutchinson, whom I often fished with.

Chris with the first of his huge predicted fish, his August 1972 common of 43lb 12oz.

Like on the night I told him I was restless and couldn't sleep properly because I knew I was going to catch a monster; yet I also said I had no need to be restless, because I was sure the fish wouldn't come till after sunrise . . . And that's precisely what happened: the carp was a common of 43¾lb.

Bob Jones, whom I also fished with at Redmire, became so impressed with this kind of thing that he would come round to my pitch every evening for a fish forecast. (Unfortunately for Bob there was often a trough of low pressure hanging over his swim.) I never predicted an event that didn't happen and I foretold when I would catch all my best fish,

73

A happy Chris holds the biggest English fish of all time, his huge Redmire common of 51lb 8oz, another capture he knew about in advance, in this previously unpublished picture of the record.

but the circumstances surrounding the capture of my biggest carp were so extraordinary that when I wrote about them in my book – '*Casting at the Sun*' (Chapter 26) – I had to make a bit of a joke about it. Though I was quite content to accept the significance and importance of a barrage of premonitions, dreams and omens I could not expect anyone else to seriously believe me – even if the result was exactly as predicted, a gigantic carp on the first day of the season, beating the previous twenty-eight year old record by over seven pounds.

As I said most fishermen have experienced the workings of the sixth sense to some degree – whether they know it or not. Those two great anglers, Dick Walker and Jack Hilton, were both convinced of its importance and their recognition of it prepared them for some of their best catches. Therefore I was very interested and amused to read in Tim Paisley's latest book, '*Carp Season*', that Jack now believes the sixth sense to be evidence of something evil! Some of his most remarkable captures were preceded by a powerful sense of

Visions of carp, a creation of Chris's mind and camera.

foreknowledge, but Jack now seriously thinks this was a sign that he was being lured wickedly from his straight and narrow path. This is surely more unacceptable than the basic premise that the sixth sense exists in the first place; a rather strange point of view for anyone to adopt, especially Jack.

Jack was, without doubt, a very gifted and technically skilful angler, but what made him great was his ability to sniff out opportunities for big fish, to instinctively recognise that there were times when he couldn't fail. It was his greatest gift, though he claimed he was only rarely aware of it. However, instincts work at a number of levels; sometimes you just get a little chivvying message from it, which at least gives you confidence; sometimes it shouts at you; sometimes it's blank; sometimes it lights up the whole world with an inescapable truth that you had previously been blind to. Jack had a very logical, rational mind, but, when he fished, he consistently intuited the potential of his surroundings.

As we know Jack's passion for angling suddenly dried up, and, having other stimulating interests in life he succumbed to one of the many religious sects that are so eager to save our souls. I don't mind creeds like the Jehovah's Witnesses, but I wish they'd keep themselves to themselves. They have ideas even more peculiar than my own and when, like the Witnesses, they teach a man to deny one of his most precious natural gifts – by saying it's evil – then I think they should be publicly censured.

However, I suppose it's understandable. Nearly all the western religions have been anxious about the seemingly powerful magic of the sixth sense. It's something that doesn't fit into their cosy view of the world. If this was the fifteenth century they would happily burn me at the stake.

Just to put the 'evil spirit' view of Jack and the Jehovah's Witnesses in a different perspective: naturally the sixth sense does not only work in fishing, or hunting. As with those coincidences talked about earlier it's working, to a greater or lesser degree, all the time. And far from being malign, as the Jehovahs believe, it can obviously be useful and benign. It even saves lives. On a number of occasions, while driving a car, or riding a motorcycle, I have reacted instinctively to a hazard that *wasn't even visible or audible* and have thus saved myself from serious injury, or even death. One such incident – while travelling at over 100mph on a motorbike – would certainly have resulted in death had I not suddenly braked, for no initial apparent reason, and so avoided a lorry that

reversed without warning out of a concealed drive. And when I've been a passenger in a car it's occasionally happened that I've shouted a warning to the driver before a potential disaster became apparent. I can't imagine how anyone can interpret such things as being proof of evil within us.

As I've mentioned religion I suppose I should say, in case you were wondering, that I don't adhere to any creed or spiritual cult. All organised religions – from Christianity to Islamic Fundamentalism – neuter a person's imagination by forcing him to conform to a fairly limited view of life. As far as I'm concerned there are no established, conventional, formalised beliefs that are truly adequate, truly equal to this magnificent, abused, awesome world. To return to our original subject the most magnificent and most awesome aspects of this world can only be viewed through the lens of the sixth sense.

I'm getting a bit rarefied now and my new friend the deer dowser has reminded me that there should be nothing other worldly about this subject. We should all be able to benefit from something that, to us, is as ordinary as our sense of smell. But just as some people have no ear for music and no eye for painting there will always be some who will never appreciate or understand this most valuable faculty. The deer dowser uses his instinct to professionally track down animals in forests and mountains, and he hopes to extend his talents so that he can offer his services to the police in their search for missing persons or wanted criminals. I sometimes find big fish merely, as Dick Walker advised, by letting my thoughts flow over the water until I realise that I'm concentrating fixedly on a certain spot. Occasionally, and for unknown reasons, it's more dramatic and spectacular than this and I know I'm going to succeed even before I set out for the water – though all the conditions might be against me, and my common sense tells me that I'm being daft.

8 Slow Mud*

Elliott Symak

With gnats in my mouth and dust up my nose, I brave the raw world for the sake of a bite. Hands scratched to shreds and dirt on my clothes, only ending my sojourn come onset of night. Well that's the way close-range fishing, the subject of this chapter, often is.

Close-range fishing: fishing off the rod tip. Terms we've come to associate with carping but which, on many waters, is unfashionable or often impracticable. As far as the unfashionable aspect is concerned, I find it sad that one of the most enjoyable facets of fishing for Cypry – the eyeball to eyeball contact, as it were – lies neglected. Ah well! Perhaps I'll persuade some of you to chance your arm at a stroll round your local lake, rod in hand, instead of sitting **all** the time behind the Optonics.

It's rather fitting that I should write this chapter as I must confess to being well behind everyone else in the technical aspects of catching carp. I'm a positive dullard when it comes to fishing at seventeen miles range with a rocket-launched lead, micro boilie and state-of-the-art gear – so I could hardly write the clever stuff, could I? I'm not knocking the distance boys, though – admire 'em really and the results they get, even if I don't do a lot of it myself.

Generally, the waters I've found myself on are small to medium sized clay and gravel pits, often deep away from the margins, the shallower ones posing weed problems.

Having fathered four children, two of them boys, it was inevitable, I guess, that the bug which has driven me on for many years would infect the boys at least, and so it has transpired, although they are afflicted with the fishing curse in rather different ways. Jay, the eldest, likes to fish for small stuff generally, catching roach with hemp being his favourite occupation at the present time. Boysie, at sixteen a veteran catcher of good fish, is the same side of the coin as myself and he's the reason I mention my sons because his pictures and some of his thoughts are featured in this section of Tim's book. In fact, Boysie's theory about carp reaction to negative flavour baits is an interesting one which, although I'm sure has been voiced before, hasn't been worked out by too many sixteen year olds. The theory in a little while.

So carp are moving about on a steep ledge on the windward side of a hole in the ground clay pit – the Gildenburgh. All around were underwater bushes, long dead, giving the carp a feeling of safety despite their proximity to the bank and the clarity of the water. I used to watch 'em from behind bankside cover, Polaroids on nose, the edge of the bank six feet above the lapping surface; or I would sit twenty feet up a large tree which had grown outwards over the water. Right above their backs I was, sitting on a thick branch. Sometimes I took a rod aloft but mostly the gear was at the base of the tree and I was upstairs, just observing, throwing in bits and pieces – floaters, sinkers, watching the fish's reaction to this alien fare. Observation; all the old-time carp anglers will

* This title concerns a Sunday, July 1989 trip to Ely Cathedral (via Friday Bridge).

77

know the pleasures (and advantages) of watching carp and seeing how they approach the matter of eating a lump of bait thrown into the water and even, more simply, how they glide about their 'safe' lairs with such effortless grace.

The Gildenburgh carp glided so! Low double figure fish – rarely one bigger. Lean, belt-buckled-in fish, but, as far as I was aware, never hungry enough to take the bait of anyone who had the gear to land them. Sometimes the time seemed ripe to try and catch these Gildenburgh carp; food was put in a line from the bank, the further ones disappearing into the mud at the bottom of the gradient amongst the detritus-coated bushes. The idea was to let the fish get the taste of the bait in their sanctuary and, hopefully, follow up the trail to a position on the slope where I dare put a hook bait without fear of instantly losing my tackle.

Now and then the trick worked – although those tigerish fish often took the line against a great, pulsing curve in the rod, round the sunken undergrowth and pinged the line like cotton. Action which took perhaps five or ten seconds after hours of patiently waiting. I landed a fish now and then, though, fish which had never before seen the dryness of a grassed bank. Even caught one on a family outing, one Sunday, against all the odds, whilst my children played in the pile of sand that I had persuaded my wife would entertain them, thus justifying the trip, with rod, to the water.

That particular water is now owned by a business man whose income is derived, to a degree, by divers - scores of 'em − who play under the surface at all times of day and night, so if permission was available to fish, I doubt very much whether these people, generally in total ignorance of our need for solitude, would ever give us half a chance to con a carp into eating a bait.

Although the Gildenburgh is a fairly large hole in the ground and offered few spotting trees, the fish were reasonably easy to locate because the only serious feature on the water were a couple of reed beds and those snags. Snags, reed beds, weed beds, overhanging trees; carp love 'em, whether they are on large or small waters and, of course, many of these features are bank-side, making them accessible to the angler. These features though, often necessitate violent action when a fish is hooked, which leads to hefty tackle, of course.

Since I began carp fishing I have been regularly using braided terylene as a matter of course. In the sixties I used Black Spider (it was black!), then, in the seventies followed Micron (white) usually of 15lb test dyed with felt-tip pen, and more recently there have been braided lines coming onto the market, custommade for the carp angler. Micron, though has not yet been surpassed to my mind. I am rather cheesed off, I must admit, to being ripped off by tackle manufacturers and sellers these days, so if I can I avoid buying terylene with some 'famous' person's name on its spool, but in the lighter strains, I have to capitulate I'm afraid and line an unworthy pocket or two.

At one stage, in the early seventies, when I found it difficult to buy the braided line I required, I bought some American braided of 25lb test which was multi-coloured and horrible. But I still caught on it!

My off-the-rod-tip line then, when there are snags or reeds about, is braided terylene. In many circumstances it is necessary to hook, hold and land a big fish in a small area; fishing within the confines of reed beds, for example, does not allow for the niceties one could fairly claim to be associated with 'standard' carp fishing.

Whatever Tim Paisley, or anyone else, says about knots, I still feel more confident of a line whose only knot is the one which secures the hook, so for this violent type of fishing you will not find my line adorned with swivels, nor will it be backed with nylon. Give me 100 per cent proof braided please. I have now settled for one

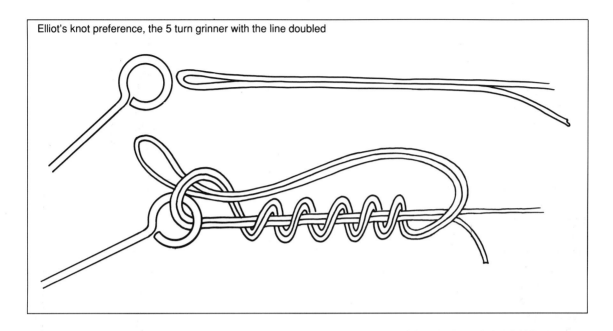

Elliot's knot preference, the 5 turn grinner with the line doubled

knot for everything – braided, nylon, multi-strand – and that is the doubled half blood (*see* sketch). Rather wasteful on line but once tested and a good one tied you are onto a winner.

Why braided line? After a heck of a lot of years using the stuff and having extracted a large pile of carp from various jungles with its help, it is not unnatural I have a great deal of confidence in the stuff. For a start, braided line does not 'go off' as nylon is prone to do, so you will not find the line pinging for no reason just as you are doing battle with the biggest carp in the lake. Terylene seems also more capable of handling rough and abrasive treatment than nylon, such as rubbing against reeds or branches when under tension. Also, there is no stretch in terylene, so those few extra inches aren't conceded to Mr or Mrs Carp which could make the difference between a fish or a tree branch. Yet another plus with terylene is the fact that if you buy the white variety, you can dye it to suit the circumstances of the swim being fished. Nylon, of course, casts much better than terylene, but fishing off the rod tip

Elliott with a 26lb plus mirror caught from a willow.

79

doesn't entail a lot of distance chucking anyway.

I was fishing a small swim, three feet of water surrounded by bushes and reeds. Several fish had been moving in and out of the swim during the course of the morning and the past half hour they had begun to take a serious interest in the few boilies on the deck. The water being shallow enough I could, initially, see the bait six feet out and all I wanted was for a fish to merely mouth the bait and I would be in. Trouble was, the bottom was very silty and every time a fish went down to feed on baits, a cloud of silt bloomed upwards, making it impossible to keep an eye on the bait with the hook in it.

The carp, being pretty canny, after years of hooks and lines slung at them, could eat all the spare baits in a swim and leave the hook bait sitting there, feeling lonely (they'd done it often enough!). They would, of course, mouth the bait, which was where the visual aspect came in, but under the cloud of silt they would eject it upon feeling the hook or line. To watch indicators for signs of a bite in these circumstances was a waste of time, as brushing against the line, which carp continually do in these swims, gives rise to false indication. What the hell do you hit?

Now there is a clever little idea called the bolt rig. Why not use that? Well, I don't want a big fish to hurtle off in self-hooked panic when the reeds are only feet away and there are sunken branches to right and left; it's hard enough playing the buggers as it is, without giving them a chance to get a move on before the strike. Who'd give Ben Johnson ten metres start?

In the circumstances so described, I often resort to the float and swan shot method. Push on a piece (½in) length of valve rubber over the hook and up the line, set a light 4in float at estimated depth, pinch on the shot, which will sink the float (won't it!) two or three inches

from the hook and keep dipping until only the tip of the float is above the surface. If the bait and shot are encouraged to rest close to a reed stem or weeds, this helps to make the set-up less obvious to the carp. Setting the float has to be done gently and slowly, but if you are quiet and keep at least some cover in front, or partially in front of you, then the fish need not be spooked.

With the carp moving about the swim, the float tends to move too. Back and forth it will swing, sometimes travelling along the surface half a foot sometimes bobbing under – surely a bite? But no, not a bite! With nerves steeled against all this dithering, wait until the float pops up and lies flat, then strike.

I've been thinking about this way of fishing, you know, and I reckon knowing when to strike is one part practical and two parts instinct. Doesn't always work, though. Sometimes the carp are spooked by the heavy terylene, although not often; sometimes their enthusiastic excavating of the bottom, lifts bait, hook and float, and the strike results in the tackle sitting in a bramble thicket behind the right shoulder; now and then the tackle will be pushed round a reed stem or sunken branch and you'll never get it back. However, despite these blights, 'tis well worth pursuing this float fishing line.

When regularly fishing where carp can be seen, it becomes apparent that (a) carp are often territorial, and, (b) some regularly patrol a 'beat'. There are ifs, buts and maybes in everything, of course, no less so in trying to fathom out the *predilections* of carp, but with enough observation, the interception points can be worked out.

Many times, when a carp is just wandering around, an interesting item of food in its path can be enough to encourage it to revisit the spot until it has the face to pick the bait up, so one shouldn't despair if a carp keeps turning its nose up at a hook bait; eventually it may.

Particularly favourite areas, literally the carp's 'dinner plates', can be identified by a reduction in the amount of debris in the form of leaves and twigs. Sometimes there are clear patches in weeded areas which the carp keep clear by their continuous rooting around. I have heard it said that carp do not worry unduly about anti-tangle tubing on the bottom, but I think this observation is made by people who have never seen a 'feeding spot' where the bottom is perfectly clear of debris. Generally, perhaps, carp don't seem too put off by tubing (although I have no doubt they are alerted), but in some spots I am sure they are. If you were about to eat your Shrove Tuesday pancake wouldn't *you* notice a bicycle pump lying across it?

I talk about seeing these carp and fishing off the end of my rod with some glibness, don't I, as if all waters can be treated the same way? Well, why not? Many waters have sanctuaries in which the presence of weeds, reeds, snags or bushes give the carp a feeling of safety from the nasty old men on the bank. Perhaps it might mean getting wet or stung to reach them, but it is well worth it. Effort! A creep around in midweek, perhaps early in the morning when most anglers are asleep in their bivvies, or perhaps late evening when tackle is being settled for the night, tea being drunk and yarns being shared, could prove fruitful. After I had just drafted the above, Boysie went down (for his first trip to the waters) to a new syndicate we had joined. Two lakes to choose from, he found that the 'in' lake had about a dozen bivvied up anglers on it, none having any action. On the lake next to it, there was no one. A period spent stalking 'em with floater resulted in a lovely 21¼-pounder. The chap who obligingly took a picture or two said he had been sitting for several days since the season had begun, without a bite. Bet he never got off his backside to do more than pee, chat, cook his meals or re-cast!

You have to be quiet and stealthful when

Stalking territory.

fishing close in and how many people can be bothered? Can you actually *be* quiet enough not to scare a carp five feet from the bank in three feet of water? Close in fishing isn't all creeping about though, sometimes a nice comfy swim can be chosen, the bed chair set up, Optonics uprighted and food and drink laid to hand. Once again though, quietness must be observed and the essential cover in front of the swim left undisturbed. Surprising how carp, who regularly patrol the margins, will not make a detour out into the lake to avoid you if they are not aware of your presence! So the margin fished baits can score again. It's fair to say, though, that if you stay in one swim for an extended period, days for example, the fish become aware of your presence eventually.

Having used rods of varying lengths over the years for stalking carp, I still cannot say 'such and such' a length is right. Conditions change from swim to swim, but, were I forced to settle for one rod, it would be ten feet long, 2lb test and an action through to the butt. Don't forget that usually strong line is required – also, don't forget the net!

There are cases, of course, where 'normal' gear is suitable for stalking, so really it is a matter of weighing up the conditions before venturing to wet a line. There is little point, though, in fishing for carp with tackle which, should a fish take the bait, proves completely inadequate for the task involved in landing it.

The stalker.

In the very worst conditions I use 30lb test braided line, knowing that with the rod bent right round, maximum pressure on and the biggest fish in the lake battling away, unless the line catches anything, it cannot break.

One point must also be remembered if you wish to treat close in fishing with any seriousness – don't go stalking without your rod! By the time you rush back to that monster you spotted feeding merrily away on the other side of the lake, she will be long gone.

And so to a close look at the favourite stalking habits of Boysie and myself; surface and sub-surface baits.

Much has been written about catching carp 'off the top', but often it seems alien to the way we fish. We live in a world where controllers rarely exist, where line on the surface is anathema, where home made baits are cooked and used without a flavour, where the hookbait is the only piece the carp have to choose from or is different entirely to the 'groundbait', where the 'floater' can well sink like a stone!

Again, weed beds, reed beds and waterside bushes are the favourite areas we look for when floater fishing, and the wind strengths and direction can have a marked effect on results. On the conventional side, there can be no dispute that floaters drifting down a lake, pushed by a steady breeze, often prove irresistible to carp, but a hookbait cast amongst them is often ignored because of the line on the surface or the way it affects the natural movement of the floater. Lilies and weed such as Hornwort flowering on the surface are interception points for wind-drifting floaters, the secret being to lay the line over the plants whilst keeping the bait on the windward edge of the plant. If your carp are encouraged to feed by the introduction of a lot of floaters, such as some of the proprietary brands of dog and cat food, then a level of pre-occupation can be achieved. Mind you, so many cat foods have gone into (onto) lakes in the past ten years or more that carp

Elliott's son Boysie with a stalked small water common of 32lb plus.

Boysie again with a mirror of 23½lb mirror.

now are beginning to drink bowls of milk and purr a lot, so they may well be cagey about hookbaits. In such a case, put in one food as 'groundbait', say Chum Mixers, and fish something completely different amongst them, say a piece of brown, home made floater. Or use 'Go-Cat' hoops as attractor and a bunch of maggots on the hook. I think, though, that just odd baits scattered around a likely looking area and the hookbait waiting on the bank for signs of feeding carp is one of the best ways of fishing. When the carp begin to take them the bait is cast to an interception point, drawn back to the weed and carefully watched.

Fishing in open water is a pain, but a couple of methods I use are as follows: the first entails a set-up as shown in the sketch. The leading bomb (a heavy one) is tied with line half the b.s. of the main line, is cast across a *bay* or

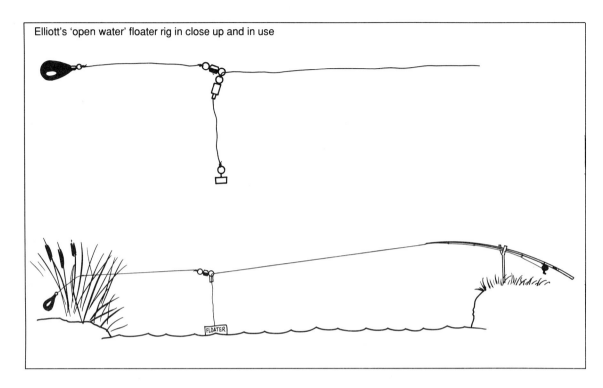

Elliott's 'open water' floater rig in close up and in use

FLOATER

narrow stretch of water to opposing reeds/ bank/bushes. The rod is pointed upwards and line reeled in until everything is tight, with just the bait resting on the surface. To reach this state of affairs may take some time and effort but on a windless day it can be quite effective. A three-way swivel can be used, although I prefer a simple swivel and split ring.

The second open water method entails sitting in a tree! I've caught quite a few large fish – to near thirty pounds, in fact – whilst sitting in the upper branches of willow trees, but it is sometimes advisable to have a netsman handy. The appeal and advantage of tree fishing are instantly obvious, of course. A good view of the lake, the facility to see exactly what the carp are up to and the chance to select the largest fish in a feeding group on 'patrol'. If the water is shallow enough, it is also possible to fish a sighted bottom bait as described earlier. Fishery rules may dictate tree fishing is out, of course,

and to be on the cautious side it *is* only for an expert (or an idiot) really.

There are two varieties of fishing trees; ones which overhang the water and ones which overlook the water. Wear trainers, not wellies or Skeetex boots for ascending them, and do take care. I've had one or two potentially nasty accidents through descending trees rather rapidly! Boysie recently fell out of a tree and lay, without the use of his legs for twenty minutes. Subsequently, he had a while off work with his bruised (not, thank God, broken) back. He won't be climbing trees again wearing Skeetex boots.

Overhanging willows are the easiest to fish floaters from; you simply dangle your floater beneath the rod tip in the spot you've decided is the best one (presumably after careful observation). Ensuring line is not touching the water is not too difficult if you've a steady hand and there is not a lot of breeze blowing. If you are prone to excitability, then the best thing to do is to somehow lay the rod on the branches until a take comes. If the breeze is strong, then you have to try and 'go with it', or put some weight on the line above the hook.

The best open water floater fishing times are when there is at least a breeze, and I suggest that you fish the bank towards which the wind is blowing; catapult out free offerings as far as possible, allowing them to drift back to you, and hopefully alerting the carp to the food. This way of fishing can be very exciting and as soon as the bait goes down the tunnel is the time to strike. Crazy game, fishing from trees, but interesting and rewarding!

Andy Little, a versatile carp catcher playing a stalked carp.

I've never standardised my floater baits. I tend to use whatever boily mix I have to hand, mixing with plenty of eggs and pouring the subsequent sloppy mix into a flat, rectangular baking tray. (I'm not saying though that this attitude is the right one.) I aim to make the bait ¼ to ½in thick. When the floater is cold and extracted from the tray I cut it into ¾in wide strips and freeze it.

Because I have always felt that a flavour at this stage is a waste of money, I don't use any in the cooking process. I believe that most of the time carp which take floaters don't give three hoots about the smell of the bait; they tend to take them regardless. At least this seems to be the case with my floaters and this is where Boysie's (earlier mentioned) theory comes in. He reckons that because our baits aren't carrying a specific label, the carp are not instantly *alerted* to danger and accept the bait that much more confidently. This idea could, of course, apply to bottom baits as well.

In a favourite pitch carp had been moving about for a while, swimming back and forth underneath the floating raft of dead reed stems which the breeze had pushed into the corner of the swim. Home made floater thrown onto and against the three foot wide swathe of reeds had been ignored by the fish, but their attitude suggested they could well be tempted to take a bait. Like one of our winter quarries, the chub, carp like cover over their heads, this roof giving them some kind of confidence, and it was onto this canopy I cast a lump of well boiled sausage. I allowed a little slack line, enabling the bait to tip off the mat of reeds and disappear from sight, then I gently pulled back until I could just feel the resistance of the bait under the reeds. Allowing a little slack line (the weight of the line on the intervening reeds holding the bait in position), I clicked over the bale arm and sat on the grass next to my rod, watching the slack line from my rod tip to the water. Still the carp cruised slowly underneath the dead reeds and my eyes kept drifting over to the spot instead of concentrating on the slack line. Suddenly, just as I'd watched a big mirror glide out of sight under the raft, I caught, in the corner of my eye, a movement of the line. Instantly I responded to the now tightening line and struck into a lunging fish which pulled, with great power, for the sanctuary of the standing rushes. The raft was torn apart in the fight, but, not allowing the carp to pick up any speed, nor get its head down, I coerced it in my direction and eventually the fight was conducted under the rod tip. Another good fish on the bank and I have caught fish under rafts more than once since.

Polaroids; black matchman's visor on forehead; ten foot through action rod; 10 to 30lb line, depending on the circumstances; strong Drennan hooks or the longer shanked Jack Hiltons; landing net and perhaps, one rod rest; rubbers; shot and spare hooks; a bag of floaters and a few boilies (just in case). Lightly kitted, able to move around even a large lake without too much effort. The line can be nylon or terylene, but usually my faithful 15lb Micron is wound on the spool. The biggest drawback with stalking gear in reeds is the modern landing net. Oh for a round one!

Quietly and slowly moving around in likely looking swims where conditions earlier described are likely to attract and hold carp. The bankside vegetation is used as cover and I am careful to watch where I put my soft shoe clad feet, as carp can be so sensitive to vibration.

In the smaller swims, I do not throw in many free offerings – perhaps one or two, maybe be none – because carp taken whilst stalking are often fish on the move; they may only be interested in taking a tit-bit here and there on their travels. Confronted with one bait (with a hook in it!) they may well be fooled, but if several baits are available, then the chances of getting the hook bait taken are reduced.

When carp are moving slowly through swims near the bank it is often difficult, in shallow water at least, to decide whether to fish surface or bottom. Knowing the water helps in this instance. For example, Redmire fish we are told, do not respond to surface baits, so it would be rather pointless nicking on a little piece of floater on such a water. Generally, though, carp will go for surface or bottom baits, so I would flick in half a dozen bottom baits and a couple of surface baits.

Although I have not had much luck with the method, I know some success has been had by presenting a bait a few inches below a float, to meet cruising carp. Also, I've failed to catch much when the bait is fished midwater, from an anchorage on the bottom (I'm talking here a foot or more off the bottom), but this method, too, has accounted for numbers of carp. This set up for midwater fishing looks like something out of a fifties war in the Atlantic movie, with the angler as Jack Hawkins laying underwater mines and the carp playing the part of a U-boat, *carefully* avoiding being blown up. Not for me! There has been much written about 'controllers' and I've even seen anglers fishing under their rod tips using them, but these floating weights used for casting out and *controlling* floaters haven't helped me a great deal over the years, I'm afraid. They are worthy of study though and can be a great asset in some conditions.

The best situation for floater fishing is against or amongst reeds, surface weed beds or at the bankside towards which a light breeze is blowing. Fishing amongst reeds is the best of the lot, I reckon, but to fish the way I do entails having the bait in sight all the time, plenty of patience and steady hands. If you are clever, you will throw baits into likely looking areas of reed beds during the course of normal fishing, letting the carp get used to finding tit-bits over a period of weeks, perhaps.

So how is the spot chosen? The waters I fish

A surface carp happily feeding under the cameraman's feet.

tend to promote the growth of Norfolk reed which carp like to get amongst; if there are areas of dead reed, then so much the better, as they thin out and manipulating the bait amongst them is not difficult. 'Round-up', by the way, is the stuff to use on reeds if they are becoming too widespread. Used at its stated dilution, and whilst the reeds are growing, this killer is perfectly 'environment friendly.' (A slight contradiction in terms!)

Look for areas near to the bank where the reeds are less dense. Sometimes you will find a clear area a yard or so across and there you will probably find carp. Observing the fish for a time, or watching their passage by the movements of the reeds, gives a good indication as to the favoured areas. Beware of cheap imitations, though. Reed Buntings, Warblers, tench, pike and eels, not to mention small fish, coots and water voles all like to move about in reed beds. The parting of reeds by a large carp is usually quite unmistakable!

Carp tend to mop up small items off the surface more readily than big ones, so my bits of floater are usually little finger to thumbnail size. The hook tied to Micron has to be strong, which means when the set up is in the water, the bait turns turtle and the hook hangs upside down, or the lot sinks; so you have to hang the line on the upright reeds, or, perhaps, if you are lucky, over a horizontal reed stem or leaf.

Only the smallest portion of the bait is nicked by the hook, then, and presuming you're not daft enough to throw it at a carp's head, the bait is swung out (almost always an underhand lob) past the intended spot. By engaging the bale arm and gently lifting the rod, it is possible to pull the bait through the reeds: when the chosen area is reached you wait for the bait to stop spinning or wafting about, then try to lower it onto the surface. Sometimes it remains in the air! By lifting and dropping the bait, though, it will eventually pop onto the surface, hopefully in the spot you wanted it. It *is* important to pick the right spot and be happy with the bait presentation, so if it takes several casts to get things to your liking, then that's the way it has to be. Your line, you will find, usually rises vertically from the bait.

Well, that's the easy bit over with, now you have to hold the rod and be patient and *vigilant*. It is often necessary to continually make small adjustments to the top heavy bait, due to wind action or even carp action! Small fish, fortunately, do not make too much of a nuisance of themselves in reed beds and if there is a problem, then the bait can be pulled half an inch above the surface of the water until the quarry is around. (If the wait is long and you don't feel you wish to hold the rod all the time, then the landing net, placed at an angle on the reeds in front of you, makes a very good rod-rest.)

Balancing the bait at times requires the steady hand I spoke of earlier, especially when a big carp pops along and shows interest in the bait! If you sensibly haven't offered any free baits to the fish, then there is no choice, is there? It's the hookbait or nothing. What happens when the fish attacks the bait varies, but if you have picked your spot well, and especially if you have been 'groundbaiting' for a protracted period, the carp may well feel safe and confidently suck the bait in. Strike! You must watch the bait intently, though, as sometimes the carp take a sideways swipe at it to see how it reacts and this can be mistaken for a take. Sometimes, too, the fish will suck at the bottom of the bait, again to see how it reacts; if you can give a little slack line at just the right time, those lips will encompass bait and hook. I've had soft baits sucked right off the hook when Mr Carp has been a clever clogs! I've had baits chased a couple of circuits round the reed stem the line is on, too, which is a bit of a pain when it comes to retrieving the tackle. Once I even had a carp trying to suck in a floater which was several inches above the water – but this tale concerns a 34lb common and can wait for another day. In clearer water, where I dare use lighter hook and line, a pyramid-shaped floater, with the hook nicked in the apex offers some stability.

Fishing these places, then, is quite a waiting game – and exciting it is too – but on red hot days, instead of moving round the reeds and (hopefully) finding your well placed floater, the carp will lie still in their chosen spot for hours at a time, or so it seems. The last resort – desperation tactics, really – is chasing the carp, which means finding the head end of the quarry and putting a bait to it. Now is the time when I'll put some kind of flavour on my floater in an effort to stimulate the fish into moving its ass instead of sunbathing. There is

quite an element of skill in dragging back to the right reed stem and lowering the floater *gently* to within inches of the carp's nose without spooking it, but it can be done, given a pinch of luck and a following wind (metaphors abound!).

I think this chapter will give some idea as to the possibilities available to anyone who is prepared to make an effort in their carp fishing. To the 'expert' who is after a special fish, there is a message, loud and clear: *selectivity*. All this work is concerned with watching carp; watching carp take baits. A day spent up a tree watching can be more rewarding than a month spent slinging a bait to the limits of your latest carbon thirteen footer.

In my book, '*Mywater*', I talk about a swim called 'The Secret Place', which was a small area on the lake people were not allowed to fish and was only accessible to anyone prepared to risk nettles and brambles, not to mention my wrath! When there was no one on Mywater, or incumbents were asleep, I used to sit in this place where the carp felt supremely safe, and feed them, waiting for the time when the biggest fish in the lake could be spotted and lured to his or her fate. As it happened, I gave up waiting in the end and settled for one or two lesser fish (read all about it in '*Mywater*') but the principle still holds good; if you can find a spot off the beaten track for your 'Secret Place' – middle of a bush, hole in a reed bed – and get the carp to regularly feed in it, you can be patient and wait until the one you want to hook comes along. Could take a month, could take two seasons, but the possibilities are there.

When the water starts rocking, the heart begins pounding.

9 The Triumvirate

Brian Garner

In his book 'The Carp Strikes Back' Rod Hutchinson says of Ritchie Macdonald that he 'has the knack' of catching big fish. Brian Garner also has that knack, and his record of big fish from the north west is second to none. He doesn't like travelling too far for his fish which means that for the most part his big fish have to be caught from his own patch, not an easy objective unless you live in one of the country's hot beds of big carp fishing. At the time of writing Brian has what must be a unique distinction – three different thirties from one north west water. The story of the captures is worth the telling because the manner of the achievement is an object lesson for any would-be big fish carp man.

I believe that Tim is writing a piece about Birch Grove and the Mangrove for his book: the events that follow took place on one of those waters – the Mangrove – and span five years of hard fishing.

I got to know about the Mangrove through fishing Birch Grove. The Mangrove was a water a number of us knew about, but we didn't know it held carp, let alone big carp. Then one day while I was fishing Birch one of the locals dropped out that Tim was fishing the Mangrove, and why wasn't I on it? I soon was! This is going back to 1985, and because I didn't know it contained carp until July, and the water closed down before the end of August, my time on it was very limited that first season. It was exciting, though, because we'd no idea what we were fishing for, and it fished well that summer.

The furthest south I've fished is a gravel pit in Buckinghamshire. The first thing that struck me when I went south was that in some ways the fishing was different from the approach we have in the north west. I've always been used to fishing over seeds and particles – where it's practical – with a good protein bait. The southern lads seemed less interested in the seed and particle bed than I am and tended not to bother with creating a feeding area. That's not meant as a criticism, but we do find the fish to be more catchable when the boilies are part of a feeding area, rather than the feeding area itself.

The kettle's on as Brian sits it out in the waiting game.

My memories of that first Mangrove summer are a bit vague, beyond the fact that it was wet and windy most of the time. I mentioned 'we', and that covers John Lilley, Roy Stallard and Steve Allcott, whom I'd known from fishing Hawkstone Park and Birch Grove, and one or two other regulars. I don't think Tim fished the water much that summer, and I certainly didn't see him or any of his friends there. When I say my memories are vague that doesn't apply to the last weekend before the shut down for shooting. I'll never forget that session.

I should just mention that in addition to the problem of the water only being open for ten weeks – which makes establishing a bait very difficult – there was, at this time, very limited angling access to the lake. Only about a third of it was fishable then, although that situation has been rectified over the last couple of seasons. So we were fishing a water crammed with natural food, that shut down just as the carp were getting interested in feeding on baits each year, and which contained plenty of unreachable areas where the fish could keep out of the way. You can see the problem, but I loved the place from the first time I went there so the problems were immaterial really.

That last weekend of my first season I arrived at the lake late Thursday afternoon. My hours were six till two, and finishing at two meant missing out on the regular overtime, and not going in Friday meant taking a day's holiday. But I'm used to the pressure angling of the north west's popular waters and take as much of my holidays as I can in the form of long weekends. Roy was fishing Reed Warblers and John was in the Field Swim. Both had taken good fish during the week but I was staggered to learn that Roy had caught a common weighing 32lb. We all had a fair idea of the potential of this very rich water but to be honest this fish surpassed everything beyond my imagination.

The wind was very strong from the west,
blowing across Roy and John into the trees on the east bank of the water. I was hoping that with the pressure they had been under the fish might have moved down with the wind and with this in mind I set up in the trees with the wind blowing directly towards me.

The first job was to get the baits in before dark. The usual method was to bait up round a marker, and we were fortunate in having the use of a boat to do this. However by the time I'd set up the wind was so strong that using the boat was not possible, so for the time being I had to make do with firing out two pounds of bait with the wrist rocket. The bait was a high quality HNV flavoured with garlic and soya oil and a spoonful of Kempy's (Geoff Kemp) liver extract as an additional smell. Stringers were attached to both rods – which were 12ft, 1½lb test curve Tricasts – and were cast into the baited area 80–90 yards out.

Once I'd sorted out the angling situation I was able to concentrate my efforts on setting up the bivvy for the three day session. I was well sheltered from the tearing wind by the trees because I was set up well back from the water. The platform I was fishing from was also well into the tree line and when the right hand rod roared off an hour after I'd set up I couldn't get a direct line to the fish when it kited. That meant I had to get into the water and wade out around the edge of the weed-bed to my right. Once out to the front of the reeds it became easier to play the fish, which turned out to be a beautiful golden common of 18lb 10oz. Photos were taken and the fish returned to the water straight away.

Darkness was setting in and I felt very confident; a fish within the first few hours of fishing was a good result. Hopefully there might be a few more out there getting their heads down. After a couple of hours without further action I decided to try to get a couple of hours sleep. During the early hours I was woken by my Optonics; a drop back, again on the right hand rod. My initial thought was that that there was an eel on the end, but when I set the hook my fears were soon dispelled; there was a carp on the end. However, getting out round the reeds proved to be no easy task in the pitch darkness, but the job was made easier by the landing net having been already positioned out in front of the swim. As with the first fish once I was out clear of the trees everything was all right; it was when the fish was in the net that the operation started to get difficult. Trying to walk back in deep silt with a landing net full of carp and a twelve foot carbon is no easy task, I can assure you. The fish turned out to be a two-tone mirror of 17lb 10oz. I stayed out by the rods for the next few hours, watching the dawn break slowly over the water, but there was no further action.

As soon I was sure we were too far into daylight for another fish I went round to John's swim to scrounge a brew. The usual carp angler's banter was taking place: 'Shh, was that Roy's buzzer?' I asked, so off we went to check. It turned out to be a false alarm, as we thought it would be; it's very unusual to get any action of any sort during the day on this water. Back we went to John's swim and back on went the kettle. 'SSShhh . . . are you sure that wasn't a buzzer?' I was at it again. 'I'm sure,' said John. 'Drink your tea.'

The day passed slowly, as days do on 'night only' waters. Late in the afternoon I decided to bait the swim for the coming night. The wind had died down by now and so I decided to use the boat. The marker float went out in the area I had been fishing the previous night and I scattered a big bed of particles round it, this being made up of groats and tiger nuts. Over the top of this I spread another two pound mix of the HNV boilies. Having done this I returned to the swim and the hook baits were cast out close to the marker, one to the left and one to the right.

During the course of the night I landed another three fish, two mirrors and a common, the largest fish going to 17lb. By morning I was well knackered, having had hardly any sleep at all. I wish the fish could arrange their feeding times around mine. I was so tired I had to get some sleep during the day, but around midday I was woken by the left hand Optonic screaming. The line was a blur coming off the spool. I jumped into the water trying desperately to keep a tight line on the fish, but it knew exactly where it wanted to go. Steve had set up in the swim to my left and it picked up both his lines and buried itself in the pads. I kept a tight line on the fish while Steve got the boat. After rooting around in the pads he eventually came back with the rig attached to one of the thick stalks. How do they get rid of the hook so easily?

I rebaited and recast to the marker straight away. It took me about six casts to get the end tackle in the right place, during which time I'd probably spooked every fish out of the baited area. To my amazement the left hand rod was away again almost straight away. I was still soaking from the previous fish so in I went again, up to my waist in horrible clinging silt. As before this fish tried to make for the pads but I had a better line on it this time and managed to turn him. After a brief scrap I put the net under a lively mirror weighing 13lb 12oz. Six fish in under two days. I was well pleased although, to be honest, I was slightly disappointed not to have made contact with one of the water's biggest residents.

Saturday evening arrived. I had already baited up the swim and was waiting in anticipation of the early hours feeding spell. I was fishing close to Steve and slipped round to his swim for a quick chat, leaving the rods out. 'Ssshhh . . . was that my buzzer Steve?' 'Don't be silly, it's a bird.' Sure enough it was my imagination working overtime again. After wishing each other luck I went back to my swim for the night's session, feeling very confident. The fish were feeding on the bait so it was just a question of keeping my fingers crossed and waiting.

It proved to be a frustrating night. The eels, which I had been dreading, moved onto the baits. During the course of the night I landed two but was kept awake by them mucking around with the hook baits. At quarter to three I had a drop back on the left hand rod. On winding down there was nothing there so I retrieved the bait and found it nearly all chewed away and the hook length covered in slime, so I replaced both. I was tempted not to recast and have a good night's sleep, but seeing this was to be my last night on the water I decided to stick it out.

I recast to the left of the marker, using a tree on the skyline as a guide, and clipped up the heavy isotope indicator at the top of the monkey climber. Almost immediately the indicator dropped back a couple of inches. I was furious; another bloody eel! I picked up the rod and struck, but on setting the hook I knew straight away that this was no eel. I waded out to my vantage point, but there was nothing spectacular about the fight. Within a few minutes the fish was safely netted, no problem at all, but I'd still no idea what it was. However when I tried to get hold of the net and lift mesh and fish out with one hand it began to dawn on me that there was something special in the net. I was all a-tremble and fumbled round in the bivvy for the small torch I carry around with me. The fish was certainly something special; the small beam revealed this black backed old monster lying in the net. By this time my bottle had gone. I put it in the weighing sling but couldn't get an accurate reading from the Avons. I needed bigger scales – and we all know that Avons read up to 32lb.

I ran through the trees to Steve's swim to borrow his big scales. I must have been in a state because Steve has since told me he heard me coming along the path shouting 'The Avons, the Avons'. It's all a blur through lack of sleep, or excitement, or for whatever reason, but I remember the fish being hoisted up on the Kevin Nash scales by Steve with me trying to read the weight in the trembling beam of the torch. The fish was a mirror weighing 32lb 12oz. I'd gone down to the water that weekend not knowing there was a thirty in there, then I learnt of Roy's new water record of 32lb, and here I was breaking that with an even bigger fish. It was one of the most exciting moments of my life and one I will always remember. That was my last fish of the Mangrove season, but what a way to finish!

By the way, John and Roy named that fish Schweppes. I wonder why?

I was proud of my result on the Mangrove and when I met Tim for the first time at a carp meeting in Stoke during the following close season I told him how well I'd done. I think I'd possibly had a drink or two that evening and I perhaps overstated the case a little bit because Tim sort of melted away with a far away look in his eye when I started telling him how good I was. I felt a bit of a prat when I woke up next morning, but I'm used to that. What I did know was that I couldn't wait to get back on the water the following season. I hadn't been as excited about the start of a season for years, and June the 15th took for ever to come round. I was going to fish the water every possible minute I could up to the close down towards the end of August.

Talk about an anti-climax! I fished every weekend, with a couple of week's holiday thrown in for good measure – 672 hours in all – for just four fish. I was fishing the same methods as the year before, using the same bait, but changing swims more than I had done previously. I could make no impression on the fish and it was just a question of soldiering on in the hope that one of the buzzers would sound occasionally. Biggest of the four fish was a mirror of 26.02, which was some consolation, but it

1985 success for Brian in the considerable shape of a fish called Schweppes.

Moment of truth in 1987; Brian holds the scales while Tim and Dave Phillips check the weight.

The fish weighed 29lb 6oz; a beautiful mirror known as Scaley.

was a let down after my winter and close season expectations. It made no difference what I was or wasn't catching, though. I loved the place and I'd got a taste of its big fish so I was going to keep going back for more no matter what happened.

Next season I did slightly better, landing five fish in 600 hours fishing. I can't recall why I fished fewer hours that year than I did the year before, perhaps my wife persuaded me to go on holiday with her, (although I find that hard to believe, come to think of it). Perhaps I couldn't duck the overtime as much as I would have liked. My two biggest fish were mirrors of

21.03 and 29.02, the latter being a carp nicknamed 'Scaley', one of the most beautiful carp I've ever seen. It had been out at 29lb plus to Roy Stallard the previous year, so we were hoping it would make thirty if it came out in 1987. It didn't quite but it had grown six pounds since Tim caught it in 1983, looked superb and seemed set to make thirty for some lucky captor in the future.

Through 1986 and 1987 I'd been fishing varying quantities of boiled baits over a bed of tiger nuts and groats. I prefer to fish HNVs when I can so the bait was the same one I described in my chapter in Tim's first book –

but I was getting increasing problems from the eels. Now I don't like eels. In fact I hate them and someone usually has to come and unhook it for me if I land one. But apart from the fact that they were a nuisance, they were also capable of upsetting the angling. Once the hook baits go out for the night I like the swim to remain undisturbed until I get a take from a carp. The eels weren't allowing this to happen, but I could see no way round the problem, short of fishing particles, which I didn't want to do. I stuck with the garlic and liver source of attraction throughout three seasons, apart from one very brief change which turned out to be disastrous. I suddenly got the bright idea that strawberry flavour and sweetener would pull me some fish, but all it did was pull the eels in a big way. That turned out to be a very short session and the new version of the bait was scrapped.

I'd become friendly with the Nutrabaits partners Tim (Paisley) and Bill Cottam by this time, and in the middle of my puzzling about a bait for 1988 I learnt of their new Ener-Vite mix, a high fat/low protein bait based on liver, yeast, bird foods, vitamin/mineral sources and a very distinctive mixed spice additive. I can't really explain why but this felt right for the Mangrove the minute I heard about it. Nutrabaits had also brought out a very pungent Mexican Onion Oil, and I decided to use this with the Addits in the Ener-Vite bait.

It turned out to be another difficult summer on the water, with everyone struggling for fish, and although I didn't exactly turn the place over I was reasonably happy with my results for the first time in three years. Most of my fishing was done from the Field Swim, and although I didn't catch for the first six nights I always knew the bait was going to work. I think this is

The Field Swim, scene of most of Brian's 1988 campaign.

an area a great many carp men struggle with: they don't have enough faith in their bait and change too soon. The fish did come onto the Ener-Vite that summer and I landed ten carp in 664 hours fishing. The biggest was a 21lb common, but I was unlucky to lose a few fish, in addition to which I had the big advantage that the eels weren't touching the bait. A number of the other anglers finished up on Ener-Vite and Mexican Onion that summer!

I should mention one incident from the last session I had on the water that year, because it tickled us at the time. It was either the last night, or the next to last night, and there were just three of us on the water, me in Reed Warblers, Tim to my left in the Duck Swim, and Ray – with the boat – across the water in the swim named after him, Stoney's. The fishing had become very mean and my run of success slowed down, while everyone else's had come to a standstill. One spot was producing, and that was a long way out from Reed Warblers – about 120 yards I would guess. Par for the course was roughly one run every three nights, so hooking a fish was a bit of an event.

This particular night I was away at about half past one in the morning. No, I had a drop back, and when I managed to make contact with whatever was on the other end I was convinced it was an eel. Tim heard the take and came round, which was just as well because I soon needed help. Now when I've got an eel on I lose my sense of urgency and don't work too hard at getting it on the bank, so I wasn't too bothered that this one was making determined efforts to disappear into the tree root jungle to my left. Tim watched my half hearted performance with interest, before pointing out that eels don't kite! He had a point and I tried to save the situation – but the tree line had been reached. Tim went round and tried to locate the fish's position, but what we now realised was that the carp was lying doggo. Tim thought he might be able to guide it out, so he

took the rod while I tried to attract Stoney's attention, with a view to him bringing the boat across to us. Have you ever tried to whisper three hundred yards in the middle of the night? 'Ray, Ray, RAY, **RAY**.' My whispered shouting increased in urgency and volume. '**RAAAY!!**' Beeeeppp. The other rod roared off! Two runs in a night just wasn't happening, and here was me with two in quarter of an hour, the second one coming while I'm standing by the rods screaming my head off! While I was playing the second fish Tim extricated the first one and I finished up with a brace on the bank, the biggest 18lb. I spent the rest of the session standing by the rods screaming RAAAYYY!

And so to 1989. I was part of the Nutrabaits team by this time, which meant that I'd no time to go fishing, but I was willing to work all hours, and as fishing was work I decided to fish all hours. Not quite, of course, but I was no longer tied to the fixed hours I'd suffered in previous seasons, and which most people have to put up with all their lives. I'd been happy with the Ener-Vite, so I stuck with that, and the Addits, but changed the essential oil to Leek. Analysing my previous season's results I came to the conclusion that most of my action had come when I'd got a lot of bait in the swim, so a lot of bait they could have. I was willing to keep making it as long as they were willing to keep eating it and get caught. Bill and I teamed up on bait, and agreed to fish the same swim all summer if possible, the idea being to gradually create a recognised feeding area that the fish would visit regularly. John Lilley and Roy Stallard had had consistent results a couple of seasons previously by adopting similar tactics.

There was one big change in the fishing in 1989. Tim was now controlling a syndicate on the water (same anglers but on a more organised, exclusive basis) and felt that baiting up from the boat should be banned. All the anglers

This 'Erehwon' fish just falls into the arbitrary 'big fish' category at just over 25lb.

A superb fully scaled Redmire mirror.

Julian with one of his many Tilery big fish.

Jan poses with a lovely Leney mirror.

Pete Springate with one of the great carp captures of all time, mirrors of 36½lb and 38½lb landed within a few hours of each other at Yeoveney in 1977.

Another big Leney fish going back to the water that Chris and his friends discovered from the late Donald Leney's records.

Thirty-two pounds of lovely Wraysbury mirror being returned.

Right: A strange after-sunset cloud effect shot from Joe's Swim on the Mangrove.

Big carp from a big carp water in France. Rod with a carp of 50lb plus from Lake Cassien.

Study of a big fish water. One of Rod's pictures of his own lake at sunset.

Pete with a magnificent brace of 32lb and 25½lb from the ultra hard Wraysbury No 1.

'Erehwon', a privately controlled big fish water which houses the biggest known living carp in this country at the time of writing. The anglers in shot are Ray Stone, Dave and Gary Morgan (see the list of forty-plus carp).

Paul Forward returns Kent's famous She to the equally famous School Pool.

A happy Chris holds the biggest English fish of all time, his huge Redmire common of 51lb 8oz, another capture he knew about in advance, in this previously unpublished picture of the record.

The beauty of a Redmire dawn caught by Chris Yates' camera as the sun slants across Greenbanks and onto the pool.

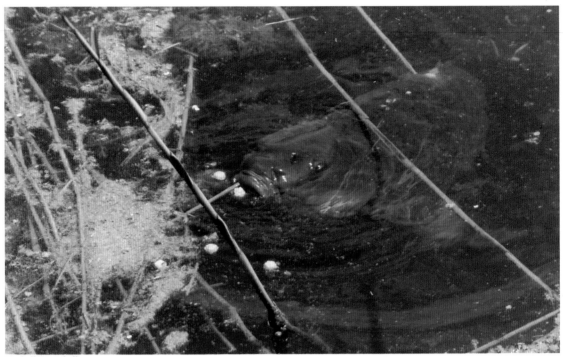

Eyeball to eyeball.

Elliott with a small water biggie.

Duck Swim success in the shape of a lovely 20lb plus common.

The fish Brian was fishing for, the common known as Trio which scaled 34lb 4oz when Brian landed her in August.

Ken looks in on the carp tight against the reedmace. He spent hours watching them feed between the two willows on either side of the swim.

Ken with 25lb 12oz of beautiful Savay Lake carp.

Dawn on a new Mangrove season.

Last night on Birch and Mary caught this unexpected mirror of 25lb 12oz. Who says there are no surprises left in carp fishing?

Not a 'big fish', but it doesn't matter one jot when the carp is a common as beautiful as this one.

Ray Stone with a mirror of 36lb plus caught on a 3in silt rig.

Lee Jackson with a stunning common of over 37lb taken on his version of the bomb on the end of the line rig.

Terry Dempsey with the second forty Longfield has produced. Rumour has it that the very difficult water contains at least one other fish that looks set to top 40lb.

Phil Harper with the Snake Pit common of 40lb plus. This magnificent fish weighed 41lb 8oz when Phil landed it.

Consistently successful big fish man Alan Smith happily poses with one of the many big fish he has landed in recent years. Alan is a great believer in making the bait available to the carp as a food source, then reaping the benefits. This mirror weighed 33lb 4oz and was just one of Alan's eleven thirty-plus fish for the season 1988/89.

Prolific catcher of big fish Rob Maylin, an angler who attaches more attention to bait than his carefree attitude would have us believe. Rob's bird food chapter in Fox Pool is necessary reading for anyone trying to come to terms with bait.

Was I after the leather? John says I was on about it all week. I was fortunate enough to land the lovely looking fish on the last morning, this carp also picking up a bait that hadn't been in the water very long.

The fish which answered to 'RAAAYYY'!

Early morning in the Duck Swim, the focal point of Brian's heavy baiting campaign in 1989.

The fish on everyone's mind, the last capture of Schweppes in 1986 when the great mirror weighed just under 35lb. Dave Phillips is the successful angler here.

been fishing for since 1985. Bill and I both did very, very well, but by the middle of August I was definitely getting a bit anxious about the biggies. I wanted the common that Roy and John had both caught at thirty plus (although I wasn't at all sure they were the same fish) and I knew Scaley had made it over thirty because John caught this beautiful fish in July. The bait was going well; the rig was still working (three inch pop-up on a fifteen inch Gamabraid 12lb hook length), in spite of the fact that Tim kept telling me it couldn't! and I felt it was just a matter of time before I caught one of the biggies. My ambition was to catch the three biggies – the triumvirate – but just one of them would have to do now.

To me one of the most exciting things about carp fishing is that you don't know in advance. Most Mangrove action comes at night, but by no means every night, so I usually go to bed and get up again if the carp wake me. I got to the water on Thursday afternoon, the 17th of August, parked at the back of the Duck Swim, my second home for the summer, and set up home. My mate John was in Reed Warblers, and Tony was on the water. Come mid evening out came the throwing stick and three mixes of bait winged their way out to the feeding area one by one. The new thirteen foot North Western Dyneemas did their job in putting the stringers and hookbaits just where I wanted them, and after the usual series of coffees, and laughs with John, I climbed into the bag.

Some runs are faster than others, and the one that woke me in the early hours of Friday morning was a screamer. Line was absolutely pouring out, which I associate with smallish fish for some reason. The fish I struck didn't exactly feel small, but it didn't feel unduly large, either. It just felt like another hard fighting carp. I don't think I had much trouble landing it, from memory, but I certainly had trouble lifting the mesh of the landing net out

weren't in agreement with this, but I was. I wanted to come to terms with the water by using boilies, and I could get these out as far as I wanted to fish by means of my throwing stick. A heavily baited (three or four 1lb mixes per night) area at one hundred yards plus, and three inch pop-ups fished in conjunction with two or three bait stringers were to be my tactics, and I would stick with this plan – unless it turned out to be disastrous. In fact it was wildly successful and I had far and away my best season on the water.

I won't bore you with the statistics (all right, I will, I had twenty-six fish in 750 hours fishing) but I landed six fish over 20lb, including two thirties – and the thirties were fish I had of the water. I knew I'd got one of the biggies then – and what a biggie. Well, you don't need me to tell you that because you've got the picture to look at. It was the common known as Trio and it weighed in at 34.04.

I must admit I was excited by the capture. I *ran* all the way up to the phone box to ring Bill at 3.30 in the morning, and there was no chance of me getting to sleep again that night. We took the pictures in the morning and I felt a real sense of achievement after all those sessions in pursuit of that fish. I didn't really look at the figures until Tim asked me to work them out to show how much effort goes into a capture like that. When I did look at them I realised I'd spent over 2,500 hours fishing for that fish. How many bait mixes that represents in total I don't know, but I do know that I put over 100 1lb mixes in during the summer of 1989.

I fished on through Friday and Saturday night with no further action, but the pressure was off on two counts. One was that I'd caught one of the biggies I was after, although I didn't realise at the time that it was the fish I really wanted. The second was that we'd got longer on the water than we'd expected, and didn't have to finish until September 10th. After all the anxiety of the previous two months I could relax and enjoy it.

I relaxed so much I got really lucky and caught Scaley at 31lb 8oz the following Friday! I had dreamed of catching those three great fish, and five years (almost to the day) after catching the first of them out of the blue I'd landed the second and third within eight days of each other. Three magnificent thirties from one northern water, I feel proud of that record. I just can't wait for next year, and I'm not

Eight days later and the trio of thirties is complete; Brian with Scaley, this time at 31lb 8oz.

joking. That Schweppes hasn't been caught for four years now, and no one's taking bets against it making forty plus when it does come out. I'll be putting in the hours to make sure I'm the one who lands it. It doesn't matter how long it takes – but then that's what I feel about carp fishing. It doesn't matter how long it takes, but if you haven't got a bait in the water you can't catch them.

10 Looking in on Carp

Ken Townley

The place, Savay Lake. The time, noon on a blistering hot July day in 1988. I was lying full length on the bank with my head and arms resting on a willow branch a mere six inches above the surface. Below me, safe in the sanctuary of the thickest snags in the swim, known as Wilson's Island, 200lb of carp flesh lazed blissfully in the heat of the noonday sun. I was shaking with fatigue from the uncomfortable position, but I daren't move for fear of spooking the seven or eight fish just inches away, in three feet of water.

I could see clearly the markings and scale patterns on these famous fish. Popeye was there, as big as a barrel with a huge pendulous belly. The fish had not been out for some time and I thought he looked fantastic; I wondered if he'd go forty? Sally's Mate, a big near-thirty pound common ghosted in and out of the swim, seemingly reluctant to come in as close as some of the others. There was a huge, dark mirror with an enormous single scale the size of an ashtray on its flank, that looked to be all of thirty-five and to make them all look small, a long, lean fish, well over a yard long with gorgeous orange coloured flanks below massive, almost black, shoulders. I wondered if this could be the elusive fish known as 'The Advert'. Last time that fish had come out was some five or six years ago and it was widely thought that the fish would go well over forty next time out. Certainly this brooding, monstrous presence, gliding gracefully through the still water below me, looked capable of breaking that magic mark; it almost instilled a sense

of fear in me; surely no mortal could catch such a leviathan.

As I watched these beautiful carp cruising to and fro beneath me, I was filled with a sense of wonder that they could be caught at all. The reason for this was that there, lying on the lake bed below the fish, was a scattering of my baits, and though the fish and the bait had been in close proximity for over three hours now, I'd not seen one fish go down for a sample.

I'd gone to Savay with my own ideas on bait very clear in my mind and, in keeping with my firmly held belief that a good bait will always out-fish a poor one, had decided not to change my approach in any way. So it was that a quality HNV base was mixed with some high fat seed ingredients and a touch of Robin Red to produce what I hoped was a good high energy/high nutritional value bait. A combination of two oils and a sweetener were added and in field test during the close season on the Cornish waters, the bait had worked a treat.

'First thing you have to do when you get in here,' said the Savay regulars, 'is to find out if the fish'll have your bait. They're very choosy.'

That's easier said than done, I thought, but then they said that there were almost invariably fish in the snags in the swim known as The Snags; I should try the bait out in there. Now I should point out here and now, that the snags are just that. In fact, they aren't just snags – they're **SNAGS**!!! Or rather, they were. Let me just explain that. The Snags can be fished from two swims along the canal bank. It is a small island some five or six yards from the

This Savay fish of 24lb took bread flake fished right in the margins.

Ken's wife Carole with a Salamander Lake twenty that was intercepted along an observed patrol route.

bank at the mouth of the North Bay. Tactics for fishing the spot were to bait the edge of the island and the main margins, away from the snags, in the hope of pulling the snag residents away from the sanctuary and making a mistake. Nobody, but nobody, would ever dream of fishing right in the snags. You'd certainly get chances but there's absolutely no way that the fish would end up on the bank. Sadly it seems as if the 'catch at all costs' attitude got the better of a few day ticket anglers, who tried to fish in the snags, and the bailiffs decided that by removing the snags they'd remove the temptation. In the close season, the work was done and one of the most fascinating swims on the lake was spoilt completely.

Happily, I had one full season of fish watching before the snags met their sad fate, which is how I came to be spread out along the bank and the willow branches, waiting for some sort of reaction to my bait.

I couldn't understand their reluctance to eat the free offerings and couldn't help thinking that I'd blown it in some way. Maybe the red stuff was no-no, or perhaps I'd overloaded one of the attractors; but surely not. The bait had worked well on other waters; what was so special about these snooty buggers that they wouldn't even deign to look at it?

It was no good. I had to stand up and stretch a bit. It looked like they weren't interested anyway. I thought they'd probably spook as my shadow withdrew from their field of vision, but as I gratefully stretched upright and crept away from the swim, I saw that the fish were unconcerned with the change in the overhead view and were still lazily cruising about. Back from the water I lit a cigarette and sat down in the comfort of the hot sun to relax and try to figure out what had gone wrong with the bait. I was in half a mind to go up to Harefield and buy some ready-mades – that's how down I was feeling.

I decided to give the carp in the snags a further hour, and crept slowly and stealthily back to my perch. The scene was unchanged; seven massive carp taking no notice of the feast spread below them. Suddenly, a smaller fish, a common of about eighteen pounds, came belting into the swim from nowhere and before my astonished gaze, fell upon the bait like a good 'un. This feeding spree on the part of one fish infected the others. First one, then two, three, four fish joined in. Soon they were all at it. I'd brought a couple of pounds of bait with me for the fish to try out and now I began trickling boilies in, a few at a time. The fish with their heads down, took absolutely no notice of the new additions, but those who were on an even keel, perhaps in between mouthfuls, seemed a bit alarmed at the fresh baits falling through the water; but not alarmed enough to spook from the area. I soon had them all feeding again and after about half an hour was able to introduce bait right over their heads without any signs of unease on the part of the fish. To say I was relieved was putting it mildly! The fish obviously liked the bait a great deal, but I was still rather concerned at their 'take it or leave it' attitude for the first three hours or so – when they'd left it!

As I watched the fish clearing up the last of the bait, I wondered just what sort of reaction the bait would produce out in the open water. For one thing, it would be absolutely impossible to introduce so much bait into so tight an area (no more than one square yard), so the bait would be well spread out. If a concentrated carpet of bait such as I'd introduced in the snag bush didn't trigger off feeding, what chance would a scattering of bait have, out there in open water? I decided to change the bait completely over to a pure HNV profile and drop the bird foods and the Robin Red, but that would have to wait until the next rota.

As I watched the carp below me finish up the last of the bait, a couple of very interesting things happened. The first was in the way the fish behaved after all the food had been eaten. I'd seen identical behaviour on another water some years earlier, when testing out flavours and bases on observable fish. Both they and now the Savay fish, showed greatly increased activity, swimming about the swim with tight turns and swirls. From time to time, one would turn on its side and tail-wash the gravel as if to try to seep some remaining food out from the stones and gravel. I couldn't help wondering if, in their earlier feeding spell, tiny bits of bait weren't lost through the gill covers and the fish ignored them in favour of the large boiled baits that were readily available. Not until all the boilies had gone did the fish turn their attention to the left-overs, as it were. I thought this rather unlikely, but what other explanation could there be? Unless it was as I'd originally thought when first I'd observed this strange behaviour those years earlier. Then I'd wondered if perhaps, while the swim was still full of carp, but all the bait had been eaten, if this peculiar display wasn't a reaction to a lingering residue of smell from the now eaten bait. That too, seems a bit far fetched, but other than sheer 'joie de vivre', I can't think of any logical explanation. There is so much we still need to understand about a carp's thought processes and behaviour patterns.

So there I was, watching these carp racing and swirling about in the swim. Gradually, they calmed down and within ten minutes all was peace and calm again. Then suddenly, they spooked. Leaves, twigs and small bits of gravel swirled around in the massive vortices caused by the carp fleeing the area. I wondered what could have caused such panic, when the fish had appeared so calm. Then, slowly ghosting into the sanctuary of the snags, swam a large, sad looking carp. It swam with a pronounced tilt to one side, and looked scarred and battle weary. I wondered if it had just been hooked and lost and then noticed that it was towing line. I could see a small, bright yellow boilie hanging from its lip and a length of line, but thankfully, no bomb. (Fixed lead advocates please note.) Could the presence of this frightened fish have caused the panic in the others? I'd read about the possible release of fear pheremones in carp and now felt sure that it

Bill Speed at Ockenham. He had excellent results there after initial observation had revealed the carp's patrol routes and habits.

was this underwater 'smell of fear' from one of their number that had caused the fish to spook.

There's a curious footnote to all this. Next day, I crept back to the swim with a handful of baits to see if I couldn't get a more immediate reaction from any fish that might be in the snags. The only fish present was the last arrival of the previous day – the one that had been in a fight. Today, he looked much more lively and I was curious to note that the yellow boilie that had been his undoing was now lying on the lake bed. The tackle looked to be still lodged in the fish's lip though. I put in some free offerings but he took no notice of them. Next day he was still there – and so were my baits, along with the yellow one. The tackle was nowhere to be seen and I guess the fish must have got rid of it in a branch or in weed, sometime during the past twenty-four hours. The fish looked

quite the picture of health now and I was amazed at this recovery rate, but the boilies stayed untouched. I called in again over the next couple of days and was very worried when the bait I'd put in remained uneaten during that time. The only resident I saw, during those three days, was the lost fish, then one day he was gone, and so was all the bait. I put in some more and waited. Ten minutes passed before the small common of a few days ago, swept into the swim. 'Doesn't this fish do anything slowly?' I mused. He was followed at a more sedate pace by dear old Popeye and these two set about the free meal with gusto. After a while three other fish joined the spree and they cleared up a pound of bait in no more than twenty minutes.

Was it the presence of the lost fish in the snag area for three and a half days that had kept the others away? Was this why the bait stayed uneaten during that time? You can understand the reluctance of this carp to try baits again, but you'd have thought that the other fish might have ventured in during the dark hours for a feed. Can it really take more than three days for the fear pheremones to clear from the water, or was the lost fish exuding them to a diminishing degree all the time he was in residence? It surely can't have been coincidence that only once the lost fish had left the swim did the others come back, and once they were back, they took to the bait like nobody's business. What about fish on the bank though, you ask? Yes, I had two out, both on the same bait I'd been putting in the snags; though neither were fish I'd seen in there, whilst feeding them!

Later in the year, Carole came up to Savay with me. We fished the swim to the left of Wilsons and I couldn't keep Carole still for more than five minutes. She was forever disappearing into the snags with handfuls of boilies to feed the fish. She must have fed nigh on three quarters of the twenty mixes I'd taken up to the fish in the snags.

Ockenham Lake, Devon, scene of a great deal of Ken's carp watching experiences.

My earlier decision to amend the bait by leaving out the high fat ingredients had been shelved and the bait Carole fed so lovingly to the snag residents was exactly the same as the previous offerings. The fish fed so avidly on the bait that I felt sure we'd get chances on baits just off the island and in the margins, but it was the bream that found the baits first and the only carp run I had, lasted less than fifteen seconds and left me attached to a large, waterlogged branch in the blinking of an eye. How **DO** they do that??

Watching those Savay fish only helped to reinforce my love of small, intimate carp waters where it is possible to look in on your quarry and judge their reactions to various baits and baiting situations. It is so easy to be over confident in one's rigs and bait and the usual excuse of 'they're not having it', is used to explain

away lack of action on the big waters with the tackle lying a hundred yards plus out into the lake. Take those rigs back to small waters and watch what happens when fish pick them up. I once had a rig I was 100 per cent sure of; it landed a lot of good fish for Carole and I, and I'd have put money on it working every time. Imagine the shock then when I watched the Salamander fish pick up and reject this wonder rig without even twitching the line. I couldn't believe it. Observing those rejections helped me amend the rig and improve it, but it also taught me not to be too blasé about things when they are going well.

I have long been fascinated with waters where carp can be seen clearly. I guess it all started for me on the Hampshire Avon in my barbeling days. Fred Crouch got me into the private swim called 'The Compound' for a few days, and a swim there, holding considerable numbers of big barbel, had me spellbound as I watched them clearing up carpets of maggots. I wrote a piece on these observations for the now defunct magazine 'Angling', and the feedback I got from that, told me that too many people go fishing with their eyes closed.

'That's easy for him to say', some of you might grumble. 'Stacks of small carp, no pressure, got the place to himself most likely! Try doing all that intimate stuff up in the carp jungle I live in.'

Fair enough, but isn't Savay in the jungle? Haven't there been some very inspired catches from ultra-hard waters resulting from patient and painstaking observation. You really can learn so much from getting down to the water's edge and really *looking* at carp. There are waters all over the country that lend themselves to such tactics. Ask Martin Gay: it was only through keeping his eyes peeled that he managed to spot those huge commons. Then, having located them, was able to trace a patrol route and intercept them. A magnificent reward for keen observation, backed up by ability, knowledge and application.

I know most of us find it harder to catch these days, compared to, say, five years ago. Most fish are wising up to feeding situations that make them suspicious. Screaming runs are getting fewer and farther between. Rod tops shaking and banging, accompanied by single bleeps from the buzzer seem to be the order of the day. We go to one of the tough waters, don't get any action and blame the fish ('they're not having it'), or the rig (it's blown'). It's easy to do and it's quite often right to make such assumptions. The thinking anglers get off their butts and try and find a reason for the silent buzzers and a way around the problem. Some of the rigs around these days are too devious for words, yet they aren't fail safe. I came back from a Savay trip in 1987 with the Looney Extension rig details clear in my mind,

having been shown it while up there as a guest; I could see the point of the rig and the way it worked, but wasn't quite sure about it, despite the tremendous run of success for the boys using it. I decided to do a bit of testing myself.

Now briefly, for those few of you who don't know the rig, it is a way of presenting critically balanced buoyant baits so as to present the bait below the hook, at the same time extending the length of the shank by means of an inch or so of silicone rubber. (Whether or not the inventors were aware of the crucial effect this shank extension would have, or whether it came about by accident, I don't know.) Suffice to say that most rigs can be improved by extending the length of the hook shank with a semi flexible piece of silicone – but you'll have to think about that one for yourselves). Anyway, back to my tests of the rig. I tied up half a dozen rigs exactly as I'd been shown at Savs, which turned out to be exactly the way it is described in Rob's book and in the 'Angling Times' piece, that explained the rig some time later. I took the rigs to a small pool close to home that holds stacks of fish, with plenty of small carp and a good head of doubles, to keep the interest going. I'd found a swim where the bottom came up from ten feet to about three feet very quickly, the top of the bar being only a few yards out and plainly visible. In the past few weeks I had been baiting the bar steadily with paste and boiled baits, whilst doing some field testing for Nutrabaits, so I knew I could get fish feeding on the bar quickly and in numbers. I was only going to fish one rod and thought I should try the rig out first using a tightly clipped up set-up, and watched reactions from a nearby willow tree. Out went the free offerings, followed by the tackle. I could clearly see the hookbait wafting gently about in the slight currents caused by the undertow. The rig was perfectly balanced to such an extent that it took about half a minute to sink one foot in tests at home in the bath.

After an hour or so, the first carp came into the swim and went straight down on the familiar baits. Three others soon joined him and it was only a matter of time before one of them approached the hookbait. Sure enough, there was a nice double confidently edging up to the hookbait. It tilted slightly down and sucked at the bait, which disappeared inside its mouth. 'Gotcha', I whispered to myself, fighting the urge to slide down the tree to the rod below. Just as well I didn't, for I'd have missed what happened next. The tip jerked a couple of times, the Optonic went 'bleep' once and the fish spat out the hookbait and fled! Funny, I thought; super duper rig, the absolute business; fish gets rid of it easily. Funny!

On went rig number two, this time on a slack line. Back came the fish – and the same thing happened. I had six pick-ups and four of them got rid of the hook. I went back home and checked that the rigs were tied correctly. Yes . . . same as the diagram. I thought about what might be happening and changed the hook from the size 6 Mustad to one of Partridge's new KM Cassien Outpoints (size 6 also) and went back for another try. Result – four out of the seven pick-ups on the bank. Slightly better but I still wasn't happy about the rig. I then decided to try my standard pop-up rig, which consisted of a size 6 barbless Hilton with a shank tied hair to hold the hook bait immediately over the hook, extending the shank with half an inch of silicone tubing. Result – five takes, five hook-ups: dump the Looney extension. In fact I did go back to the rig at a later date on a big silt laden water and there it worked very well indeed, but because I was fishing at range I'd really no idea how many chances went undetected. It must be the same with a great many rigs. I recall Hutchy saying that all hook holds are a chancy business. I can certainly back that up after watching fish pick up tried and tested rigs and ejecting them with ease.

There is one ray of light on the horizon for me at the moment in the form of a bottom bait rig that I've been playing around with using the new Partridge Arrowpoint barbless hooks. I've been messing around all summer with these hooks and have found a way of putting a properly balanced bait hard on the bottom rather than having them popped up two or three inches. The rig is basically the Swimmer Rig favoured by Rod Hutchinson. After tying in the small power gum loop and supergluing it in place I leave a small tail of power gum to which I attach the counter balance weights. (I use tungsten olivettes and tungsten putty). I have found that by having the counter weights close to the hook these strangely shaped hooks get a firm hold in the bottom lip more often than not. I can't claim it's 100 per cent successful but I've watched fish get hooked on it enough times to know it works well.

It was while trying out this set-up that I saw for the first time the antics a hooked fish can perform without bolting in panic when it first feels the hook take hold.

I was at a small club water near my home and was convinced the fish were having the bait, but I wasn't getting the sort of action I had expected. I decided to bait up a margin swim that is only fished on rare occasions by the few members who like to go stalking their fish. Over a week or so I carefully built up the swim. The bait introduced the previous evening was all gone the next morning, and trickles of bait introduced during daylight hours saw the odd fish come along for a brief feed. I decided it was time to fish the swim and set up two rods fishing down the edge about four feet out in three feet of water. The free baits, about fifty of them, were scattered around the swim and I sat back to await developments. Three hours later and not even a twitch. I climbed the lower branches of a sturdy oak tree that overhangs the water. Through the polaroids I could see the gravel bottom very clearly and it was

Ken's favourite end rig which has worked well on a number of waters. The fine tuning to balance the bait is critical.

obvious that all the bait was still there. As I watched a large fish of over twenty pounds swam into view. I recognised the fish as one of the largest inhabitants of the pool. He'd made plenty of mistakes in the past but from what I could gather talking to other members the fish had not been out for a long time. Slowly the fish inched down on the baits, picked one up in its lips and moved back very slowly. I could see the boiled bait quite clearly, held tightly in the lips. The fish moved four or five inches, then spat out the offering with great force. I watched as the rejected bait fell back to the bottom, and it had no sooner touched down than the fish went down again and ate the bait very confidently. He then left the swim for ten minutes or so before returning, this time accompanied by two other fish. These three fish seemed reluctant to feed at first but eventually it was the biggest fish, the original visitor, who again played the 'now he's got it, now he hasn't' trick. The pattern was exactly the same. Mouth bait . . . eject . . . watch it drop . . . eat it when it hits bottom. Then all three fish began feeding in the same way. It was very cautious stuff and each bait was closely tested

before being picked up. I watched one of the fish approaching my hook bait — and it froze! Up came the dorsal fin, the pectorals spread out and the whole fish seemed to quiver with urgency. I jumped straight out of the tree and was on the rod in a split second. The strike hit empty space: the fish was gone. I climbed the tree again and to my surprise the other two fish were still there. 'Next time I'll wait for the run.' I said to myself.

The fish didn't appear to be spooked by the sudden departure of their mate but they still fed very gingerly. At last one came up to the second hook bait and sucked it in. The whole fish seemed to twitch and I saw the line tighten and heard a single bleep from the buzzer. He'll be away and running now, I thought, he must be well and truly hooked by now. Then I saw the carp's mouth working frantically. It was sucking and blowing with such force that the line was twitching constantly, but the fish didn't run. I watched in fascination for about thirty seconds then, to my astonishment, I saw the bait come flying out of the carp's mouth and the fish rushed out of the swim, without the end tackle. How could it possibly have got rid of what was obviously a pretty fair hook hold, all the time staying almost stationary, moving only its lips in great powerful jerks as it struggled to expel the hook.

Until I watched this incident I can honestly say I did not believe such a thing could happen. Now I know better.

When I joined Savay they told me that sometimes the fish would inspect a hook bait many times before making a mistake with it. I heard a tale of a bait that was left out there for three days before it produced a run. That shows an awful lot of confidence in both the bait and the tactic and to be honest I thought it a bit far-fetched. Yet the angler was convinced that carp had been for a look at the bait on many occasions, had marked its position to the inch, and only made a mistake after convincing itself that the bait was safe. If the bait had been brought in and a fresh one put on, and then recast to more or less the same spot he was convinced that the carp would know this was a new source of danger (possibly due to a stronger smell, or the altered position) and it would maybe take another three days – or more – before the bait was again considered safe enough to eat. Can you believe that?

I couldn't come to terms with the idea, but how can you be sure it isn't happening? I decided to see for myself on a local water. I made up two end rigs comprising of pop-ups finely balanced. Instead of the bait being firmly attached to the hair by a stop, or tied on, I mounted it on a piece of match stick. I cut the hook away at the bend and tied the two rigs to quite heavy stones. These were then dropped into two adjacent swims about thirty yards away from my bivvy. While the experiment was under way I would be fishing nearby for three nights and two days. I knew there was no chance of the fish getting hooked up on the rig, and felt sure that the bait would slip off the match stick easily enough if a taking carp came along and picked the bait up. I know it sounds pretty crude, but I can assure you it works. When we first started fishing a new big fish water we used similar tactics to find the fish, chucking out lines with baits on match sticks all around the pool and inspecting the lines at regular intervals. The ones that came back empty had been visited by Mr Carp, therefore fish visit that swim. Simple eh?

Anyway, back to the test. The water con-cerned is a hard one and the fish are cute in the extreme, but I felt positive they'd come along, see a single hook bait and suck the bait off the match. All I had to do was keep inspecting the baits regularly. In fact, during the first night one hook bait was taken, but the other was still there at first light. It was still there at mid day, and during the heat of the afternoon I decided to reel in and go and watch the swim for any carpy comings and goings. It was about four in the afternoon: the bait had been out almost twenty-four hours. A good fish came slowly along the margins emerging from the cover of a nearby snag tree. It came up to the bait, looked at it for a few seconds, then swam away. An hour later the same fish repeated the inspec-tion, again without any attempt to eat the bait. From what I could see the bait was still behav-ing as a normal hook bait would. Maybe it had taken on a bit of water, but not enough to upset the fine balancing to any extent. I put my hand in the water and wafted a current of water towards the bait. It rose nicely off the bottom and danced enticingly in the current before slowly settling down again. All was well there.

I looked in just before dark. I thought I could see a fish there inspecting the bait, but maybe that was just a trick of the light. Next morning the bait was still there. I began to wonder if the bait hadn't swollen up to fit too tightly onto the match stick, and cursed. If that were so it made a lash up of the whole thing. Carp could have been in there all night tugging frantically at the sweet smelling morsel that didn't want to be eaten!

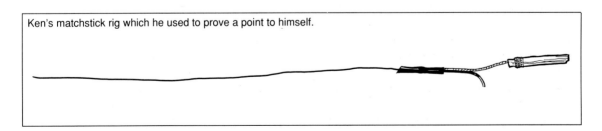
Ken's matchstick rig which he used to prove a point to himself.

I looked in again mid morning, and got very lucky indeed. At about 11am that same fish I'd seen the previous day came into the swim and checked the bait once more. I had seen this fish look at it four times now, and maybe it had also paid a few short inspection calls during the two nights the bait had remained untouched. The carp then made as if to swim out of the area when suddenly it turned around, swam straight up to the offering and neatly sucked the bait in. The stone acted like a lead and the line went tight. The fish turned, felt the line, and fled taking the bait off the match in the process. The bait had been in the swim for forty-two hours! I'm convinced that it hadn't been mouthed by a carp during that period as the bait would have come off (as the other one did on the first night). Heaven knows how many times the fish that eventually took it had actually looked at the bait. There were almost certainly other fish giving it the once over while it was in there but I only saw the one fish approach the bait. I have since repeated the experiment, this time moving the bait six feet within the swim after two days – the bait being renewed at the same time. The fish took four days to actually take the bait. Next summer, when the fish are once more to be found in the margins I'm going to try the same tactic with plenty of other free offerings about the swim. But I have a feeling this won't work at all. This is a water where I've seen fish spook in blind panic when confronted with a carpet of free offerings.

Talking of which I thought I'd close with some interesting observations on the subject of carp's reactions to varying amounts of groundbait in a swim.

As if there weren't enough variables to take into consideration these days we must now accept the fact that on some waters carp are getting very suspicious of groundbait. It doesn't matter whether it's particles or boiled baits that are being used, sometimes too much bait means any quantity more than the hook bait alone. There are certain variables, such as time of the year and water temperature, and these factors certainly have their effect on the reservoirs down here in the West Country. On these waters where close season fishing is allowed the fish will eat just about anything at any time in any quantity during the warming up months just prior to spawning. I've put two thousand boiled baits in as an initial bait up, and topped up with two or three hundred after each fish – and still had fish within the first three or four hours. They are out there cleaning up at a vast rate of knots when you get this sort of action. On the other hand we've found as the season goes on that they'll tolerate fewer and fewer baits in the swim. One of the starkest examples of that was last season (1988) when my mate the Big O spent five days at College and had eighteen fish out, plus other non-productive takes. All the fish came from two rods chucked long with no freebies at all. His inside rod at about seventy yards never produced a run, and this one had been heavily baited. There were quite a few other anglers on the water at this time, including myself. Everyone was putting a fair amount of groundbait in, but I doubt if we put half a dozen fish on the bank between us.

I've been closely associated with a nearby water that holds a few decent fish for several years now. I've been able to chart the carp's increasing awareness of bait over the years, from the early days – when they'd take anything that was chucked in there, to modern times, when single baits and small stringers are the order of the day. Last year a couple of newcomers made the mistake of filling the whole water in with thousands and thousands of baits. They were there for six runless days and it wasn't until a few days after they'd gone and most of their baits came up to the top and were attacked by the swans and the gulls (how can they eat that stinking stuff?) that the place gradually started to fish again to single baits.

One of Ken's many big carp, a College fish of 31lb 3oz.

On the same water, where I did most of my experimenting for the 'Coarse Angler' articles, I watched carp bow waving out of the swim we called The Aquarium on coming across a scattering of tiger nuts. Now tigers last a long time in the water. They had caught a lot of carp over the previous two seasons, but now the carp were exceedingly wary of them. That bait remained uneaten in The Aquarium for nearly three weeks. When the nuts did finally disappear I wasn't convinced that carp were the culprits. There was a breach of the dam at this time and the water level dropped quite considerably, thus allowing the resident swans to browse the area. I truly believe that were it not for the swans the tigers would have remained uneaten indefinitely. Tigers have not produced a take for two years, to the best of my knowledge: how's that for a memory for danger?

The more I observe carp, watch their feeding patterns, the way they react to rigs and baiting situations, the more I realise that I'm damned lucky to catch any fish at all! I can't help feeling that my compulsion to try and improve my results through close season observation sometimes costs me fish rather than the other way round. I know there are anglers who thrive on the big waters where the bait goes out a hundred and fifty yards, and doesn't come back till there's a fish on the other end, and usually a great big one at that. Me, I no longer have the patience for that kind of fishing. The truly dedicated big fish man knows he has to put in the hours to gain his reward. I'll stick to my little pools and the intimate relationships I have with their inhabitants. I've learnt so much from them through watching their behaviour, and I know I'll never tire of looking in on carp.

11 Big Fish Summer

I took control of two carp waters in the spring of 1989, which was exciting. I suppose the timing of obtaining the rights to run them was somewhat unfortunate, as it was partly responsible for setting back the compilation of this book by some few months! Never mind, it's an ill wind that doesn't blow, and my experiences at the two waters are worth recounting, not really because of the fish that were caught, but because of some of the hard earned lessons learnt through the glorious months of our first real summer for years.

The two waters are known as the Mangrove and Birch Grove, and although they are only half a mile apart and are both carp waters they have very few other similarities. The Mangrove is a very rich mere of eighteen acres. It holds a good head of fish ranging from low doubles to very big, and is a difficult water to catch carp from. The fish are not heavily pressured, but they seem to know what's what. In addition they have so much natural food to go at that they seem to look on baits as an optional extra – in the case of the more co-operative fish – or ornaments, in the case of the majority of the fish.

Birch Grove isn't a true mere. It's a three or four acre farm pond carved out of rock, a feature which may well date it back to the time of the formation of the meres (the Ice Age I'm told), but which gives it little in common with them. Birch is deep, dropping quickly down to twelve feet and showing depths of almost twenty feet in places. The bottom is silt of varying depths rich in natural life judging by the prolific bubbling that occurs most days. The water is well stocked (both waters were

stocked by Ray Stone and his brother Reg in the seventies) and while the water had been closed to general fishing for three years (Tony Murtagh had exclusive fishing rights from 1985 through to 1988) it had been very popular with numerous north-west carp men in the early eighties. My friends John Lilley and Brian Garner had fished the water up to 1984–1985 and they informed us that it wasn't a difficult water and a big double had been an exceptional fish in the early eighties. Compared to the Mangrove it had to be considered an easy water, and for that reason we didn't take the fishing particularly seriously. Perhaps that's not accurate. Because of the theme of this book I wanted to catch a twenty-five plus fish so my thoughts were centred mainly on the Mangrove. Birch was looked on as real pleasure fishing, made all the more enjoyable by the fact that the fish are strong surface feeders.

After starting on Birch, catching some nice fish, and renewing my acquaintanceship with the joys of floater fishing I turned my attentions to the Mangrove towards the end of June. Both waters close down at the end of August for duck shooting so I had two months to achieve the hoped for twenty-five plus before having to move onto other waters.

There is a big question mark over bait choice for the Mangrove, because of the massive head of eels the water contains. Brian Garner is an HNV man but his experiences of the previous seasons had driven him onto Ener-Vite to avoid the dreaded wrigglers; he hates them, and if he does hook one another angler is summoned to deal with it. Eels or not I was after a biggie so I was going in with the protein/fat

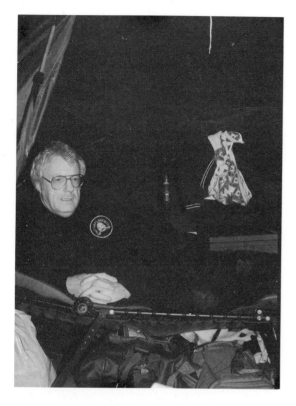

The waiting game, willing the indicators to move.

Early season success for Bill Cottam with this mirror of 27lb 6oz.

combination I feel happiest with. I made up a bait, determined to stick with it until my biggie was on the bank. In the meantime Brian and Bill Cottam went in with Ener-Vite, with the Addits, and with a new oil, Leek, as the label. Brian had used Ener-Vite the previous season with fair results. John Lilley also chose Ener-Vite, with his smell being Mexican Onion Oil. The other lads were on a variety of baits and tactics. Here is the recipe I was using:

16oz	Hi-Nu-Val	3ml	Ultraspice
1oz	egg albumen	2	drops Spanish sage oil
3grm	Addit-Taste and Addit digest	1	drop Spanish thyme oil
1ml	Sweet Cajouser	6	size 2 eggs

I had a long think about presentation. Over the previous seasons all sorts of permutations of balanced and buoyant hookbaits had been used. The carp would be used to having a fair amount of latitude for their examination of the bait. I'd had some success using bomb-on-the-end-of-the-line bolt rigs (I'll refer to it as the silt rig for brevity's sake) with a braided hook length of just three inches during one of my Mangrove seasons and decided to go back to this set-up for these wary silt-feeding carp. I was using a 15lb shock leader and felt this was adequate to withstand the stresses thrown on the end length of line when playing a fish, provided the bottom knot was adequately protected. This was the presentation I'd taken

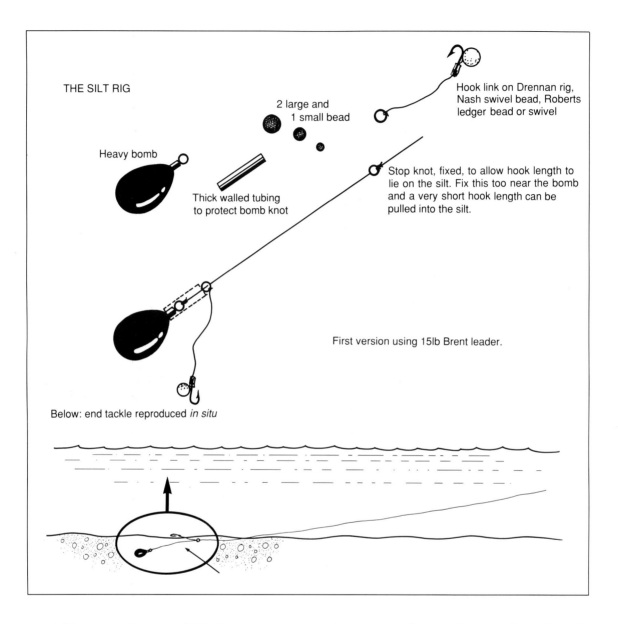

THE SILT RIG

2 large and
1 small bead

Heavy bomb

Thick walled tubing
to protect bomb knot

Hook link on Drennan rig,
Nash swivel bead, Roberts
ledger bead or swivel

Stop knot, fixed, to allow hook length to
lie on the silt. Fix this too near the bomb
and a very short hook length can be
pulled into the silt.

First version using 15lb Brent leader.

Below: end tackle reproduced *in situ*

good fish on previously and I had no reservations about using it.

I was a fortnight behind the other lads going onto the Mangrove and so didn't really expect action for the first couple of nights. I was happy to get the bait going in and to be back in the lovely atmosphere of the water. I started in Reed Warblers and the first two night sessions lived up to expectations; not a bleep. Actually that was better than expectations because I def-

initely expected a few bleeps – from the eels. No eel action on Hi-Nu-Val? What was going on?

The following week I'd got three successive nights fishing, and I moved into the Field Swim. First night actionless, but I put three mixes out so that wasn't a surprise. (Three mixes of HNV was probably over-baiting, but I don't like baiting up when there is anyone else on the water so I had to do my baiting up while I was fishing.) Second night I'm away at three in the morning on the right hand rod. I set the hook and whatever was on the end came in on a straight line offering little or no resistance. It had to be an eel; sod, they'd caught up with me. The rods were on the right hand side of the swim platform; I'd got a bed of reeds to my immediate right. The eel came in to the edge. I'd not dropped the other rod tip and wondered if the eel was going to be small enough to swing in over the other line. I was using Carbomatics and had shut the fightin' drag down as I struck the run – and anti-reverse was on. I was playing an eel, why wouldn't it be? It all happens a bit quicker than you can tell when it does happen, but it wasn't an eel, it was a carp which suddenly took off down the margins and I had no way of giving line, quick as I was getting the anti-reverse off. It was too late: the 8lb Gamabraid didn't stand a chance. Disaster number one. Yes, the loss was a stupid one, but I was certain I was playing an eel, which was why I was so casual.

The next night was undisturbed. I woke to a flat calm morning and a sun that was hot the minute it climbed above the trees to my left. It was so unpromising that I brought the car down to the back of the swim and started packing up at half past six. At quarter to seven a cooling northerly breeze blew in over my head, hitting the water about ninety yards out – on the baited area. I carried on packing up but knew I'd got to give them another hour with the change in conditions. Ten minutes was enough. I was stowing gear in the back of the car when that most glorious of all sounds carpy – a screaming buzzer – had me rushing back into the swim. I landed my first Mangrove carp of the season, a common of 11lb.

I was back the following week for a four nighter, this time across the water in the woods. I was on the same HNV with maple peas as a back up to create a particle bed. I was avoiding the eels and I felt that single hook

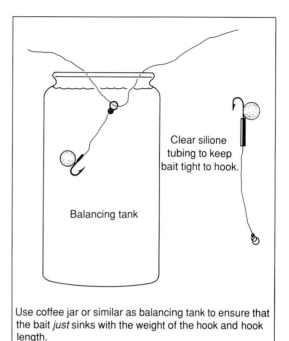

Use coffee jar or similar as balancing tank to ensure that the bait *just* sinks with the weight of the hook and hook length.

baits over particles with the loose feed boilies spread over a widish area might keep eel interference to a minimum. I should explain that the swims in the woods are difficult to fish because they are fronted by dense lily pads, but they do give reasonable access to the fish at times. I put a couple of pounds of maples out with the bait dropper, then set about balancing the hook baits. I was using three inch hooklengths which could slide up to a stop bead, an arrangement that enables you to tighten down with the hook length on top of the silt. The position of the bead is fixed according to the estimated depth of the silt. The bait is balanced to neutral buoyancy, a rig I explain in greater detail in the presentation chapter.

I balanced the first bait and cast it sixty yards onto the maple bed. I'd got no indicator needles in position yet, but this was the Mangrove and there was certainly no hurry. I balanced the second bait and cast it out just off the particle bed, to the right and behind it. If you watch carp feeding on a bed of floating particles they tend to work the edge away from the bank, which was why I positioned the second hook bait thus. I was just putting the rod in the rest when the baitrunner on the first rod whined briefly. I looked out and the line was dropping slack on the water – and there was a bow wave heading my way off the particle bed. I wasn't ready for the confrontation and had my second disaster of the season. I got the rod up, put the pressure on and the carp swung left, towards a reed bed on the edge of the pads. It was travelling fast and swung into the pads at the last minute. I'd got to keep the rod up and wind fast to keep in touch with it, but it confused the situation (meaning it confused me) by swinging out of the pads at the last second and heading back for the open water. There was a sudden terrific pressure, the fish turned over on

Bigger, but not big. A breakfast time mirror of 19lb 3oz.

its side, and the hook pulled out. It was a good fish, without a doubt, and I lost it through bad angling. The hook had opened out, but if I'd been in conrol of the situation it shouldn't have done. I was so keyed into the lily pad situation that I just wasn't able to give line when the fish did an about turn.

One of the dangers of the silt rig is that the hook is prone to open out unless you understand what is happening and take precautions. I'd known this, but felt that provided the hook was sharp enough it would penetrate to the bend and the problem would not arise. Did I treat the hook straightening as a one-off and ignore it, or take it as a warning and act accordingly? I was using size 6 Gamakatsus, superb hooks, but were they right for the bolt/silt rig? I put the rods out, had supper, tried to dismiss the loss as a one-off, but couldn't and started rooting through the tackle box. I'd no strong pattern spade end Au Lion d'Ors, the hook I would have been happiest with. I did have some Terry Eustace Super Strong hooks, eyed hooks based on the Lion d'Ors. I retied the hook lengths with Terry's in-turned point hooks and retackled each rod in turn.

It was one in the morning by the time I'd finished and I didn't expect any further action until around first light. I was wrong, and the middle rod roared off at two o'clock. The run caused a moment's mega stupidity. Up to that point of the season I'd been bivvied tight to the rods, with the sounder box immediately below the buzzer head. The new swim meant fishing bivvied five or six yards from the water, with the control box remote from the rods. I staggered our from the bivvy and homed in on the flashing LED: another disaster; the rods had gone! I told the unimpressed woods as much, but then noticed another green LED flashing at the water's edge – where the rods were. Sanity returned and I pulled into the second carp of the night. It plodded around for half a minute or so then the leader line parted about a foot up

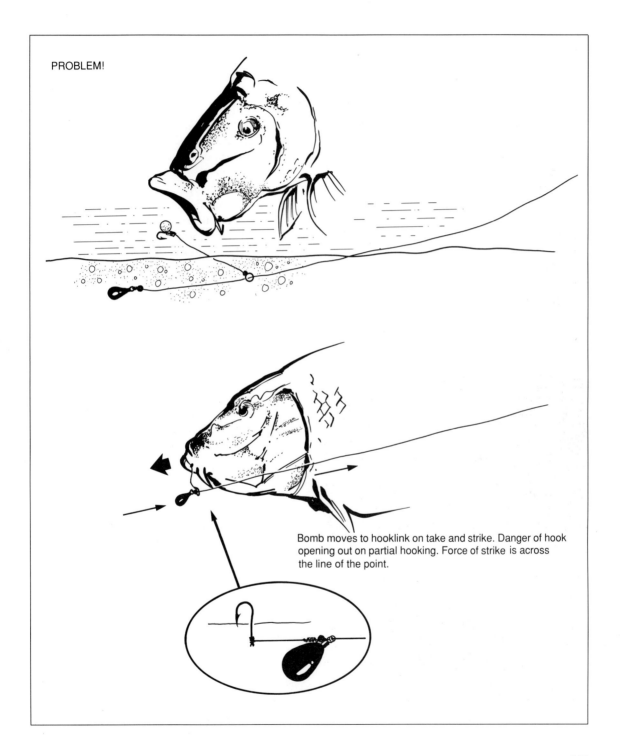

PROBLEM!

Bomb moves to hooklink on take and strike. Danger of hook opening out on partial hooking. Force of strike is across the line of the point.

Steve Wilde out in the boat at Birch Grove. I later went out in it – and fell in!

Clive Gibbins with one of his Mangrove fish from his first season on the water. This typical Mangrove common weighed 21lb 6oz.

from the bomb. I reeled in, sick as a parrot and tried to work out what had happened. I really was gutted. Four Mangrove carp hooked and three lost. The line below the stop bead felt rough. My mind went back to early evening when I'd been spodding. The constant retrieving had attracted a pike into the swim and it had struck at the bait dropper – and at the actual fishing lines as I retrieved them after casting out to position the leader knot. Had a pike grabbed at the line and weakened it? I couldn't believe that I hadn't noticed the roughening as I tied the hook length on, but it was the only reasonable explanation for the state of the line. (I'm not at all sure about that now.)

I retackled the rod and recast it towards the skyline tree marker. I was pleased by the amount of action but shattered by the loss of fish. You just don't get enough chances on the Mangrove to blow **any**, let alone seventy-five per cent of them. It became eighty per cent at five o'clock! I was away on the middle rod again, pulled the rod back over my shoulder, briefly felt the surge of power, then the hook pulled out. I could have cried. I reeled in and found that I'd got another opened-out hook, this time the Eustace Super Strong. Had I hit the run a bit too strongly? Had the hook hit bone? Probably a combination of a bit of each. I'd got to sort it out in my mind or I'd have to scrap the method. I thought about it over a couple of coffees and decided I had to treat the latest occurrence as one of those things and ease the hook home, rather than strike. There is a terrific difference between striking a silt rig set up and a standard hooking arrangement with the hooklink beyond the lead. I'd got another problem. I'd spent years not fishing a clutch: with the Mitchells I'd been able to fish with the anti-reverse off and have instant control. The Shimanos were new, strange weapons and I'd got to harness their technical excellence to the actual fishing. I had my fourth run of the session at half past nine in the morning and waited for it to drop off. It didn't and I landed a common of 12lb 12oz. Bigger than the first. Just over half way to the target weight, in fact.

I settled for the Eustace hooks, carefully checked and rechecked the end length of line before the baits went out and settled in expectantly for the following night. I was away at half past one and ten anxiety-wracked minutes later I landed a common of 18½lb. In the glow of the torchlight it looked to be a beautiful fish, and it looked even better next morning when we took it out of the sack for Bob Tapken to take the pictures. I get a glow of pleasure every time I look at the pictures of that fish; it really was very special.

I moved the next day and spent two blank days in Stoney's Swim. There were big fish showing in front of the swim so the move wasn't quite as daft as the end result suggests. I did have some action, too. I was away within half an hour of casting out, but there was nothing there, then I had another run in the early hours, the strike again meeting fresh air.

You can't 'miss' a run on the bare hook rigs so I put the occurrences down to a fish trailing line. Looking back it wasn't very bright to move out of a producing swim, but I wanted to explore the potential of three or four swims as early as possible – and Stoney's had been the most productive in terms of big fish the previous season.

All my non-fishing hours were being spent working, so I didn't have time to make any of the going bait for the next session, which was to be one of a week. I wasn't too bothered about not having the bait with me; I wanted to fish maples to see if a steadily baited particle would get me to the bigger fish in the water. I wasn't unhappy with the build-up of action on the HNV but fish were being caught on boiled baits on a regular basis, but there had been just two twenty-five pluses caught up to this time. Both were 'regulars', which come out each season. That is no slight on the anglers or the fish: Bill Cottam had landed 'One-eye' in his four fish one night haul the first week and John Lilley had landed the beautiful Scaley at 31.08 one lovely July evening. Bill and Brian were both catching consistently on their steadily applied Ener-Vite bait but it wasn't producing the bigger fish. That isn't to suggest that it wasn't going to, but I felt my chances of a twenty-five plus might be better on particle in the limited time I'd got available to me before the shut down of the water. (As it turned out we got an extra two weeks and I should have carried on with the HNV.) There are a great many big fish in the water that are very rarely caught, and weren't showing. If we could fish through to October and November I would just keep putting the HNV in and waiting for the biggies to show, but we never have that time.

Fred J Taylor and his friend John Mason spent a couple of days with us on Birch Grove over the weekend prior to the week's session, and it gave me the chance to fish the water

First real biggie of the Mangrove summer fell to that fine young carp angler John Lilley, who poses here with the magnificent Scaley at 31lb 8oz.

with bottom baits. Up to that time our Birch fishing had been mainly on top. I used the Mangrove bait and presentation for Birch, mainly so I could get confidence in both. The Mangrove undermines your thinking when things aren't going right there – as any water will – and I needed blind faith in my method to sit it out on that difficult mere. The three inch hooklinks and the balanced HNV baits worked well at Birch and I had a run of good fish over the three days with Fred and John. Mary was fishing more and more and she fished orthodox set-ups on her rods – and she didn't have a bleep over the three days and nights.

On Sunday Fred J and John departed south, Mary went back to Sheffield to keep the business running smoothly ('*Carpworld*' was due out that week and she had to supervise its despatch) and I moved onto the Mangrove for seven days. I went into the woods swim that had produced so much action on the previous session. Having thought long and hard about tactics I'd settled on a bed of maples and buckwheat with maples and tigers as hookbaits. I was putting the bait out with a bait rocket, using a beach caster rod purchased specially for the purpose. I found this method very hard work, suffered recurring damage to the tip section of my index finger, and lacked confidence over the amount of feed I should have in the swim at any one time. I also suffered too many crack-offs on the bait dropper rod, these usually occurring just when I was baiting up last thing in the evening, with dusk half an hour away, and me left with no means of getting loose feed out without going for the boat, recovering the bait dropper and starting again. (Baiting up from the boat is banned.) After that trip I made sure I had a supply of bait droppers with me, changed rods, using the North Western 2¾lb Dyneema for future sessions. Since then I've also been convinced that Silkworm 25lb braided line is superb for shock leaders, and I think my bait dropper problems are over. No,

Birthday fish. 6am 14 August and my last Mangrove fish of the summer at 15lb. I pulled off after this in the interests of work and enjoying myself!

not quite. I've still got the gradual disintegration of my right index finger to contend with and I'm going to have to look at the casting buttons that are used on some of the tournament casters to get round this difficulty. The finger damage was only occurring over a period of days when I was creating a big bed of bait over seventy yards out each day.

I juggled around with presentation a bit on this session, as we had done at Birch, and without a doubt the silt/bolt rig was hooking fish that were *picking* the bait up, as opposed to sucking it in from a distance. On the occasions we lengthened the hook link to five or six inches we didn't hook fish. I had a long hard rethink about the best hook for this rig prior to these sessions and settled for the Drennan Super Specialist, either in size 6 or 8. I think these are brilliant hooks and I've used them a great deal, and while I wasn't certain that a straight point hook was perfect for the silt/bolt rig I felt that the priority was to get the hook set to the bend. The hook straightens out when it isn't set properly, and the danger is increased with the silt rig because of the direct pressure you are able to put on the hook and, I think, because you change the angle of pull quite markedly on the strike. I'd already learnt not to strike hard with this presentation and felt happier with the Drennans.

Back to the Mangrove. I had a common of 16½lb the first night, a fish hooked right in the margins at quarter to three in the morning. I was actually standing by the rods when this one roared off. I lost a fish at around breakfast time the following morning, the end length of line again parting, this time as I played the fish against the far side of the lilies, but with no great pressure on it at all. In fact I was just holding the rod waiting for the carp to clear itself of the pads when the line went. That was a big fish and I felt very frustrated by the loss. Again the line had parted a foot from the bomb, and again it had a badly roughened feel as though a pike had had hold of it – which was a possibility along that margin at that time of the day. It sounds dumb but I didn't know I had a technical problem at this stage. The set-up had worked a dream at Birch without a single break, and I'd used it very successfully in

Mangrove evening from Stoney's Swim.

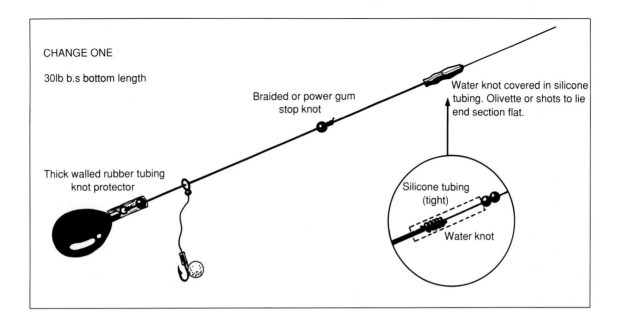

CHANGE ONE

30lb b.s bottom length

Braided or power gum
stop knot

Water knot covered in silicone
tubing. Olivette or shots to lie
end section flat.

Thick walled rubber tubing
knot protector

Silicone tubing
(tight)

Water knot

the past. The leader line was 15lb Brent, the bomb knot was very well protected, the rig was hooking fish, but things were going wrong. Pike striking at the end length of line had to be the cause. I was becoming a bundle of nerves though, and when the very same thing happened again that evening I knew I'd got to think it out again. The fish was hooked on balanced tigers fished over the maples and looked to be a mid-double. Again it came in against the other side of the pads, but it was on top so it was just a question of easing it through. The line parted a foot up from the bomb as I did so.

I was an hour away from dark and I had to accept that changes would have to be made. What alternatives had I got, other than going back to a more orthodox set-up? I'd got a spool of 30lb line in the tackle box, so I tied a three foot length of this onto the end of the leader line by means of a water knot. I switched to the Kevin Nash swivel bead with this set up, having experimented with Gardner beads, Drennan rings, and standard swivels. At about the time I was having these problems Lee Jackson published his version of this presentation in '*Coarse Fisherman*', and I later experimented

with thin tubing over the bottom length of line. I'm not sure which version I prefer; I think the thirty pound line one because we've had no problems whatever with this rig.

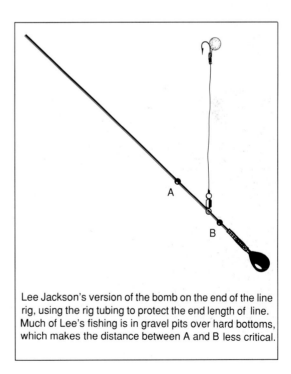

Lee Jackson's version of the bomb on the end of the line rig, using the rig tubing to protect the end length of line. Much of Lee's fishing is in gravel pits over hard bottoms, which makes the distance between A and B less critical.

123

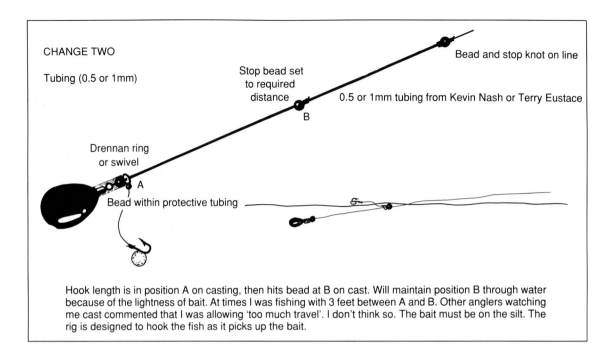

CHANGE TWO

Tubing (0.5 or 1mm)

Bead and stop knot on line

Stop bead set
to required
distance
B

0.5 or 1mm tubing from Kevin Nash or Terry Eustace

Drennan ring
or swivel

A

Bead within protective tubing

Hook length is in position A on casting, then hits bead at B on cast. Will maintain position B through water because of the lightness of bait. At times I was fishing with 3 feet between A and B. Other anglers watching me cast commented that I was allowing 'too much travel'. I don't think so. The bait must be on the silt. The rig is designed to hook the fish as it picks up the bait.

I landed one other fish that week, an immaculate mirror of 19lb 3oz, and lost two more, one being just one of those things, and the last one being down to a combination of bad angling, an increasing fear of the fish because of the mauling they were giving me, and plummeting confidence. If Mary hadn't had the car I would have packed up a couple of times that week, not through lack of guts, but because I knew I wasn't on top of what I was doing. I'd lost a number of fish because of a technical problem I didn't know I'd got, and some more because the Mangrove apparently didn't like me very much (for the third season running, I should add). I wanted a big fish, but I didn't want to fish on in uncertainty, in addition to which I really do think carp fishing should be a pleasure: although I was enjoying being there I was beginning to dread the buzzer sounding.

The last loss of that session was one of the cruelest I'll ever suffer. I moved across into Stoney's on the Thursday morning. Clive Gibbins had fished the swim on Sunday and Monday nights and had caught four carp, the biggest twenty-one plus. After he had gone the fish had shown very strongly over his baits and while I thought they would move back across the bay onto my baits they didn't and I sat through a couple of days of inactivity. I moved, lost a fish Friday morning, lost one Saturday morning, and couldn't wait for the session to end on the Sunday. Sounds daft, doesn't it? But the compulsion was keeping me there, while common sense was telling me that I'd got to think it out again.

There hadn't been a fish out over the weekend, which made the Sunday morning feeding spell make or break. Half past four to half past five was action time in Stoney's, and when the right hand rod roared off at half past five I pounced on it, quaking with joy. There was nothing there! The run was on the balanced tigers so it took no time at all to recast. The water was swathed in mist and I could only just see the marker, but I could see it, and the end tackle dropped just right first cast. There was nothing to see, nothing to photograph, and it was very cold out on the exposed swim, so I did what I hardly ever do, and went back to bed. I woke up about eight, saw the mist had given way to brilliant sunshine, groaned and must have gone back to sleep again. I could have been up and starting to pack but I was weary with disappointment. At quarter past nine the recast rod howled off again! At quarter past nine on a flat calm, brilliant sunlit morning? I didn't question my good fortune because the memory of striking nothing a few hours earlier was fresh in my mind. I panicked out in my stockinged feet and without my glasses. The line was running straight away from me across the bay. I eased the hook into the fish and there was a huge swirl. I'd got pads to my right and I prayed that the fish would swing left, not putting any great pressure on it until it had made a move. The line started to swing left, into the open water.

I crammed on the pressure and the fish started to come, grudgingly at first, then at a great rate of knots. I struggled to keep up with it: the course it was taking would bring it very close to the last bunch of pads. If it missed them I'd have no problems, but even if it hit them I should be all right. I wasn't as calm as I usually am with a fish on, though; there was too much anxiety in my efforts. I managed to get enough pressure on to get the fish up on top as it hit the pads, and it stayed on top. It was a big fish. A bit of give and take should ease it clear, and if it didn't I'd have to get the boat. Whereupon the hook pulled out. End of session. Go home Tim, the water doesn't want to know you.

I'd got a month of fishing left on the waters, give or take a few urgent commitments. In fact I put in one more four day Mangrove session, which yielded one fish of fifteen pounds, and I then got side-tracked into fishing for pleasure. I was going to plod on with the Mangrove, but Mary was starting to get very enthusiastic about her carping and I started doing some fishing with her on Birch. Ener-Vite was the going bait on Birch, so I decided to see how quickly the fish would start falling to the HNV bait. I didn't catch for thirty-six hours, in which time

Mary had three good fish, and lost two others. I was beginning to feel past it. Then the HNV started producing, starting with an 18lb common, and I finished up with six different 19lb mirrors out of eight fish in two three-day sessions. Mary had two 18lb commons, a 17lb 12oz mirror and a couple of other fish. (She was still using Ener-Vite.)

The close down for duck shooting was on September 11th. The Mangrove produced some good fish over the last three weeks, Brian Garner having the big common at 34lb 4oz, and Scaley at 31lb 8oz a week later. On the next to the last night of fishing Joe Bertram had both fish within an hour of each other, fishing Stoney's swim. Apart from One Eye falling to Bill early on the only two fish to come out at over 25lb were the Big Common, known as Trio, and Scaley. Joe had had an even bigger

Next to the last evening on the Mangrove and Joe Bertram netted this brace of Scaley at 31lb 8oz and Trio at 32lb 8oz within three quarters of an hour of each other. These were Joe's first fish over twenty pounds from the water in three years of hard fishing!

mauling from the Mangrove that I'd had over his three seasons and his big brace was a just reward for persistence and determination. I'm beginning to think that as long as your bait and method are proven and reliable, persistence and determination are two of the greatest ingredients in the big fish catching recipe.

I smiled when Brian Garner told me about Joe's brace and reminded Mary of something I'd said when I started on the Mangrove for the season: I'd just got to stick it out in Stoney's and one night a couple of big fish would come rolling into the net and ease all the frustrations away. I hadn't stuck it out; Joe had, and he got his big fish reward. One of my favourite expressions about carp fishing is 'Just because it hasn't happened doesn't mean to say it isn't going to'. I could probably add to that 'As long as you're sure of what you are doing', because you need confidence and belief to stick at it successfully.

Mary and I stopped an extra night on Birch, just to savour the atmosphere after the comings and goings of the magnificent summer. At half past nine she had a run and lost a hard fighting fish under the rod tip. A ten o'clock she had another run and brought a good fish to the net after a protracted, anxious scrap. It came in at the first time of asking and looked good. I made to lift the mesh, and laughed; it was the feel I'd been waiting for all summer on the Mangrove. The fish was a mirror of 25lb 12oz and we celebrated into the early hours.

Mary thinks she was lucky. On the Mangrove just once or twice I felt I was unlucky, and we all feel like that periodically when we are fishing for the big fish. But when I sit down

and analyse it all dispassionately, the noticeable thing is that my bad luck almost always comes when I'm not really on top of what I'm doing. An 'unlucky' season is often the prelude to a very, very good one, as long as you learn from the experiences and the frustrations you suffer. When you switch methods, or bait, the 'fine tuning' can make all the difference between success and failure. There are a great many very successful, very experienced carp anglers who haven't caught a twenty-five plus fish, so I suppose Mary was lucky to catch one from a water that we didn't think contained one! But if she goes ten years without catching another that will be bad luck: but then big fish carping is like that, and if you give up on it because of a bad season or three you don't deserve a biggie.

Note: I make reference to the technical problem I decided I'd got with the silt rig. I was using the baitrunner device on the Carbomatics for the first time, which I think may have kinked the line. I've had no disasters with 15lb leaders on this set-up in the past, but I had a number on the Mangrove – as you will have gathered. Using 30lb line for the bottom three feet completely solved the problem, as has using tubing. I now think that the roughening was from the line shattering under pressure through twisting and then being unable to untwist itself. The line seems to be all right until it comes into contact with another surface when it is suspect, presumably because its abrasion resistance is decimated by the kinking. I may be wrong about this but can think of no other explanation for the series of breakages. The line was in perfect condition.

12 Presentation – Cause and Effect

I've already written at length about presentation ('*Carp – The Quest for the Queen*' and elsewhere) so I was going to get someone else to write this chapter, but changed my mind. Why? Because the more you write about a subject as confusing as presentation the more certain you become that you haven't put it across *quite* as you wanted to, but that the all-clarifying work on the subject is on the tip of your pen. I think the long chapter I contributed to *Quest* will have helped a great many people, but that was written a few years ago now and the pressures on carp have been changing over that period. In addition I think I could have laid more emphasis on certain points.

It may seem a contradiction at the start of a chapter of a few thousand words to ask the reader to keep presentation as simple as possible, but it is sound advice. This is a book about big fish and it has to be accepted that many of the big fish in this country are being fished for all the time, season after season. They are aware that in the course of their feeding they are going to encounter baits that are a source of danger: therefore they feed circumspectly – much of the time. The more confidence they have in the bait, or the more they want it, the less caution they will show in trying to identify the rogue baits. Therefore the effectiveness of your presentation will always be proportionate to the effectiveness of your bait, within the guide lines we'll later look at for a successful bait.

The pressure on waters varies with access-ibility and numbers of anglers on the bank. In addition I'm almost certain that in some waters carp that are subject to heavy non-carp fishing pressure learn to cope with rogue baits better than carp in waters where there is no non-carp angling pressure. That's worth thinking about because it emphasises the necessity for thinking your way to your own presentation conclusions for your own water. Carp that have learnt to avoid being hooked on 1lb bottoms may be a different proposition to boilie-oriented carp to which 8lb Gamabraid is fine.

I may appear to be labouring this issue of the differences in pressure on the carp, but I'm doing so for a good reason. We are nearly a decade into the general use of the heavy bombs and bare hook rigs – and the widespread use of boilies as a food source for carp. If your bait is anything like effective you can be sure that your hookbait is at least being inspected, and very probably picked up. A starting point on presentation is to not fish fixed bomb and take the line out of the clips. If you are getting no indications of any sort on a fixed bomb, clipped up set-up you are likely to think that the problem is the ineffectiveness of the bait. Yes, I know the problem because I've been through it all. If you are fishing running lead unclipped and you get a steady lift of the indicator that stops, you curse yourself for a missed opportunity. Would that have produced a hooked fish if I'd been fixed bomb, or clipped up? Dismiss the thought. Fishing like that you wouldn't even have known that the bait had been picked up. Don't worry too much about false pick-ups: in fact be reassured by them. You know that the carp are interested in the bait to the extent that they will pick up the hookbait. It's more than a starting point to catching carp: you are more than halfway there.

You're getting twitches. What next? Change the rig? Change the bait? Stop and analyse. Big carp fishing is a game of patience and logical thinking. It may be as simple as this:

a) You are five bait mixes short of the twitches becoming strikable indications.
b) You may have too much bait in the swim for the carp to need to pick up the hookbait.
c) The fish just might not be feeding strongly enough on that day to get themselves caught; exactly the same situation might catch them another day.

Tactically, over the short term, there is one thing you can do to remedy the situation when you have had a twitch. Leave well alone for ten minutes then reel in and recast. Unless you really have to *don't change the bait*. All you are doing is moving the bait slightly in the hope that the carp will reinvestigate it, and, hopefully, get itself hooked. I feel quite certain that a bait that has been in the water a long time is a safer bait to a carp than one that has just been introduced. When a bait has been tested and 'sussed' it may as well have a notice standing by it reading 'Unsafe; do not eat under any circumstances'. When you recast you are moving it away from the notice and inducing an involuntary reaction of 'There's one I've missed here' on the carp's part. When I'm recasting I'll often tie a fresh stringer to an old bait, hoping to create a greedy suspicion about the new free offerings and confidence in the older hook bait. On some mornings at Birch Grove this is the only way I can get a take, and on that water I always recast after any sort of inexplicable buzzer indication.

I know this chapter is about presentation, not bait, but the line between success and failure is very fine at times. So fine that I'll give a couple of examples of cases where bait was the problem: I could give dozens. Back at Snowberry Lake in the seventies: the first day of the season and I'm getting twitches. You had floaters and bottom baits, bolt rigs and confidence rigs in those days so the fine tuning lay in the length of the hooklink. The effectiveness of your rig was actually the effectiveness of your bait. I was fishing tough balls of bread paste – and getting twitches. (You can sneer, but how do you *know* it won't work now?) I'd got some tins of luncheon meat from the previous season in the tackle box. I opened one, cut off some cubes and cast one into the twitching area – on the set-up already in use. I caught four carp in the next hour or so, including my first, second and third doubles! The change of bait produced lovely, unhurried lifts of the bobbin to the rod (takes in those days).

Mark Summers was fishing the Tip Lake. He'd got the bait established *after two weeks of catching nothing but tench and pike on it* and knew it was working well. He also knew he'd got fish showing strongly over the baits because he could see them, but the weather was warm and the baits he was using were eighteen hours out of freezing. He wound in, shot home for a fresh frozen mix, cast out and had a twenty on both rods at the same time within ten minutes. They were feeding on the first mix, but not strongly enough to get caught on it. Apparently the turn on from the new mix was strong enough to make the difference.

a) If action on a bait is tailing off re-establish it by rebaiting with it.
b) If the fish are interested be patient and keep the bait going in.
c) If you are sure all the other aspects are right, that you are in the right place and the carp are feeding strongly on your bait and you

Fresh baits were the successful rig in this capture. Mark Summers with two twenties hooked within seconds of each other.

are still not catching then you are going to have to put your thinking cap on regarding presentation. But don't look at presentation as the relationship between the hook and the bait – yet. We'll examine that aspect when we consider anti-eject rigs later.

After bait effectiveness the length of the hooklink and the material it is made of are usually the two most vital aspects of presentation.

If you are fishing one water regularly you can appraise the presentation problems over a period of time. You can discuss it with others, pool ideas, get some idea of the tactics that are accounting for the downfall of the carp, appraise how successful your bait is in comparison to others in use – and so on.

Tactics. Before you even come to the hooklink and hooking arrangements consider the validity of anti-tangle tubing. I've no direct evidence one way or the other on tubing, and I'm quite happy using it – which isn't to say I'm right. It will be more obvious in some situations than it is in others, but even then it will take some time for the carp to associate the presence of tubing with danger, I would have thought. But if the evidence before your eyes is that the carp you are fishing for are spooking off tubing, don't use it.

Are the fish coming out to single hookbaits fished in splendid isolation, or are they coming out when they are feeding strongly over big beds of bait? This single hookbait thing is an important issue and a more complex one than many anglers seem to think. A bait starts going in and fish begin to get confidence in it, and get caught on it. The confidence in the bait is the direct cause of them starting to get caught on it. Because they are familiar with it they can be caught on single hookbaits, and as a rule single hookbaits start to be used because the angler is casting to a hot spot that he can't get his free offerings into. The single hookbaits will possibly go on working for as long as free offerings are being introduced, even though the baiting up may not coincide with the angling. But the moment free offerings stop being introduced the life of the bait becomes strictly limited. Single hookbait fishing is a tactic, not a baiting philosophy!

Are boilies over seeds or particles producing the goods? Are the carp preoccupied on hemp, or maggots, or natural feed? If the latter is the case keep putting the bait out there and go back in October and November.

Why aren't you catching? Are you getting it wrong, or just waiting?

When you have looked at every angle and have finally convinced yourself that it is the actual rig that's the obstacle to success attack the problem with logic, and don't heave out some elaborate hooking arrangement that's going to reduce your chances rather than increase them. If you're fishing for big fish you are chasing a limited number of spooky carp. What has gone before? What are the big carp you are fishing for *conditioned to avoiding*? Cause and effect. Conditioned reflexes.

Take the average presentation as a starting point: heavy bomb, nine or ten inch hooklink, bait on or just off the bottom. Bottom baits will have been done, but then again the carp is conditioned to picking up bottom baits. Does it make sense to fish with a hookbait that is anything other than just another bait they will encounter, pick up and swim off with? Does the answer lie in the hook length material if the

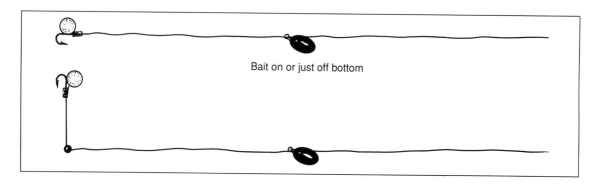

Bait on or just off bottom

carp is picking up the bait and not getting caught? There are now hook lengths available that are far harder to detect than mono or heavy dacron. When you are fishing for big carp the presentation problem is exaggerated because of the strength of the tackle needed to keep these big fish out of some of the spots they make for when hooked. An 8lb or 10lb hook-link is a minimum for big fish, so any material that gives you an edge and lets you fish finer with an adequate breaking strain is a bonus.

Because of the inevitable time lapse between the writing and publication of a book, and the startling rate of development of new carp fishing products I'll not over-praise any particular line because there may be something even better by the time you read this. Have a look at the adverts in the specialist magazines to keep abreast of developments and ask for recommendations at the nearest specialist tackle shop. More importantly, check out everything you think may make a good, hard-to-detect hook length. If you can come up with a material that only you know about you will be able to develop your own personal edge – and most carp men who are consistently successful in catching big carp have an edge of some sort. Multistrands (Kryston and Gamastrand), fine braids (Gamabraid and Silkworm), fine monos, wool, kite string, dental floss, dacron, industrial threads. Come up with the finest, most reliable line you can find of the required breaking strain then fish it with confidence. I've been using Gamabraid in 12lb and 15lb breaking strains this summer and have total confidence in it, but do read this recommendation in the context of the chapter on knots (Chapter 13).

What Can Go Wrong at the Bait End of the Line?

When you fish a finer line that may be sufficient change to turn twitches into takes. I don't think carp can detect hooks even when they are pulled into them. They run, or stop because they feel resistance. This is why fixed leads become less effective and why it doesn't pay to automatically fish monkey climbers. Fixed leads and monkey climbers are designed to create resistance, and they now seem to be an integral part of all carp fishing set-ups. Accept that they can be a hindrance at times and choose an alternative arrangement if necessary.

Here's a stunning statistic. Nine out of every ten carp men fish a hook length of nine to twelve inches. Honestly. I could say 'it is my experience that' to qualify the assertion but I've been on so many waters where hooklinks of that length were in general use that I've got to assume that the statistic is accurate. Given the universal nature of the standard hooklink how difficult do you think it is for the carp to think its way round the presentation? To arrive at the right presentation for a fish, or a particular group of fish you've got to try and get inside the carp's head so you can work out how the carp will react to a given set of circumstances.

Given that most captures arise from set-ups involving two and a half ounce bombs, nine inch hooklinks, size six hooks, and tight lines if you are not catching carp with an effective bait your alternatives for a more productive presentation are numerous, and include the following:

1) Heavier bomb or lighter bomb.
2) Longer hooklink, or shorter hooklink.
3) Smaller hook to aid penetration and reduce chances of the hook being shaken out at the pick-up stage.
4) Larger hook to exaggerate the shock tactics and reduce the chances of ejection.
5) Fish a better hooking arrangement.
6) Fish an anti-eject rig.

I'm not going to dwell too long on any of the alternatives. If you can't come to terms with

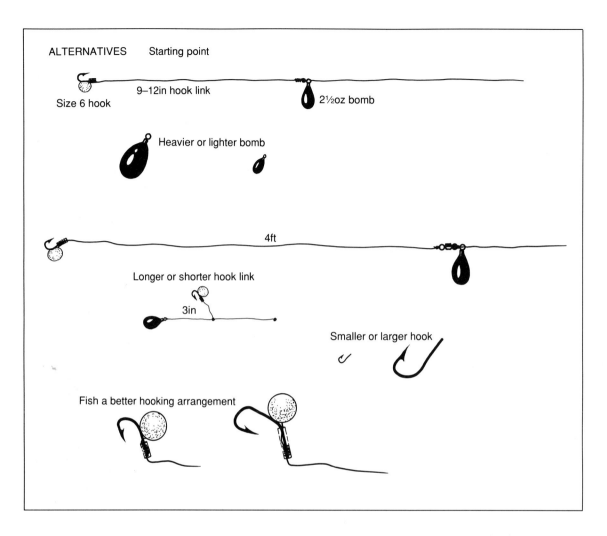

ALTERNATIVES   Starting point

Size 6 hook

9–12in hook link

2½oz bomb

Heavier or lighter bomb

4ft

Longer or shorter hook link

3in

Smaller or larger hook

Fish a better hooking arrangement

the basics of presentation in your mind from the outline given you will struggle. The important thing to grasp is the idea of cause and effect. A situation that results in carp being caught is a very temporary state of affairs and you have to have alternatives ready. The alternatives will ultimately depend on what has gone before.

If carp have been caught regularly on quarter ounce bombs they won't be used to hooking themselves on two and a half or three ounce leads. And vice versa. A carp gently pulling for the resistance from a three ounce bomb may find a quarter ounce weight negligible and start to move off.

A carp starting to move is a carp at risk. There is a point of no return in a carp's mind beyond which it can no longer keep control and will be spooked into running. You are probing for that point, and the more absorbed the carp is in its feeding the sooner the point is reached, however conditioned the fish is to avoiding being caught.

If carp are conditioned to nine inch hooklinks you can either go much longer, or much shorter. Much shorter because on a three inch hooklink the carp's first slight movement with the bait may result in its being hooked beyond quickly shaking the hook out again. A smaller hook with a small, but well defined barb may be best with a heavy lead and a short hooklink.

When you are using heavy resistance the important thing is to get the carp to drive the hook home itself. I've described the use of the silt bolt rig at some length elsewhere and I prefer to fish heavy indicators with a foot drop when I'm fishing this method. It's easy to imagine that with a three inch bolt set-up and a heavy bomb the first indication will be a screaming run or a sudden drop back. It's not the case at all. I first used this set-up on the Mangrove in 1985 at a time when the fish can't have been over rig-conscious. In the middle of a very wet night I had a roach-like take about midnight with the indicator tightening slowly to the rod, slackening off to its original position, then tightening up again. I lay in bed looking at what was happening and feeling well sick. The bed of baits was seventy yards out; carp feeding time was coming up and I was going to have to move one of the hookbaits to unhook a roach. Reluctantly I crawled out into the wet night – and discovered a double figure common on the end of the line. It might have screamed off eventually, or it might have got rid of the hook. If I'd been clipped up tight I might never have known that I'd had a visitor!

I'll re-emphasise the danger of opening the hook when you are using straight pointed hooks with very short silt rigs. The strike is across the line of the hook point, so if the carp is only lightly hooked a strong strike can open the hook out.

Long hook lengths work. They are known as confidence rigs because they give the carp confidence to move off with the bait. When the sudden resistance of the bomb is felt long after the point of no return the carp bolts. If the carp can't detect the hooklink then the confidence rig may be difficult for it to think its way round. If it can detect the hook length a very short link may be best because it may be unwilling to move far.

Fineness of line, weight of bomb, length of hooklink, sharper, smaller hook, better bait.

What are the other alternatives if your biggie steadfastly refuses to be conned into getting caught?

Suspended baits? I can't rationalise suspendeds in the way I can other forms of presentation. What I do know is that they are far more effective than my mind tells me they should be, which means I'm missing something obvious. Perhaps the obvious thing is that they are far easier to find than bottom baits, or it may be that the source of attraction is much stronger because the bait is off the bottom. Suspendeds fished at all depths and in all manner of presentations have caught big carp so try different methods if you aren't getting success. Pressured carp aren't likely to fall to a bait fished directly off the bomb – but that doesn't stop the method working! It does mean it's a method I have little or no confidence in and one I don't fish. This last summer I found takes very hard to come by if I fished the bait more than an inch off the bottom. That's not to say I didn't try going higher because I did, but with little or no success. My strongest action came through fishing balanced baits on the bottom, or suspended balanced baits fished an inch off it. Having spent quite a while waiting for the indicator to move with the bait three inches off the bottom I was fairly convinced that the balanced bottom bait was the best presentation. I don't think a big carp can distinguish between a

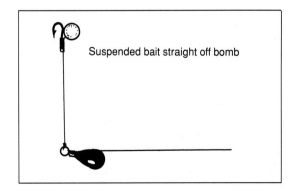

Suspended bait straight off bomb

bottom bait and one fished an inch up. On the other hand it does pay to ring the changes. I had one morning at Birch when I knew I'd got fish in the swim and couldn't get a take; a switch to two inch pop-ups brought immediate action and a couple of fish. The following day they wanted it back on the bottom!

With a heavily prebaited bait it is possible to argue for or against pop-ups. If they are used to taking baits off the bottom why risk the chance of arousing their suspicion by popping the bait up? Or on the other hand once they have confidence in the bait they will take it wherever they find it. Brian Garner feels that he gets a much better hook hold with a popped up bait, which is obviously a factor to be taken into consideration.

There is room for experiment here so I'll not take it further, but I will leave pop-ups with a warning. They have been enormously effective, and continue to be so on a number of waters; but I can't believe that fish are going to go on picking up pop-up baits indefinitely. I heard it said of a number of waters this year 'Pop-ups have blown'. Be warned.

Anti-Eject Presentation

Because of the danger of false pick-ups the presentation trend is for baits to be fished ever closer to the hook. A carp that picks up the bait and doesn't take the hook into its mouth isn't going to be hooked, which is the reasoning behind making sure the hook and bait are going to be picked up together. It's how I fish, because I lack the confidence to fish the bait well off the hook, but I know that in certain situations the method reduces my chances of hooking fish, rather than increasing them.

Read Ken Townley's superb chapter (Chapter 10) and you will soon realise that some of the rigs designed to reduce the chances of a successful ejection do nothing of the sort. They

As big as an orange. Remember that when you are picturing the carp ejecting the bait.

can't whenever the bait is fished close to the hook. Look at a carp's mouth. I've got a mug of coffee in front of me and the circumference of the carp's mouth is at least equal to the circumference of the mug. About the size of an orange. Now imagine the carp sucking in and blowing out a bait through a hole that size – its mouth. With the bait tight to the hook and chances of the hook pricking the carp aren't remote, but they are very much smaller than they would be with the bait a couple of inches away from the hook. I think that's unarguable, particularly when you think that with the hook independent of the bait the weight of the hook will cause it to drop down into the bottom of the carp's mouth.

When we first fished the hair we used very fine line and had the baits a couple of inches away from the hook. It worked brilliantly on the majority of waters it was used on BUT the whole issue of why it worked so well was obscured by the fact that two whole new principles came into play at the same time. *The two principles were a fine line hair and a bare hook.*

On some waters one or the other might have been enough. It all depended on just how the carp had been testing suspicious baits prior to the introduction of the new rigs. As it turned out bare hooks were enough on many waters, and the hair got shorter and shorter. But in fact there were probably three principles at work in the initial hair form, and these are the three, spelt out:

1) *Very fine line* at the bait. What happened if a carp 'fanned' the bait or picked it up in its lips? In the first instance it would act naturally; in the second it would feel natural. Within months those two major pluses were scrapped.
2) *The hook was bare*, and it was smaller and lighter. We used to get twitches before the hair, which must have come from carp straightening the hook length out to feel for resistance. These carp started hooking themselves and bolting. This advantage became the major consideration behind the use of the bare hook rigs.
3) *An element of anti-eject*, which had to have considerable significance with the bait fished two inches off the hook whether the carp was sucking and blowing or mouthing the bait. The fine line gave the hook bait credibility if it was mouthed, but the set-up made blowing the bait out harder. A carp sucking and blowing was more likely to blow the hook into itself if it was two inches off the hook than if it was tight to it.

I was fortunate enough to fish with Lenny Middleton a couple of years after the hair was publicised. He was still fishing it, but he wasn't using it as a bolt set-up with a six to nine inch hooklink and a half inch hair, he was using it as a confidence rig with a two foot hook length and a two inch hair. If you think about it there is a direct ratio between the length of the hooklink and the length of the hair, but as this

This big carp has clearly got rid of the bait, but not the hook.

section is on anti-eject I'll not dwell on the confidence aspect.

Anti-eject is only valid when the carp is taking the bait cleanly into its mouth – which it has got to do at some stage if it's going to take the bait. The carp takes the bait in, then decides that it isn't at all sure about what it's just picked up, or it blows the bait out anyway just to see how it acts. *The more independent the hook is of the bait at that stage the greater the chances are of the carp blowing the hook into itself when it tries to eject the bait.*

You want the best of both worlds, the bait and hook going in together, and the bait coming out on its own. The principle is best used for suspicious carp that are reluctant to move far enough to get hooked when they pick up a bait. If the fish are feeding confidently on your bait this type of set-up may not be necessary. If they are spooky and spending a long, long time examining baits it may help.

There are a number of rigs designed specifically for situations such as this, and I'll go through them briefly.

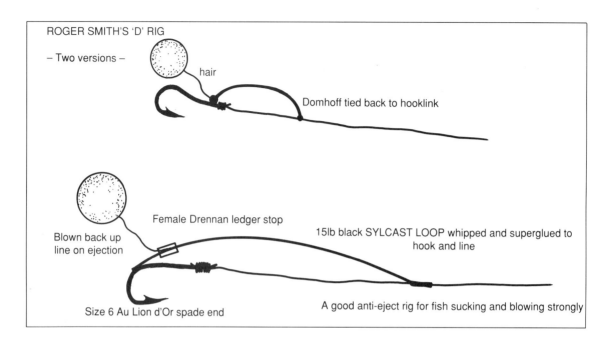

ROGER SMITH'S 'D' RIG

– Two versions –

hair

Domhoff tied back to hooklink

Blown back up line on ejection

Female Drennan ledger stop

15lb black SYLCAST LOOP whipped and superglued to hook and line

Size 6 Au Lion d'Or spade end

A good anti-eject rig for fish sucking and blowing strongly

Tim and one of a brace of big fish caught on the version of Roger Smith's rig shown here, fished in conjunction with a six bait stringer.

Roger Smith's D Rig

Roger had terrific success on Savay and other gravel pits using this rig. It fulfils all the necessary criteria for a successful hooking arrangement when the carp are sucking and blowing, the bait carrying the hook and line into the mouth when the carp sucks, and letting them separate when it blows. I've shown the arrangement I used when I fished this rig, which isn't as Roger fished it – but it worked successfully on the Tip Lake and helped me catch a couple of big fish.

Rod Hutchinson's Sliding Hair Rig

This is a good anti-eject rig when you are on a water where the carp tend to pick the bait up rather than suck at it. You can fish the bait very close to the hook, and make allowance for the hook and bait to separate once they are in the carp's mouth. It is most effective on waters where the fish feed in silt, and where there is no interference from eels or other nuisance fish. A small fish getting hold of the bait without the hook can destroy the presentation.

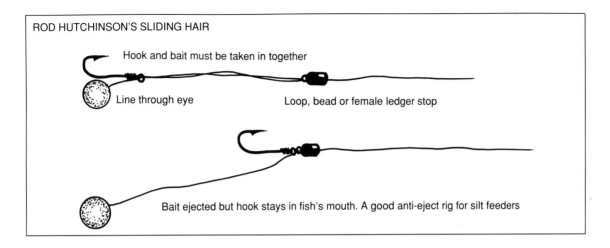

ROD HUTCHINSON'S SLIDING HAIR

Hook and bait must be taken in together

Line through eye

Loop, bead or female ledger stop

Bait ejected but hook stays in fish's mouth. A good anti-eject rig for silt feeders

Don't make the sliding hair too free-moving. It works best over silt because silt feeders tend not to suck from a distance and the hook bait won't be as free to slide clear as it would be over clean gravel where the baits may be moved around a great deal by fish moving over them.

Long Haired Pop-Up

This rig can't work. I told Brian Garner that on the Mangrove three years ago. He caught Scaley on it at 29lb 6oz that night! It's worth looking at, and thinking about, and fishing with

confidence – if you can talk yourself into it. As long as you fish it on a long hook length it fulfils all the necessary criteria for a successful presentation. Why on a long hook length? Because if the fish does pick the bait up in its lips it won't feel any line; if it then moves with it to feel for resistance you must make allowance for that movement. At some stage the fish is going to have to decide whether to take the bait or leave it. As a carefully balanced bait sucked in it will be difficult to eject, with the three opposing forces of bait, hook and shot complicating the issue. I used this rig at Cuttle Mill with

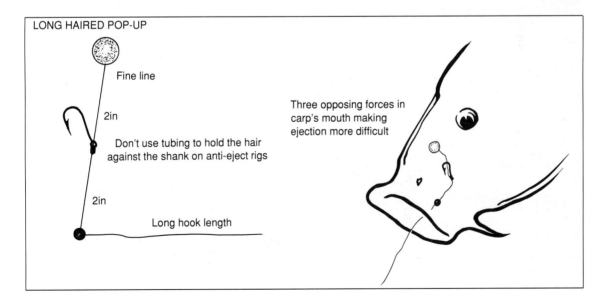

LONG HAIRED POP-UP

Fine line

2in

Don't use tubing to hold the hair against the shank on anti-eject rigs

2in

Long hook length

Three opposing forces in carp's mouth making ejection more difficult

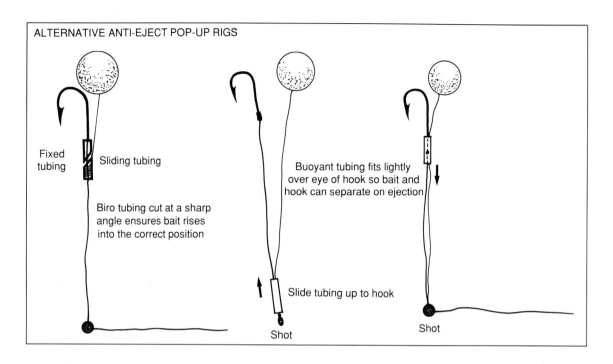

ALTERNATIVE ANTI-EJECT POP-UP RIGS

Fixed tubing

Sliding tubing

Biro tubing cut at a sharp angle ensures bait rises into the correct position

Buoyant tubing fits lightly over eye of hook so bait and hook can separate on ejection

Slide tubing up to hook

Shot

Shot

some success, but haven't used it since. It works but I don't have the confidence to use it.

Sliding Pop-Up Rigs

I've drawn two pop-up rigs which work well on the bait/hook separation basis. I think they are self-explanatory.

Presentation Conclusions

The majority of bare hook presentations are designed to hook the fish when it moves off with the hook bait (the anti-eject rigs and some versions of the bent hook rig being the exceptions). When you are deciding on your presentation for a water don't consider the rig in isolation, look at it in the light of the strength of the bait, the wariness or confidence of the fish, the way in which the carp feed, and the strength of tackle you are having to use to cope with hooked fish. Presentation is an exercise in logic, but it is also often the subject of considerable misconceptions on the part of the angler.

Fine tuning. It just isn't possible to lay too much emphasis on those words. If you look at the rig I was using for most of my fishing last year you will see how small the margin for error was. I was fishing a balanced bottom bait which would waft up with a gentle suck. If I gave the fish room to back off with the bait it would feel the resistance and get rid of it. The fish were used to having freedom of movement with the baits. The shorter the hook length, the more effective the presentation was. The carp's carelessness was likely to occur in the first moments after picking up the bait. The difficulty was having the confidence to fish short enough, but the rig was at its best with a balanced bait and a three inch hook length. I could have done without the technical difficulties but I knew the principle was right, and if I'd managed to get the rest of it right I would have had an exceptional summer.

I'm using what I was doing as an example. Choose the presentation you think will suit your fishing best then fine tune to get the best results from it, basing your fine tuning on the reactions of the carp.

13   Knots and Hooklengths

Knots are vital. Well that's a pretty obvious statement. Of course they are, and the bigger and harder the fish you are fishing for the more vital they become. It never ceases to amaze me that anglers are still willing to go and fish for carp without first ensuring that the knot they are using suits the line they are using and will withstand the rigours of being stressed by a hard fighting carp. In the last couple of years such progress has been made in producing finer, limper hooklengths that the hooklength knot aspect has taken on a new significance – and that is one of the areas that will concern us here.

Blood knots are dangerous. Multistrands and the new braided lines marketed by Kryston and Kevin Nash are stunning materials compared to the braideds we have been using over the last few years. I'm not going to enter into a braided versus mono debate here because I haven't used mono hook lengths enough in recent years to comment, but I do know that I am more than happy with what I'm using – which is Gamabraid. I have listened to people moaning about their lack of success with Gamabraid and Silkworm, and these moaners have admitted that the line was going at the hook knot, and that the knot they were using was a blood knot. *Don't they read?* (If they don't these words are wasted!) Blood knots strangle many dacrons, braids and multistrands and drastically reduce their breaking strain. The time to discover that alarming fact is not when you have just hooked the big fish you have been fishing for for half a season, is it? If you take your carp fishing seriously you will check every aspect of your tackle at the start of the season, or in the close season and know in advance that your tackle will answer any demands you make on it. It really does amaze me how little trouble some people who consider themselves serious carp anglers will go to to *get it right*.

There are two very reliable knots for dacrons, braids and multistrands, the five turn grinner and what I know as the clinch knot. I've illustrated both, and they have both appeared frequently in magazines and books over the last two years. I should add that the clinch knot is one I learnt from a 1970s Jim Gibbinson article, but it isn't the knot he shows as the clinch knot in '*Big Water Carp*'. I think he used to refer to that knot as the jam knot, but that's immaterial. The knot illustrated here as the clinch knot is tremendously reliable, as is the alternative, the five turn grinner. Dave Chilton and Jim Gibbinson both make the point that if you have any doubts at all about the strength of any of your knots you should tie them with the line doubled. That doesn't mean passed twice through the eye of the hook or swivel – which you should do with all your knots anyway – but with two thicknesses of the line throughout the knot. I'm quite happy with the knot strength the clinch knot gives me, and I've used this knot since the mid-seventies with complete confidence.

The knots discussed above are for connecting your line to the eye of a hook or swivel. The next knot I'm going to look at is the best knot there is for tying a spade end hook – the Domhoff knot. There will be big fish situations in which you need the strongest possible hook with the least possible weight. I'm happy with Drennan Super Specialist hooks for most of my

FIVE TURN GRINNER

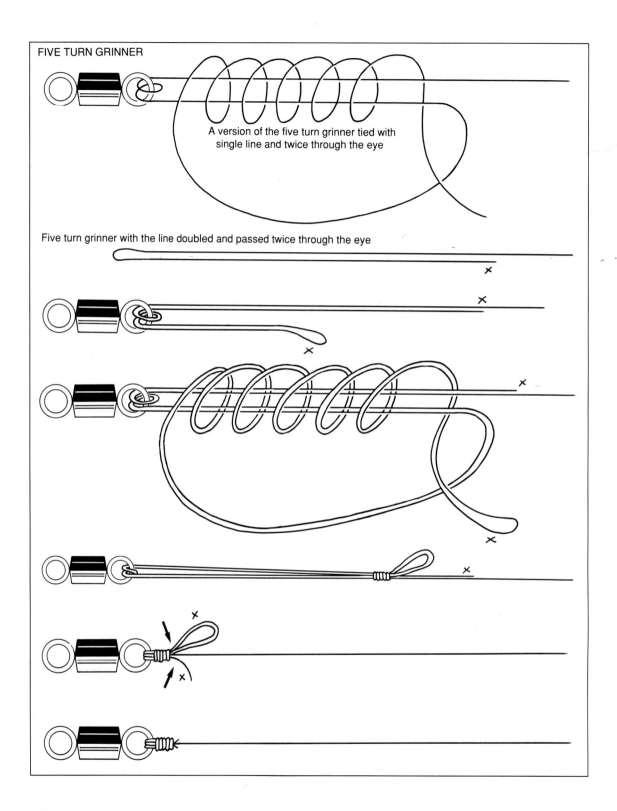

A version of the five turn grinner tied with
single line and twice through the eye

Five turn grinner with the line doubled and passed twice through the eye

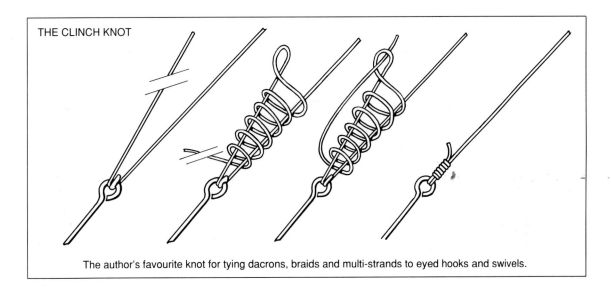

THE CLINCH KNOT

The author's favourite knot for tying dacrons, braids and multi-strands to eyed hooks and swivels.

fishing: I like the bent hook rigs and have confidence in the Drennan Lure Hooks I use with this rig: I like the Terry Eustace Super Strong hooks, which are an eyed version of the Au Lion d'Or spade end hooks; but in any situation where the prime consideration is that the hook goes in and stays in, particularly where I'm fishing near snags and know that I may have to exert extra pressure, and slacken off at times, I'm happiest with the extra strong pattern Au Lion d'Or spade end hook – which is best tied with the Domhoff knot.

I've seen a number of drawings of the Domhoff knot in print and I couldn't understand them. I have never seen any directions from which an angler could learn to tie this difficult knot, so I hope the drawings and the description that follows enable the reader to come to grips with this vital weapon in the big fish angler's armoury.

The Domhoff Knot

1) Take a loop of line. Let the end of the line protrude just beyond the bend of the hook and grip the top of the loop and the extension of the hook length against the shank with the thumb and index finger of the left hand. The loop itself is taken in the right hand, as shown.

2) Use the loop to make a turn of line around the hook shank and line as illustrated. This first turn, which has to trap the line firmly is difficult to make and needs some patience.

3) Continue whipping up the shank with the loop, ensuring that the turns are tight against each other, but not gripping the line against the shank too tightly at this stage.

4) Make up to ten or twelve turns around the hook shank and line with the loop. I'm not sure that many turns are necessary but I prefer the finish given by this number.

5) When you have taken the required number of turns grip the end of the line and pull the loop through the whipping, gripping the top of the knot to ensure the required finish. If you've bedded down too tightly when you are whipping you will have problems achieving this pull through. Use your teeth if necessary.

6) Finishing the knot off correctly is vital. Ease

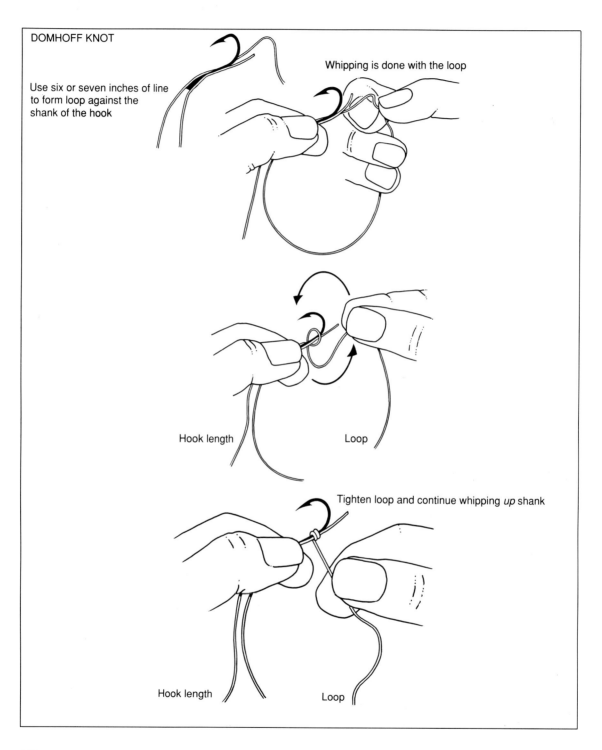

DOMHOFF KNOT

Use six or seven inches of line
to form loop against the
shank of the hook

Whipping is done with the loop

Hook length   Loop

Tighten loop and continue whipping *up* shank

Hook length   Loop

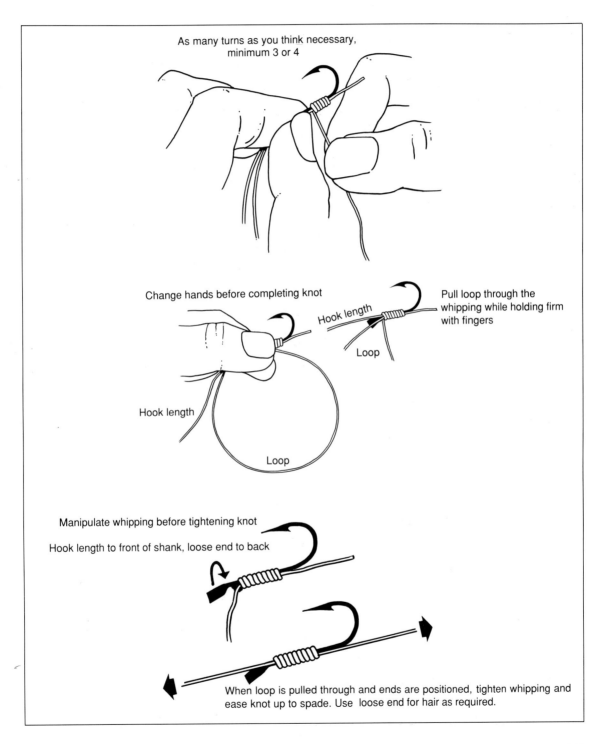

As many turns as you think necessary,
minimum 3 or 4

Change hands before completing knot

Hook length

Hook length

Loop

Pull loop through the
whipping while holding firm
with fingers

Loop

Loop

Manipulate whipping before tightening knot

Hook length to front of shank, loose end to back

When loop is pulled through and ends are positioned, tighten whipping and
ease knot up to spade. Use loose end for hair as required.

the knot back up to the spade before you pull the two ends of line to really tighten it down and manipulate the knot so that the loose end is behind the shank and the hook length runs across the middle of the spade. The hook length positioned thus ensures that the angle of pull on the line is at its most effective for taking full advantage of this in-turned point hook. Check it out. The loose length of line can be used to tie the 'hair'.

You can have complete confidence in this knot with all types of line, but if you have misgivings about the effect of the spade on the hook length apply some superglue where the line joins the hook, or use a length of tight rubber tubing to achieve the same end. I have seen a recommendation that the hook length should come from behind the shank but to me this gives the wrong angle of pull altogether.

The Water Knot

I'm including this knot because there may be situations in which you will need it, the two main ones being:

1) In tying Harry Haskell's combi-link, which is a non-tangle method of fishing multi-strands.
2) For tying shock/snag leaders where every ounce of breaking strain is necessary.

Harry Haskell's combi-link is shown in the Cause and Effect chapter (Chapter 12). As regards shock or snag leaders I usually use a three turn double grinner to connect the leader to the main line, and this simple knot is normally perfectly adequate for my purposes. However there may be situations where you will be best advised to take advantage of the slight added strength given by the water knot, which I think is the strongest knot for connecting two lengths of line. Where you want to employ hit-and-hold tactics, and need the lightest possible main line so you can cast a long way I think the water knot would be advisable.

The water knot is easy enough to tie. You simply overlap the two lengths of line by about a foot, form a loop, pass both lines through the loop four times, then bed the line down, ensuring that it is wet as you do so. The main problem the knot presents is that one of the lengths of line will be too long to pull through the loop with ease. I once wrote a slight send-up of this

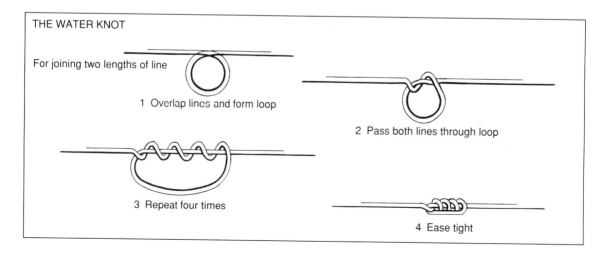

THE WATER KNOT

For joining two lengths of line

1 Overlap lines and form loop

2 Pass both lines through loop

3 Repeat four times

4 Ease tight

knot, describing the difficulties of pulling a five or six yard Sylcast leader through the loop when the Sylcast is being bloody minded about the whole operation. One or two readers kindly wrote explaining the simple way to cope with the long length of line: leave it on the spool until you have tied the knot, a solution I had worked out some years before, but advice I was grateful for, nonetheless. This is a very simple knot, as the drawings demonstrate, but it can be invaluable.

And that's it on knots. A reliable eyed hook and swivel knot for use with any type of line: a reliable spade end knot with the same pedigree: the most reliable knot for connecting two lengths of line. What more can a carp man need?

14 Bait

A number of people commented that they would have liked to have read more about bait in 'Carp Fishing'. There wasn't more because in a general book about carp fishing I felt it would have been wrong to lay any undue emphasis on what is to many – to start with anyway – just another aspect of carp fishing. There are too many different types of carp baits to attempt any kind of in-depth analysis in an introduction to carp fishing, but there does come a time when *the bait* acquires an increasing significance. Having said which, it has to be conceded that for some a bait is a bait: if it will catch a carp it will catch any carp. That's not so. We all know that bait can be sub-divided into the obvious categories of seeds, particles, boilies, paste baits and so on. We'll look at those categories, but only insofar as they reflect on the further sub-division of:

Baits which will catch carp.
Baits which will catch big carp.

Baits that will catch big carp? Some of you will recognise that such a state of affairs exists: others among you will be downright sceptical: it will not have occurred to a great many more that the actual bait can have that sort of significance. I'm getting ahead of myself but the basic theme of this chapter is that the thinking behind any carp bait is influenced by an established set of principles: understand those principles and you will have a clearer concept of how you go about selecting the bait you require for a particular set of circumstances.

We'll start with the basic bait concepts of preoccupation, attraction and nutrition. A bait's effectiveness can depend on the degree to which a carp becomes preoccupied in its eating, the intention being that it becomes preoccupied to the extent that it forgets itself, makes a mistake and gets hooked. You'll all have fished on the basis of preoccupation – with maggots if with nothing else. How often have you fished with one maggot on the hook in splendid isolation? Very rarely, if ever. If you are fishing close in you'll keep a carpet of maggots in front of you by throwing them in, or catapulting them there, and if you're any sort of an angler you will probably supplement the flow of maggots with groundbait. If you are fishing at range you'll build up the baited area through the constant recasting of a swimfeeder. You are trying to achieve preoccupation in the fishes' feeding to the extent that they move far enough with the hookbait to give a strikable indication, or hook themselves. You can attempt preoccupation with any bait. Seeds and particles lend themselves to this type of fishing, as do boilies, mini-boilies or bricked paste baits boiled hard and chopped up to the required size. There are a minimum of three vital factors to consider when you are attempting to achieve preoccupation, and they are as follows:

1) *The desirability of the bait.*
2) *The size of the individual food items.*
3) *The quantity of bait available at any one time.*

I've caught carp on baits the size of a tennis ball. They were hungry carp feeding strongly. It isn't a tactic that's been consistently successful for me, but the bait mix would catch on most carp waters. The bait has the potential to catch carp: the manner of presentation hasn't. Given the same tennis ball size of the same bait its potential as a carp catcher is far greater if we make it into twenty individual baits; almost certainly greater still if the tennis ball becomes one hundred individual baits. The end tackle might not have changed; the bait is still the same mix, the quantity of bait available is just the same, but its potential as a carp catcher has become far greater.

There are two interpretations of pre-occupation though. It can be achieved by the immediate application of enough individual food items to induce a lack of caution in the carp's feeding, or it can be achieved by making the carp dependent on, or confident in the bait by steady, unpressured application over a period of time. I have seen both methods achieve success to a desirable extent, and we have recently had two very public examples of preoccupation being achieved through pre-baiting over a period. So many Richworth Tropicana and Tutti-Frutti baits went into Harefield over a couple of seasons that they encouraged a degree of pre-occupation, or confident feeding by the carp. The same thing has happened on the famous Darenth complex over the last two seasons, in this case the pre-occupation having been achieved to a startling degree by the wholesale use of fish protein/fat based baits. Those of us who fished the Tip Lake four or five years ago cannot relate to the sort of catches the lake is yielding this season: fish meal baits have become the carp's main diet. They are not small food items; in fact Paul Selman, one of the most successful anglers on the Tip this season uses baits far bigger than those being introduced into most waters at the present time. But the carp have eaten sufficient of these baits to become dependent on them and careless in their feeding. They are not examining each individual food item as closely as they would with a bait they were indifferent to, or suspicious of. In addition the steady application of protein/fat baits has resulted in a stunning growth rate being achieved in carp that should be long past the time in life when any sort of growth can be expected. I'm sure that those anglers who have suffered on Harefield in the past have also been surprised at the way the fish in that hard water suddenly started coming out regularly on boilies.

The fact that the successful bait is common knowledge at these waters has resulted in a massive pre-baiting exercise that still continues. Pre-baiting will only be consistently successful if the food value of the bait is high enough for the carp to recognise it as a food source and

Bait dealer Martin Locke is helped in the landing of this 32lb plus Savay mirror by Keith O'Connor, himself no stranger to big carp.

Mickey Sly with a Tip Lake fish caught during the first week of the season on an established protein bait.

feeling on a hit-and-miss application of the bait. More recent observation suggests that the more the bait is used on a water the better the results become, and that the bait's effectiveness increases dramatically the further into the season you progress. People say that hemp is a warm water bait, but there's more to it than that. Hemp isn't easy to fish as a hook bait and it is usually used as the groundbait with another bait fished over it. It is difficult to determine how much of this bait you need in the swim at any one time. Rod Hutchinson reckons that with too much there is a danger of preoccupying the carp to the extent that they don't take the hookbait. I don't honestly know. I fish a number of night feeding waters and I rather get the feeling that hemp put out before dark is often taken quite soon into the hours of darkness. We've had premature feeding activity on a number of occasions when we've put a lot – up to ten pounds of hemp out – and no indicator activity in the usual early hours feeding period. Either they were preoccupied on the hemp in the early hours, or the hemp had all gone and they didn't come back into the swim. Incidentally don't dismiss this idea of the carp being preoccupied on one food item to the exclusion of another as nonsense. My friend Colin McNeil has observed carp feeding on a hemp/tares bed with boilies over the top of it. The carp weren't only ignoring the boilies, they were ignoring the tares, too! They were picking the hemp seed out from the tares. Don't make the mistake of dismissing hemp as a potential feed because it has been used before on a water, or because it must have been in use for too long to warrant consideration. It's a mistake I keep making, then someone else's results forcibly remind me that I'm wrong again. Carp are so rarely caught on hemp itself that it doesn't seem to alarm them, even if they have been caught 'over it'. I've put 'over it' in inverted commas because you can't always be sure that the capture did come over hemp,

keep on eating it. That sentence is necessarily vague at this stage but we'll consider the full implications of 'food value' later. This consideration applies equally to seeds, particles and boiled paste baits, and it is therefore important to understand which baits will go on working and which tend to have a short life.

Seeds

I think the best of the seeds is **hemp**. For a long time I was inclined to look on it as not being a big fish bait, but I now think I was basing that unless it happened soon after the bed was put down! It's possible that you don't catch a carp from the baited area until the hemp has all gone.

In addition it is worth considering that a very low percentage of the carp that come and feed on hemp actually get caught. To them it becomes another food source to be visited in the course of their feeding.

'Just another food source' opens another line of thought. Much of my fishing is done early in the week, following on from the weekend. We have few secrets between us on the waters I fish, so I usually know what everyone else is fishing. Two groundbaits in particular appear to have fish coming back into the feeding area over a period of days, long after the swim has been vacated, one being hemp and the other being tiger nuts. This probably applies to other particles and seeds but the rolling over previously baited areas has been very pronounced on the two baits I've mentioned. In fact it is worth mentioning a comment by Dr Bruno Broughton on this aspect. When I asked him about the possibly damaging effects of particles accumulating on a lake bottom his view was that an accumulation of seeds/particles would be responsible for the creation of *a new concentration of natural food*. He makes the point that all forms of pond life will feed on the breaking down baits and result in more regular visits of carp into the area. There are clear angling implications in that new natural law, but they are complex ones.

Oat groats are considered to be second, or first, in the seed league table by regular users. I haven't used them and so cannot speak from personal experience, but I have seen a number of big fish caught by anglers fishing over them. In addition I've seen carp caught a long way away from groats beds leaving strong evidence in the sack that they had been feeding on groats before they were hooked. Other users have commented that this is another feed on which

Paul Selman, a northerner who enjoyed extraordinary success on Darenth Tip Lake using Premier Baits fishmeal baits. Here Paul poses with the mirror known as Scar Bar at 32lb 4oz. The fish had made a weight of 35lb plus by October.

it is possible to preoccupy the carp to the extent that they don't take the hookbait. Groats are very cheap to use and very easy to prepare, but they are light and can only be used at range by the use of a bait dropper or boat (if rules permit). Like hemp groats seem to have a long life season to season, but results can slow down during the course of a season.

Results over groats and hemp are so outstanding, and these seeds are effective over such a long period of time, that I won't go into the other seeds in detail, although there are some effective ones. Go for food value, or fat value when you are selecting a seed, because that is the nutrient value that is attractive to carp. **Dari seed** has had some good publicity in carp circles, and Kevin Clifford had some good results at Redmire and elsewhere on them, but our results have been inconclusive. They work on some waters, don't on others. **Rapeseed, niger, sunflower seeds** are all worth trying if you are looking for something different, but don't overlook the obvious – that you might be better fishing what others are using. Familiarity breeds carelessness is a useful maxim to bear in mind when it comes to planning the downfall of big fish. The more addicted they become to a food source the more careless they are likely to become in their feeding. But the dividing line between familiarity and fear can be a fine one where there isn't much feed being introduced. If a carp gets caught every time it gets its head down over groats it will soon start to associate them with danger. Assess your baiting on the evidence available to you and keep considering the likely effect on the carp. Results don't come quickly with big carp so there is a great deal of patience involved in planning and applying a baiting programme.

Particles

When you start to use a bait you can often get a very quick result that turns out to be misleading. In these circumstances I've got a feeling that the result came about because of the difference: a new food source with no danger associations became available so the carp took advantage of it – then found that it wasn't really what it wanted, or wasn't what it seemed to be. **Soya beans** tend to produce that sort of explosive result, but no follow through, and they have no big fish track record as far as I'm aware.

Broad beans are another bait with a brief,

sometimes prolific, life, and they have accounted for some big fish. I've a feeling this bait must smell like something it isn't, so instant is the turn-on, and so total the turn-off. Well worth a try, but don't persevere with it.

Sweetcorn is a big fish bait. It is so instant, and so prolific that its life tends to be limited by its own success. Kevin Clifford proved at Redmire that its life is not quite as limited as people think – as did Yatesy over again some years later when sweetcorn accounted for the record. Chris's other Redmire monster also fell to sweetcorn. This was a breakthrough bait in the seventies, preceding the general use of protein baits by a few years. It is different enough, and attractive enough to be successful over again and is well worth considering when you are planning a baiting campaign. It will have lost its effectiveness on many waters because it is a good roach, rudd and tench bait, but there will be many waters on which it will still work.

Maize has accounted for some big fish and has enough food value to work after prebaiting. I've got reservations about it as a consistent catcher of big fish, but on waters where it does work it can produce electrifying results. Maize must have a good food value for carp because it works well after very heavy prebaiting campaigns.

Black-eyed beans are highly rated by a number of carp men for whom I have the highest possible regard. I've had no success with it, and so can't comment, but Rod Hutchinson and Jim Gibbinson say it is at its most effective after being boiled in tomato soup. These beans have a good food value and should benefit from a pre-baiting campaign – but they are also considered to be an instant bait.

Hazel nuts are a strange bait. They are very difficult to use because they take so much preparation, but I'm inclined to think of them as a big fish bait once they are established. Again they are fairly instant, but I have seen them

Paul with another familiar Tip Lake resident, Chubby Chops at 29lb plus. This fish was also a mid-thirty by October. All the carp in the water were significantly up in weight after two seasons of quality baits.

succeed over a period of time, which suggests they should stand prebaiting – as any nut should do – being high in attractive fats.

Brazil nuts work on some waters, but not on all. Some of them float, others sink, so test them before you start introducing free offerings. Any nut is worth trying, including **walnuts** and chopped **coconut**.

Tiger nuts are an astonishing bait. They are instant, prolific, and very, very long lived – and they are a big fish bait extraordinaire. I know of

no other bait that works over as long a period as tigers, and I can only conclude that they contain some nutrient vital to carp that isn't available from their other food sources. Most baits you have got to cross off the list of possibilities after one or two seasons on them, but not the tigers. The carp may become a bit more wary when they feed on them, but they do continue to feed on them whenever they are being introduced into a water. Tigers are banned on some waters, so check before you use them. If you want them to go on being sucessful don't introduce them in large quantities. When they are piled in at the start of a season they work exceptionally well – for a while. The water then seems to die almost completely, and the fish can become extremely difficult to catch on anything. In addition there is a strong, if unproved, connection between heavy feeding with tigers and a high mortality rate the following close season. The connection between the tigers and the deaths is unproved, but very strongly suspected, and this is the reason for them being banned on some waters. Dickie Caldwell had terrific success on Savay with tigers – fishing close in – and he is reported to have used no more than a few pouchfuls at a time. Use the bait sensibly and you will have success without causing any problems, but the bait can be dangerous.

I can't really write about particles without mentioning the dreaded **peanuts**. They are also banned on many waters, and as far as I'm concerned there should be a total angling ban on them. They are potentially dangerous on two counts. In the first place any type of peanut can endanger the carp's health if used in large quantities. We have checked this out scientifically, and it is a fact – but this danger only exists if peanuts become a significant part of the carp's diet. This is only likely to happen on waters where the carp are dependent on baits, and where peanuts become *the* bait. In these circumstances a characteristic unique to peanuts can cause a chronic vitamin E deficiency in the carp resulting in weight loss, listlessness and, in extreme cases, death. This is the 'only' danger from human food grade peanuts, but the trouble is everyone doesn't use food grade nuts. Peanuts available as bird food are *dangerous* – full stop. They are carcinogenic and shouldn't be used under any circumstances. The above remarks don't represent my opinions, they are documented scientific fact. It astonishes me that after all the bad publicity

peanuts have had I still see leading carp anglers advocating their use. Mercifully they are banned on many carp waters: I hope this reminder of their dangers results in them being banned on some more. Is the necessity to catch carp so great that we've got to endanger the carp's well-being to an even greater extent than we are doing already?

One final point on peanuts. As a rule a carp will stop feeding on a food source that is of little use to it, or which makes it ill – as with baits containing excessive flavour levels. But the metabolic processes involved in the vitamin E deficiency syndrome are apparently too complex for the carp's system to cope with. Peanuts are not a natural part of the carp's diet, and their effect is unique. Mother Nature cannot have envisaged their availability, and provided no defence mechanism in the carp's system.

Specials, Pastes, Boilies

Even before we get on to paste baits, paste particles, boilies and so on there is an underlying theme to this section that we'll have to meet head on at this stage – and that is that carp have an instinctive awareness of the nutritional value of a food source. I think I'm right in saying that this hadn't occurred to anyone – in the carp world at least – until a science buff/ carp angler from Kent by the name of Fred Wilton publicly theorised that carp, in common with many other creatures, have a natural instinct which enables them to 'recognise and take advantage of the best available food source'.

This natural law is so commonly accepted by those authorities whose domain this is that I'm not going to argue the case to any great extent here. I have a long chapter on food recognition in Rod Hutchinson's book 'Carp Now and Then', and a chapter entitled 'Why HNVs Work' in Kevin Clifford's book 'Carp'. In

Martin Locke, consistently successful on his own baits which he markets through Solar Baits. Here Martin poses with one of his many Savay successes, a mirror of 30lb 6oz.

addition I always refer enquirers to Fred Wilton's very explicit chapter in George Sharman's book '*Carp and the Carp Angler*', because Fred states the case in a nutshell. If carp had no instinctive food recognition system they wouldn't be able to feed, and that observation can be applied to any creature that must survive from the first moment of its existence without parental guidance. I'll just make reference to one other book source here, and that's Jim Gibbinson's recent book '*Big Water Carp*'. In it Jim credits me with the theory that carp can make an instant assessment of a food source prior to consuming it. Well, I'm grateful for

the credit, and even more grateful that Jim agrees with the theory, but I think all I've done is rationalised and drawn attention to the workings of a natural law. How does a carp know what to eat if its olfactory system doesn't spell it out for it? It is a necessary natural instinct. Food is food. The best seeds are the most nutritional ones; the best particles are the most nutritional ones; the best paste/boiled baits are the most nutritional ones – in the long term.

Here's the confusion. With the aid of modern attractors and bait additives it is possible to produce a silk purse from a sow's ear. You can fool the carp into believing that the bait you are offering is something it isn't. A bait which attracts superficially – smells like the real thing but doesn't have the nutritional quality to fulfil the olfactory promise – may evoke a strong initial response, then fail to live up to its promise. Such a bait can be useful if your time on the water is limited, but self defeating if you are engaging in a baiting up programme. Now it's no good talking generalisations when the reader wants specifics, and I'm well aware that many readers *do* want specifics – mainly, I think, as a confidence booster. So we'll talk specifics, as far as that is possible with bait, but the reader must bear in mind that however exact we try to be about this subject all the guidance available can only result in the laying down of inexact principles along which the angler can work. Pressure causes changes in carp. I don't know what the fish in your water have seen and have been caught on. It is no good me saying 'This bait will work, that bait should work' when the angling and baiting situation existing on a particular water rules the promise right out of court. (In addition I should make it clear that when I talk about a bait I'm talking about its food content, not its smell.)

There was a time when I could confidently give someone a bait recipe for Darenth Tip Lake knowing that it would catch fish – if fished correctly. That same bait would now require a heavy prebaiting programme by three or four anglers to achieve consistent results on the water. The carp are feeding confidently on a common bait, and almost all the captures are coming to that type of bait (fishmeals). If four anglers undertook a conscientious baiting campaign with a milk protein/fat based HNV it would gradually start to account for its share of the fish, but it would take time. In all honesty the best current advice would be to recommend the use of fishmeals. A bait is a means to an end, not an end in itself.

We've already looked fairly briefly at the principle of preoccupation. The rest of the bait chapter will be devoted to the principles of nutrition and attraction, *but* the comments about preoccupation can be applied with equal force to any type of bait, including attractor baits, nutritional baits, protein baits and HNVs – High Nutritional Value baits. I'm going to deal with attractor baits last because until we've really looked at the principles of nutrition it isn't easy to come to terms with the practicalities of attraction as a separate principle.

Nutrition

What is nutrition? If you don't understand how food values are assessed you cannot relate the food value of your bait to the carp's needs. I cannot claim 100 per cent accuracy in this section because there is no existing authoritative work on the finer points of carp nutrition to the degree that we have tried to refine it in carp baits. That is not to say that what follows is *not* 100 per cent accurate, just to concede that on occasion an apparently perfectly logical conclusion may contradict a natural law which hasn't yet been proved. But what follows is not mumbo-jumbo: it is based on a logical assessment of information gleaned from biochemistry books, works on fish physiology, scientific

papers based on experiments with carp – and other fish – and works on human nutrition (which is at variance with fish nutrition in some important areas).

Nutrition is not the eating of food, it relates to the body's use of nutrients from food. A great deal of the food that is ingested passes through us as waste. What isn't waste is converted into tissue or energy, a process started by enzymes. The body is very functional and in most of us the enzymes will convert more nutrients than we require. For instance carbohydrate and fats are energy sources, but the body has to have reserves of energy to take us from meal to meal. Energy reserves are built up, but when the tanks are full we start to build up fat. Physiologists are able to make an exact measure of the amount of energy used by the average man in every act he undertakes, and can quantify that act in terms of the measure of nutrients required to fuel it (calorie measure). For most of us eating more than our calorie requirement results in weight increase of the wrong sort (fat). Weight increase of the right sort (growth) can only be achieved by the intake of protein, vitamins and minerals, with the energy fuels of fat and carbohydrate being balanced by the required amount of exercise. All the subdivisions of nutrients are mentioned there. Protein, carbohydrate, fats (which are divided further into saturated and unsaturated fatty acids), vitamins and minerals. I'll try and describe the function of each division as simply as possible.

Protein

Proteins are built up of amino acids, Table 1 (*see* page 155) showing the relative quantities of man's eight essential amino acids in a cross section of proteins. In nutritional terms 'essential' means that it must be ingested in that form and cannot be manufactured within the system. Twenty amino acids occur regularly in proteins: they are all essential in the sense that they

Table 1   The amounts of essential amino acids in certain proteins (expressed in mg per gram of nitrogen)

Amino acid combination estimated as ideal for man	isoleu-cine	leucine	lysine	phenyl-alanine	methio-nine	threo-nine	trypto-phan	valine	protein score as measure of excellence
	270	306	270	180	144	180	90	270	100
Egg protein	428	565	396	368	196	310	106	460	100
Beef	332	515	540	256	154	275	75★	345	83
Milk protein	402	628	497	334	190	272	85★	448	80
Fish	317	474	549	231	178	283	62★	327	70
Oat protein	302	436	212★	309	84★	192	74★	348	79
Rice protein	322	535	236★	307	142★	241	65★	415	72
Flour protein	262★	442	126★	322	78★	174	69★	262	47
Maize protein	293	827	179★	284	117★	249	38★	327	42
Soya protein	333	484	395	309	86★	247	86★	328	73
Pea protein	336	504	438	290	77★	230	74★	317	58
Potato protein	260★	304	326	285	87★	237	72★	339	56
Cassava	118★	184★	310	133★	22★	136★	131	144	22

The table indicates how cereal proteins lacking in lysine can be supplemented with soya and other bean protein: the 'score' of each protein given in the last column is based on some inexact tests of what biological excellence is. These values are derived from a variety of feeding tests, some carried out on experimental animals and some on people. There are two difficulties in measuring in exact terms the nutritional quality of any particular protein. The first is that 'essential' amino acids are only essential because the rate at which they can be manufactured in the body is too slow to keep up with the need for supplies of them to combine with those which are more readily available, in order to make up a pool of amino acids which contains the proper proportion for building up the proteins the body needs. The second difficulty is that the biological value of a particular protein will be affected by the *total* amount of the protein present in the diet. Obviously, if very little protein is available, what there is will serve the body best if it contains the right proportion of amino acids. If, however, there is ample protein in the diet and some to spare, there may be sufficient of any particular amino acid, simply because of the quantity of protein eaten.

must be present for the protein to be complete, but those that aren't labelled 'essential' can be synthesised from the essentials.

Carp have ten essential aminos. The significance of the amino acid profile is that when proteins are eaten it is the aminos that are the source of the protein nutrient. The food is the amino acid donor and the eater the acceptor. The amino acids from the donor are reassembled by the metabolic system of the acceptor. Each amino acid requirement has to be fulfilled, which is why some proteins are better than others — as Table 1 (above) will readily confirm. The amino acid deficiencies stand out in the table and it is immediately obvious that vegetable proteins are not as valuable as those from animals. But on the other hand combining vegetable protein with animal protein may be necessary to arrive at the ideal amino acid profile.

But keep remembering that nutrition is not what is eaten, but what is used by the system — the digestibility factor. Beef is top of the protein table — for humans. In terms of amino acid

Table 2   The protein percentage in a range of foods

	g per 100g			g per 100g
MEAT			**PULSES AND NUTS**	
Corned beef	22.3		Soya flour	40.3
Rabbit	21.0		Peanuts	28.1
Chicken	20.8		Lentils	23.8
Whale	20.6		Dried peas	22.1
Veal	19.2		Haricot beans	21.4
Calf's liver	16.5		Brazil nuts	13.8
Beef (fresh)	14.8		Walnuts	12.5
Lamb	13.0		Desiccated coconut	6.6
Pork	12.0		Chestnuts	2.3
FISH			**CEREALS**	
Lobster	21.2		Oatmeal	12.1
Whiting	19.9		Wholemeal flour	11.6
Crab	19.2		White flour	10.0
Salmon	19.1		Maize	10.0
Cod	18.0		Wholemeal bread	9.6
Herring	16.0		White bread	8.3
Haddock	15.9		Rye	8.0
Plaice	15.3		Barley	7.7
Eel	14.4		Rice	6.2
DAIRY PRODUCE			**FRUIT AND VEGETABLES**	
Dried egg	43.4		Green peas	5.8
Dried skimmed milk	37.2		Cauliflower	3.4
Dried whole milk	26.6		Spinach	2.7
Cheese	25.4		Potato	2.1
Egg	11.9		Dates	2.0
Condensed milk	8.5		Cabbage	1.5
Evaporated milk	8.2		Bananas	1.1
Liquid milk	3.3		Turnip	0.8
Butter	0.5		Apple	0.3

In considering these percentages it is important to consider the quality of the protein

profile it is for carp, too, but only in theory. In practice carp would find it impossible to digest. We have a stomach containing hydrochloric acid and the acidic enzyme pepsin, and all our food, however tough, passes into the intestine as an emulsion. Carp don't have a stomach, or hydrochloric acid, or pepsin and their digestive system wouldn't cope too well with a fibrous

protein like beef. In other words we have to pay some attention to the physical properties of food when assessing its suitability as a bait, or in bait, and not just its theoretical food value.

Protein is the carp's major source of nutrition. It is the only nutritional source which rebuilds tissue, gives growth and is an energy source, too. But, paradoxically, for a carp to

Table 3   The essential amino acid requirements of 4 species of fish

Amino Acid	Chinook Salmon[a]	Japanese Eel[b]	Carp[b]	Carp[c]	Rainbow Trout[c]
Arginine	2.4 (6.0/4.0)	1.7 (4.0/42)	1.6 (4.3/38.5)	1.52 (3.8/40)	1.40 (3.5/40)
Histidine	0.7 (1.8/40)	0.8 (1.9/42)	0.8 (2.1/38.5)	0.56 (1.4/40)	0.64 (1.6/40)
Isoleucine	0.9 (2.2/41)	1.5 (3.6/42)	0.9 (2.5/38.5)	0.92 (2.3/40)	0.96 (2.4/40)
Leucine	1.6 (3.9/41)	2.0 (4.8/42)	1.3 (3.3/38.5)	1.64 (4.1/40)	1.76 (4.4/40)
Lysine	2.0 (5.0/40)	2.0 (4.8/42)	2.2 (5.7/38.5)	2.12 (5.3/40)	2.12 (5.3/40)
Methionine	0.6 (1.5/40)	1.2 (2.9/42)	1.2 (3.1/38.5)	0.64 (1.6/40)	0.72 (1.8/40)
	Cys = 1%	Cys = 0%	Cys = 0%	Cys = +	Cys = +
		0.9 (2.1/42)	0.8 (2.1/38.5)		
		Cys = 1%	Cys = 2%		
Phenylaline	1.7 (4.1/41)	2.2 (5.2/42)	2.5 (6.5/38.5)	1.16 (2.9/40)	1.24 (3.1/40)
	Tyr = 0.4%	Tyr = 0%	Tyr = 0%	Tyr = +	Tyr = +
		1.2 (2.9/42)	0.8 (2.1/38.5)		
		Tyr = 2%	Tyr = 1%		
Threonine	0.9 (2.2/40)	1.5 (3.6/42)	1.5 (3.9/38.5)	1.32 (3.3/40)	1.36 (3.4/40)
Tryptophan	0.2 (0.5/40)	0.4 (1.0/42)	0.3 (0.8/38.5)	0.24 (0.6/40)	0.20 (0.5/40)
Valine	1.3 (3.29/40)	1.5 (3.6/42)	1.4 (3.6/38.5)	1.16 (2.9/40)	1.24 (3.1/40)
Total	12.3 (30.49)	14.8 (35.4)	13.7 (35.8)	11.28 (28.2)	11.64 (29.1)

Sources: [a] Mertz   [b] Nose   [c] Ogino

The table shows the carp's ten essential amino acids (as against eight for humans) expressed as grams per 100 grams of food (dry weight). The figures in brackets are ('1'/'2'): '1' grams per 100 grams of protein. '2' percentage of dietary protein.

The 'extra' essential aminos are Arginine and Histidine, which are present in all proteins.

obtain optimum benefit from available protein it requires a balancing direct energy source. It is a stated law of physiology that the first requirement to be fulfilled is the energy requirement. We'll look at the full implications of that later but in bait terms the law equates to this: a 100 per cent protein bait will be wasted, in the sense that it will be used as an energy source, until the energy requirement has been fulfilled. The carp's system will then start to make use of the protein for maintenance and tissue repair. A protein/high fat bait will achieve a better balance. The fat will fulfil the energy requirement and 'spare' the protein for its proper use. In human terms fats and carbohydrate perform a similar energy supplying/protein sparing role – although even in humans fats are 100 per cent more efficient than carbohydrate, gram for gram. It isn't clear that that is the case with carp and we'll look at this anomaly more closely under 'Carbohydrate'.

Fats

When I was studying nutrition it took me a long time to come to terms with the two basic sub-divisions of fats – polysaturates and polyunsaturates: my mind kept closing whenever I

Table 4   The fat content of certain foods

	g per 100g
FATS AND OILS	
Frying oil	99.9
Lard, dripping, cooking fat	99.3
Margarine	85.3
Butter	82.5
MEAT	
Bacon	28.2–61.1
Pork	23.2–50.3
Lamb	20.4–52.5
Beef	10.5–32.1
Duck	23.6
Calf's liver	8.1
Chicken	6.7
Veal	2.7
FISH	
Fatty Fish:	
Herring	18.1
Kipper	11.4
Mackerel	8.5
Canned salmon	6.0
Non-fatty fish:	
Plaice	1.8
Sole	1.3
Cod	0.5
Haddock	0.5
DAIRY PRODUCE	
Cream	48.0

	g per 100g
Cheddar cheese	34.5
Gorgonzola cheese	31.1
'Processed' cheese	30.0
Edam cheese	22.9
Eggs	12.3
Condensed milk	9.2
Milk	3.8
CEREAL PRODUCTS	
Oatmeal	8.7
Wholemeal bread	3.1
Barley	1.7
White bread	1.7
Spaghetti	1.0
Rice	1.0
Cornflakes	0.5
FRUIT AND NUTS	
Dessicated coconut	62.0
Brazil nuts	61.5
Almonds	53.5
Walnuts	51.5
Peanuts	49.0
Olives	8.8
Avocado pears	8.0
All other fruits	trace
VEGETABLES	
Potatoes	trace
Green vegetables	trace
Peas and beans	trace

encountered those two awful looking words. In fact the terms are chemical definitions and meaningless to most of us. The bottom line is that saturated fats aren't nutritional; unsaturated fats are, and are a valuable energy source. More than that they are *the best energy source*. Although both types are present in all fat source foods Table 5 shows that vegetables, nuts and seeds are the richest source of the polyunsaturates from which the carp draws its energy, oleic and linoleic acid. Animal and fish fats are also rich in polyunsaturates but are also more concentrated sources of saturates. The latter are digestible but aren't nutritional; they are deposited as fat in the recipient system (and are a dangerous cholesterol source for humans). The explanation of the butter/margarine debate is the presence of saturated fats in butter, while the best margarines are based wholly on unsaturates. You will often see fats expressed as chemical carbon chain formulae, so I've included these references in case anyone encounters a scientific paper where only formulae are used (which does happen).

Table 5   The percentage of the principal fatty acids in various fats and oils

| | Unsaturated fatty acids | | | | Unsaturated fatty acids | | | |
	lauric (C_{12})	myristic (C_{14})	palmitic (C_{16})	stearic (C_{18})	oleic	linoleic	lino-lenic	arachi-donic
VEGETABLE FATS								
Coconut oil	48	17	9	2	6	3		
Cottonseed oil		1	29	4	24	40		
Linseed oil			6	4	22	16	52	
Maize oil			13	4	29	54		
Olive oil			16	2	65	15		
Palm oil		1	48	4	38	9		
Peanut oil			6	5	61	22		
Sunflower oil		8		3	13	75	1	
Sesame oil		10		5	40	43		
Soya-bean oil		11		4	25	51	9	
Sunflower-seed oil		11		6	29	52		
Wheatgerm oil		13		4	20	55	7	
ANIMAL FATS								
Beef fat		3	25	24	42	2		
Butterfat (cow)	4	12	29	11	25	2		
(goat)	6	12	28	6	21	4		
Lard		3	24	18	42	9		
Mutton fat		5	25	30	36	4		
Fat in egg yolk★			32	4	43	8		
MARINE FATS								
Cod-liver oil		6	8	1	20	29	25	10
Herring oil		7	12	1	12	20	26	22
Menhaden oil		6	16	1	15	30	19	12
Pilchard oil		5	14	3	12	18	18	14
Sardine oil		6	10	2	13	14	26	29
Whale oil		9	16	2	14	37	12	7

★ Fat in egg yolk also contains 13 per cent of a C22 saturated fatty acid. The fatty acids as equations, which is how they are often expressed.

Rod Hutchinson and I have talked a great deal about fats and something Rod said made me rethink some aspects of them: I'm inclined to think that for a long time I may have been overlooking a significant point (but this is conjecture). The breakdown of animal and fish fats makes it clear that polysaturates are present in significant quantities, and it's got to be conceded that a number of low protein/high fat baits are more effective than one might expect them to be. Luncheon meat, Bacon Grill and fish all have a significant saturated acid content, a content which will be deposited as fat in the carp's system. As carp don't wear clothes is it possible that saturated fat deposits are their 'clothing' and that they are therefore as important a part of their diet as proteins, vitamins and minerals?

Carbohydrate

I started my 'serious' carp fishing on a hungry crust water, which led me to believe that carbohydrates were of great significance to carp. I no longer believe that because the science and fish physiology sources I refer to suggest that carbohydrates have a limited nutritional significance for carp.

There's a conflict between practical observation and logic and the teachings of science here but I'll try to rationalise the conflict. Carp are diabetic in the sense that they don't have the hormone insulin. This means that they can't oxidise carbohydrate to direct energy use (as we do), but can only metabolise it by storing it as glycogen in the liver – the usual energy reservoir. Starvation tests on carp have shown no reduction in the liver glycogen levels, which has led fish physiologists to suggest that carbohydrates are of little or no value to carp as a source of nutrition.

I'll rationalise that a bit further by suggesting that the starvation tests weren't made over a

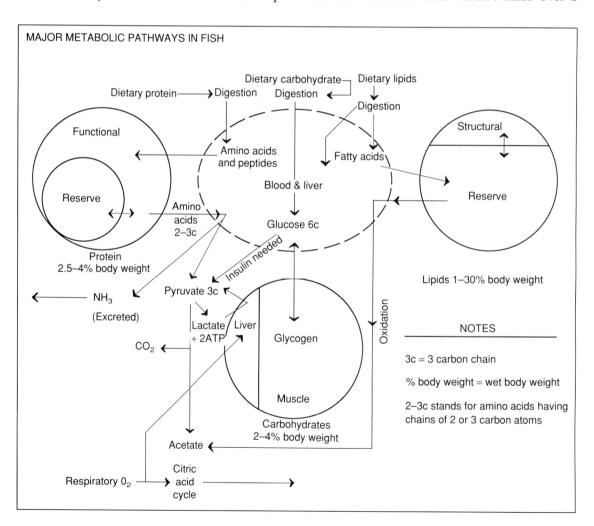

long enough period, and weren't complete enough either. Aksakov at the end of Ransome's *Rod and Line* described the carp spawning migration at the end of a long hard winter freeze up.

Closer to home carp are most 'crust conscious' through the close season and early summer. That may be due to angling pressure, or it may be because of the timing of the nutritional need for carbohydrate. In many waters carp will have little or no natural food supply through the winter and early spring, then go into the rigours of spawning when their energy reserves are possibly at their lowest ebb. That being the case the liver glycogen reserves may be drawn on long after the scientist's three-month trial period and the intake of carbohydrates become a valid nutritional necessity for a while.

This is a complex, slightly controversial area but as the boffins are very dubious about the validity of carbohydrate in the carp's diet I've got to pass those doubts on.

The following is a comparison of the relative efficiency of the energy sources for humans:

Fats 9:1
Protein 4:1
Carbohydrate 4:1

Nutritionists give the same figures for carp, subject to the reservations about carbohydrate, so whatever your feelings about carbohydrates, fats/oils are the prime energy food for carp.

Vitamins and Minerals

The vital extras, required in such minute quantities that it's easy to think they don't matter. They do: very much so, and for a number of reasons. Vitamins and minerals can be important foods in their own right, or they can be of great significance in enabling the system to make proper use of other nutrients. Some of the B vitamins, for instance, play an important role as co-enzymes and assist the main enzymes to function efficiently.

The following table shows the carp's vitamin requirements *per kilo of dry feed* and are reproduced with the kind permission of Roche Vitamin and Chemical Division, upon whose research they are based, and Nutrabaits, in whose catalogue they were first published.

Nutritional Baits

It isn't necessary to have any understanding whatever of nutrition to catch carp, but I'll go

Table 6   Roche Chemicals Vitamin/Mineral Division research figures for the Vitamin requirement of carp. Figures per kilogram of dry feed

A	D	E	K	B1	B2	Niacin	Pantothenic
IU	IU	mg	mg	mg	mg	mg	mg
8000–12000	1500–2000	200–300	6–12	10–20	15–20	80–120	40–50

B6	B12	Folic Acid	Biotin	Choline	C	Inositol	
mg	mg	mg	mg	mg	mg	mg	
8–12	0.02–0.05	3–4	0.5–1.0	800–1200	150–300	100–150	

IU = International Units   mg = Milligrams

Table 7   A summary of the vitamin requirements of carp showing reference sources

Vitamin	Deficiency Avitaminosis Signs	Suggested Dietary Level (parts per million)	Recommended Intake (mg/kg/day)	Reference
Thiamine (B₁)	poor growth, anorexia, loss of colour, hyperaemia of fins and skin	60ppm	–	Aoe *et al.* (1967c, 1969)
Riboflavin (B₂)	anorexia, disorientation, mortalities, skin and heart haemorrhages, necrotic kidney	40–62ppm 70–100ppm	0.11–0.17 0.23–0.33	Aoe *et al.* (1967a); Ogino (1967)
Pyridoxine (B₆)	poor growth, loss of balance, epilepsy, abnormal swimming, oedema, exophthalmia	20ppm	0.15–0.20	Ogino (1965)
Pantothenic acid	anorexia, weight loss, inactivity, exophthalmia, haemorrhages, anaemia	30–40ppm	1.0–1.4	Ogino (1967)
Inositol	anorexia, poor growth, skin lesions, haemorrhages, skin erosion	440ppm	7–10	Aoe and Masuda (1967)
Biotin	poor growth, changes in haemopoietic tissues	10ppm	0.02–0.03	Ogino *et al.* (1970)
Folic acid	no signs	15ppm	–	Dabrowski (1979)
Para-amino-benzoic acid	no signs	200ppm	–	Dabrowski (1979)
Choline	poor growth, accumulated hepatopancreatic fat	2,000–4,000ppm	60–120	Ogino *et al.* (1970)
Niacin	anorexia, poor growth, skin haemorrhages, high mortality	28ppm	0.55	Aoe *et al.* (1967b)
Cyanocobalamin (B₁₂)	no signs	0.09ppm	–	Dabrowski (1979)
Vitamin A	anorexia, weight loss, loss of colour, fin and skin haemorrhages, warped operculae, exophthalmia	2,000 i.u./kg	4,000–20,000 i.u./kg/day	Aoe *et al.* (1968)
Tocopherol (E)	low weight gain, muscular dystrophy, exophthalmia, lordosis	100ppm 300ppm	–	Watanabe *et al.* (1970a,b)
Ascorbic acid (C)	no data	2,000ppm	–	Dabrowski (1979)
Menadione (K)	no data	40ppm	–	Dabrowski (1979)

Table 8   Mineral requirements of carp

It has only recently been confirmed that carp have a mineral requirement. Tests over fifty days were inconclusive, but recent studies have shown that carp on mineral-free diets display deficiency symptoms after eight weeks, including lordosis, loss of muscle tone, reduced growth and food conversion efficiency, and reduced haemoglobin, haematocrit and mean haemoglobin concentrations.

Minerals which can be shown to have biological functions include calcium, phosphorus, magnesium, sodium, potassium, sulphur, chloride, iron, copper, cobalt, iodine, manganesem zinc, molybdenum, selenium and fluorine. (Lall 1978).

Calcium and Phosphorus:	The major mineral nutrients are considered to be interdependent. Requirement: Phosphorus 0.6–0.7% of diet. Calcium 300 parts per million.
Magnesium:	0.04–0.05% of dry diet.
Iron:	Essential but quantitive data lacking
Cobalt:	Has a biological role as a component of Vitamin B12 cyamocobalamin
Zinc:	Requirement of dietary zinc in carp found to be 15–30ppm
Iodine:	Sufficient in plant proteins to meet carp's requirements
Other Trace Elements:	Copper, sulphur, fluorine, manganese and molybdenum – no data

on from the basic description of nutrients for many readers who love the complications, whys and wherefores of making their own nutritional bait. It's essential to grasp the significance of nutrition and to accept that what the carp eat has a massive, measurable effect on their well being. The main argument against nutritional selection on the part of the carp is that they can't think, therefore they can't know. But the same people who argue thus will offer the observation that carp like sweet things. That's questionable. Liking is partly a thought process; nutritional awareness is an instinct. We are taught what is good for us (and largely ignore the guidance): carp are wild creatures and feed by instinct. We do have some instinct for food in that we can identify many foods by smell, but a carp's senses are far more sharply honed than ours are when it comes to the location of, and assessment of, a food source.

Compared to the very complex nutritional instincts present in some wild creatures I don't think the carp's feeding instincts are particularly complex. In an article written in the seventies I pointed out that some ants have to eat one food which provides them with the necessary enzyme to eat their main source of nutrition. For most of us the problem is that we understand so little about nature and biochemistry that even their simplest workings can seem incomprehensible.

It is possible that for carp 'hunger' is only triggered by a food source representing a nutritional requirement. There is some evidence to suggest that there is a link between the olfactory and the enzyme systems. The significance of that is that any hunger message would be a direct link between the potential food source and the recipient enzyme. When the carp's system had received sufficient of the required food source the enzyme would stop 'receiving' its nutritional message through reaching saturation. The link between amino acids and the carp's receptors is well documented, although Hara, who has done most of the pioneering work in this area, cannot precisely locate the receptor site. All the evidence points to it being the enzymes, or an enzyme linkage.

Now many of you who have read thus far, largely the bait buffs and those getting ready to pounce, will have a number of questions waiting to be asked, and I know the form most of them will take.

First, I think it is essential to consider the carp's diet as a whole entity, rather than trying to convince yourself that an HNV bait will be the answer to all your carp fishing problems. It is very difficult to imagine a water where there won't be deficiencies in the carp's diet. Early in the season the most marked deficiency is likely to be suitable energy sources. Very few people include an adequate energy provision in their protein HNV baits, for example. If the carp's nutritional awareness *is* deficiency-orientated energy baits *will be* high nutritional value baits. I have never subscribed to the argument that only protein baits are high nutritional value baits, and I don't think that was the basis of Fred Wilton's original theory. There will be times of the year when protein/vitamin-mineral baits will represent the greatest nutritional requirement; in autumn and winter, for instance. Early season? How about bird food baits (energy sources); how about ready mades (semolinas and soya flour = energy source); how about particles and seeds (energy sources)?

It is no good arguing against nutritional awareness, and then throwing up strong evidence of the manifestation of that awareness as an argument against it by citing baits which are nutritional and claiming they aren't!

It would be wrong to suggest that the nutritional deficiency case is that simple though. Any bait satisfying a nutritional requirement to whatever degree is a nutritional bait. The need might be a very minute, temporary one soon fulfilled (as a vitamin or mineral deficiency is likely to be), or it might be an ongoing one, as with energy, maintenance and tissue repair. If you don't approach the problem with an understanding, open mind you are likely to be confused by the evidence before your eyes and not comprehend what is happening with your own carp on your own water.

Fred Wilton's theory is 'A carp will recognise and take advantage of the best possible food source'. Until the carp man cometh that food source will be natural food; no argument. If there isn't sufficient natural food carp will take advantage of any additional food sources, however unsatisfactory in nutritional terms. Angling pressure and bait competition will complicate the issue. Baits that *smell* like ideal food sources but are in fact nothing of the sort will complicate the issue even further. Increased angling pressure will lead to better baits, better smells, better rigs. It will become more and more difficult to get it right from the angler's point of view unless he remembers those two words 'food source'.

Have you ever stopped to define those two words 'food source' to yourself? When it comes to fishing for the big fish you've got to. If you are fishing a water with 20 or 30 twenty plus fish in it how much of a bait will have to be introduced before it starts to be accepted as a food source? Don't ask me, I've no idea, but I'm sure that when it comes to wary fish familiarity breeds acceptance. If your bait was good enough last season don't change it, because it is likely to be far more acceptable the following year.

Where nutritional value becomes a factor in the effectiveness of a bait it can do so for two reasons. One is that the bait competition on a water where baits are the main food source can make the degree of nutritional excellence important: to establish a bait long term it has to provide something natural foodstuffs and other baits aren't providing; it doesn't replace the existing food sources but complements them. Alternatively a high nutritional value bait can be a necessity on waters where it is difficult to interest the carp in baits at all; where there is such an abundance of natural food that the carp don't have to eat baits as part of their diet.

Grasp the principles behind the use of nutritional baits and don't be seduced by the magic word protein; high fat baits are just as effective as high protein baits. Concentrated fat sources, like bird foods, seeds and particles often fulfil a nutritional requirement not met by protein-rich and natural food sources. I've often seen bird food baits described as 'crap baits' (the usual expression for low food value baits) when they are nothing of the sort. They are fat and vitamin-mineral rich.

But protein is an essential part of the carp's diet and a high fat bait will rarely catch *to the exclusion of* results on a well balanced fat/protein/vitamin-mineral bait (based on milk/egg or fish proteins). In fact a fat source bait will increase the effectiveness of the protein bait; as we've already seen fats will increase the nutritional effectiveness of protein when the two are used at the same time – *and that doesn't necessarily mean in the same bait*. Baits in competition with each other can actually complement one another!

If you accept that there is great significance in bait then try to grasp the principles behind the issues we are discussing here; they are scientific nutritional fact, not bait gobbledygook, and what we are going the long way round to arrive at is the concept of the all-fulfilling HNV; the high nutritional value bait based on good quality food grade proteins, convertible fats, and vitamins and minerals. And enzymes. Oh no; not them. Well ideally, yes.

Carp have no stomach and the nutrients from their food intake have to be extracted by the carp's enzymes as the food passes through the intestine. A carp's system is designed by nature to cope with the food it encounters in nature, and the naturally occurring proteins carp eat are mainly live mixtures of amino acids and proteolytic enzymes. The carp's enzymes are complemented by the enzymes in the food source (maggots, worms etc will all have enzymes) helping the digestive tract cope with the nutrients passing through.

Protein based baits are a more complex food source than natural protein and don't usually have the enzyme factor present in natural foods. So the presence of proteolytic enzymes in the bait can help the carp's system break down the comparatively complex proteins, making them a more convertible food source. Bromelain is an efficient acidic enzyme; trypsin an efficient alkaline one (occurring in the intestine). Nutrabaits make both enzymes available at safe levels in their product Addit-Digest. I've used quality HNV baits with and without enzymes and I'm convinced that the use of enzymes at the right level make the baits more instant and far more effective over a long term.

Anglers do have problems with protein and HNV baits, so it's perhaps as well to have an idea of what can go wrong; an insight into the possible pitfalls makes them easier to avoid. Here are some of the pitfalls:

1) It is easy to underestimate the importance of high quality ingredients, but they are the cornerstone of a nutritional bait.

2) Fresh baits are essential. We freeze our baits as soon as they have dried out after boiling, and then use them within twenty-four hours of thawing. On the other hand it is worth experimenting with drying your baits out and seeing whether they mould or not. Baits that don't mould can increase in effectiveness, but I've experimented with baits not straight from freezing and I have no confidence in them.

3) Attractor level is crucial to the success of these baits. However good the base mix the carp may not continue to eat your bait if you overload it with the flavour, the oil, or any other type of attractor. Getting the attractor level right for a long term bait isn't easy. Start too low, rather than too high, then increase the level slightly if results are disappointing. You need some source of attraction to ensure that the fish find the bait. What you are trying to achieve is the highest level of attraction the carp will accept and still go on eating the bait.

4) Some flavours are just not acceptable to

carp; be careful to steer clear of these. Use an essential oil at the recommended level, a low level flavour/essential oil combination or a nutritional attractor like Sense Appeal, Nutramino, Minamino if you are in doubt.

5) The availability of the bait is just as important as its nutritional value. If you use a food bait you must make it possible for the carp to feed on it. A long term bait works best on the basis of long term preoccupation. Make the carp dependent on your bait. Don't just put it in when you fish with it. Build up the carp's confidence. Familiarity breeds content.

6) Try to get some idea of how many baits you need in the swim at any one time to give you the best chance of catching the fish you are after. This is one of the hardest aspects of carp fishing and one on which you will get all sorts of advice. In his smashing book '*Big Water Carp*' Jim Gibbinson recommends a maximum of two ounces of free offerings at any one time. I know successful anglers who aren't happy unless they've got two or three mixes out in front of them! Experience and observation will guide you to the right level in differing circumstances, and I honestly wish I could be more specific about this – but I keep changing my mind about it. Seasons differ, fish change, pressure alters angling considerations. I've seen terrific success achieved through very heavy baiting this season, and have fished sessions during which I was sure I'd got too much bait out.

I think that if you are fishing for a number of big fish you can keep a fair amount of bait in front of you, but if in doubt use your HNV sparingly over a bed of seeds or particles. Provided you have established the bait the carp will take it and you aren't taking the risk of fulfilling their nutritional requirements before they come to the hookbait.

Nutritional baits are consistent big fish catchers, whether the main source of the nutrition be protein or fat. Provide the fish in the water with a steady supply of quality bait and they will come to accept it as part of their diet. Once they are feeding on it you can then set about planning the downfall of the fish you are after. It is the most reliable method of catching big carp that I've seen. Use it with confidence.

Attraction

Attractors in carp baits occupy the thinking of anglers as much as any other aspect of carp fishing. Go into any tackle shop, or watch the crowd round a bait stand at a carp conference, and you will see a steady stream of sniffers assessing the potential of the hundreds of smells on offer. And while a list of all the known carp attractors would fill a chapter in this book they all have one common denominator – they are designed to attract the carp to the bait. Some achieve that end better than others but that is their purpose.

A carp finds its food sources through receiving 'here is food' messages via the olfactory system (smell). In nature a carp's food is buried in the silt, suspended in the water or clinging to the weed. There are some individual food items, like water snails and swan mussels, but most big carp will have food larders available to them which they exploit in the course of their feeding – and their feeding will involve the intake of various particles of food, along with some of the underwater habitat – be it silt or weed, the waste from which is immediately rejected by the carp's digestive system. The carp's enzymes will only act on those nutrients they were designed by nature to act on.

A carp feeds by smell and taste, the initial seeking out being by smell. Its senses recognise a food source: the carp feeds on the food source until its system is satisfied. I've more or less said all that before, but I'm repeating it because at this stage we will have to look at one of the most confusing areas of carp bait lore:

An attractor, or combination of attractors, can be used to fool carp into 'thinking' that something that isn't a good food source is one – because it smells like one.

In other words a bait doesn't have to have any nutritional value whatever to catch carp, as long as the smell fools the carp into thinking it is food to the extent that it picks up the bait and gets caught.

You've got a problem using this attraction only method if you are fishing for a specific big fish – or a mere handful of them. If you pre-bait an attractor bait you risk blowing it out before the fish you are fishing for picks it up. If you fish hookbait only you have to be very sure of the location of the fish you are after. You may draw a fish into an area through regular pre-baiting with a nutritional bait but you are hardly likely to draw a fish off course with a single attractor hookbait.

I'm not suggesting that attractor baits aren't valid for big carp fishing. It is possible to make a compromise between food value and attraction. Some very potent attractors have a long enough life for you to come up with a bait which may not have the life of an HNV, but will go on working long enough for you to aim for a short term result. If you are going to Waveney D Lake for a few days a high attractor/low food value bait may be a viable proposition. You haven't got time to establish a food bait but there are enough big carp in the water for you to be fairly sure that at least one or two of them will be curious about the bait you are offering, and feed on it.

The big problem with attractor baits is that you have to come up with something new, or something that worked long enough ago for the carp's memory to have forgotten that it

represents a danger. Permutations are better than single smells, because some of the best attractors can be used in a mix without the carp recognising a known danger. The surprise element is an essential ingredient in a successful attractor bait, which throws up a problem for the reader. Any sure fire attractor, or combination of attractors, that is published will immediately be fished by a certain percentage of the readership. In addition if it is sure fire it must have a successful track record, which may have already reduced its effectiveness on some of the pressured waters. You are going to have to use your initiative to come up with an attractor that is unique to your bait, but there are so many substances to work from that a little experimentation should give you your own personal water-emptier.

Where the main strength of the bait lies in the quality of its attraction there are a number of factors to consider:

a) If you are fishing single hookbait tactics, either in isolation or over a bed of seeds, particles of boilies, the taste of the bait doesn't matter, so in these circumstances you can overload the bait. (That isn't an irresponsible suggestion because the carp isn't going to eat the bait.)

b) If you are fishing for a known big fish, or a number of such fish, you have to be careful to avoid a source of attraction that may have blown.

c) Some smells have a proven track record for catching big fish, others haven't. It isn't possible to go to too much trouble over bait, so ask someone who understands attractors before you put your bait together if you don't have full confidence in what you're doing.

d) The more complex the mixture of smells the less chance there is of offering the carp an attractor it can identify as a source of danger.

e) Use a base mix that will hold together for a long time in the water. With some mixes it is necessary to make the hookbait from a slightly different mix from the free offerings, particularly bird food baits (which break down more quickly than protein baits).

f) If you are using a combination of smells divide the recommended dosages by the number of different smells you are using, otherwise you will get a heavily overloaded and possibly unattractive bait.

g) Understand that there is a level at which attractors will be most effective. An overloaded bait can locate the bait in the wrong position. A carp will search for the bait at that point where the food message is strongest, which may be feet, or yards away from an overloaded bait. I've observed this phenomenon and it is frustrating seeing carp obviously excited by the smell of the bait and not getting within feet of it!

Conclusion

Coming up with a successful attractor bait that will pick out the bigger fish can be a matter of luck, finding out, being told, or painstaking trial and error. Coming up with a food bait that will give you a chance at the bigger fish is a far more predictable operation. It is my experience, and that of many of my friends, that the better the quality of the bait in terms of its food value the more selective the bait will be in terms of big fish captures. That will sound a bit fanciful to some of you but it has been proved time and again that if you will go to the trouble of establishing this type of bait as a food source, and persevering with it, the bigger fish will feed on it – and fall to it. Sometimes the blind faith needed for this type of fishing is beyond many of us. Brian Garner is one of the best carp men I have seen for single minded perseverance with

a bait he knows should work. Sometimes his first capture on the bait is long after many of us would have given up on it – but he finishes up getting the biggies on it.

Know the bait is right then believe it is going to work, and it will sooner or later. The experiences Ken Townley recounted in his 'Big Daddy' chapter in 'Carp Fishing' mirror those of many HNV users, and it should be added that Ken has since had the same fish on a number of occasions since the capture he described. Each time the fish fell to the same base mix – but with a different essential oil label.

Why should bigger fish fall to nutritional baits? Well, perhaps some of our big carp are big because they have a better developed sense of nutritional recognition than many of their lesser brethren. Yes, some of our bigger carp will be one-offs, genetic freaks which were always going to finish up big – like human giants. This is probably the case where you get one fish in a water that grows far bigger than any of its fellow carp. But even given that isolated big fish are freaks they still have to keep eating to maintain that size, and to keep eating their senses have to recognise every available food source.

Where you have a mix of sizes in a water experiences repeatedly indicate that the smaller fish are more inclined to feed visually where baits are concerned, while the bigger fish seem more inclined to feed on the better food value baits. Results on particles can include some good bags of smaller fish while those same fish don't show up on HNV and protein baits at all. On the other hand some HNV baits only produce bigger fish. I'm not imagining any of this; there is a predictable, oft-repeated pattern to captures from carp waters. I made the suggestion that there is a connection between food recognition and big fish in Kevin Clifford's book, to which he replied that big fish are big because they eat more. But they don't eat more of *anything*, they eat more of those food sources that their finely tuned sense of smell recognises as food: coincidentally, those food sources that the lesser fish either don't recognise, or don't bother with.

I've caught a carp on all types of bait, and at one time I was as sceptical about nutritional baits as anyone. I now believe in them because I think they enable anyone to catch big fish. Now that isn't to suggest that you should use HNVs but if you lack the confidence to go out and catch big fish a reliable HNV may just give you the required confidence to make you believe you are going to succeed. There are baits and there are big fish baits. You may fluke the very occasional biggie 'when it's your turn' on just any bait, but for consistent success with the bigger fish you need them consistently feeding on your bait, not picking it up once in a blue moon.

Bait Make-Up

Nutritional Baits

The list of possible ingredients for your bait is endless and potentially confusing. However, if you consider each *nutrient* you wish to employ you can gear your ingredient selection on the basis of nutritional value. When you are first concocting a bait ingredient selection tends to be a random affair and the nutritional value of the bait very hit and miss. At that stage the most important consideration is that the bait binds together as you want it to. We've all come up with brilliant theoretical recipes that wouldn't bind, wouldn't boil, broke up when boiled and were generally not in accordance with our original intentions. A bait mix has to score on a number of counts, and I'll list them:

1) The bait must appeal to the fish.
2) The ingredients must be compatible and mix together.

3) If the mix is to end up as boilies the paste must produce hard baits when boiled.
4) If they are to be used at range the baits must withstand being catapulted, or fired out with a throwing stick.
5) Size of the finished bait will be a consideration, small to achieve preoccupation, larger if they have to be fired out to extreme range.

I think it is because a bait mix has to have these properties that many carp men fight shy of making their own baits, or prefer to work with tried and tested recipes if they do make them. I'm used to making up baits from scratch; it is one of the great pleasures of carp fishing for many carp anglers. When you are putting together mixes for the commercial bait market, as we do at Nutrabaits, the mix has to be spot on and there is a great deal of trial and error in arriving at the finished product. I'm quite happy using base mixes I've helped design because I've been through all the stages of the bait development, but I can understand both points of view: the need to have a made up mix, and the desire to create a personal bait.

For those who do like to come up with mixes of their own the following brief notes might help clarify some of the more frustrating bait aspects. The more you mess about with bait the more you learn about the whys and wherefores of it.

Your first bait tends to be put together on the basis of an ounce of this, an ounce of that, simply because you have read somewhere that the powders are useful bait ingredients. Baits put together on this basis are usually very nondescript affairs with a high, largely unconvertible carbohydrate content, a low poor quality protein content, little regard for the fat content, and no regard at all for the vitamin/mineral content. The bait is just a carrier for the smell, which is useful when you are putting together an attractor bait, but useless when you are trying to concoct a nutritional bait. Such baits are a waste of time, but they are part of the process of learning and show that the angler is having a go and is willing to think for himself.

We've already considered in detail the major types of nutritional baits, these being high fat baits, high protein baits and high nutritional value baits. We'll consider the possible make up of these categories in terms of the nutritional and physical properties of their usual ingredients.

High Fat Baits These are usually based on bird foods and other high fat ingredients, like full fat soya flour, almond and peanut meal, high fat calf milk and any other powder that will contribute to the fat content. Getting these mixes to bind can be a problem where a combination of fatty substances are used. Eggs are an essential part of these baits, as binders; caseinate and egg albumin can absorb some of the fats and help with the binding. Wheat gluten is a popular binder but I've never used it because of its lack of nutritional quality. (There's really little need to worry about a single ingredient to that extent because the undigested part of the bait will simply pass through the carp's system.) Concentrate on the polyunsaturated fats for high energy baits. If you can add an extra liquid fat source direct, in the form of olive, sesame or rapeseed oil do so, but the more fat you have in there the more difficult it becomes to bind the bait. If you have problems coming up with your own high fat mix that will fire out of a throwing stick try adding some egg albumen to the mix; this can help produce a harder, more stable bait. Add a vitamin/mineral supplement to increase the nutritional value of the bait. *See* list (page 173) for a list of high fat ingredients and sample bait recipes.

High Protein Baits The main ingredients used in these baits are fish, milk, soya and egg protein. You will encounter other ingredients in the bait dealers' catalogues and price lists, but some of the additional proteins are a bit gimmicky and nutritionally dubious. The main line of attack is to make up a bait based on either the fish or milk proteins, with egg albumen added to harden the bait, and a binder thrown in if the physical make up of the mix warrants it. If you can add to the nutritional value of the bait with the binder do so, and one of the best binders on the market for doing this is Nutrabaits' Nutrapro. Again wheat gluten can be used to bind, semolina or egg albumen to harden, and eggs to bind the mix together, and a vitamin and mineral supplement to enhance the nutritional value of the bait. Protein ingredients and sample recipes are shown in the protein list (*see* page 173).

High Nutritional Value Baits (HNVs)

'High' as it is used here is part of the description of the bait principle given to this type of bait. It is comparative: the baits we have already looked at are high in nutritional value. An HNV bait lays no particular emphasis on any nutritional aspect but is designed to fulfil all the carp's nutritional needs in one food source. To achieve this end it must have a good protein content, a high fat content, and the best possible vitamin/mineral profile. In addition many HNV buffs now add an enzyme source to increase the nutritional value of the protein by making it more available to the fish. When a high fat *and* high protein content are required in a milk/egg bait the fat source is more likely to be liquid. Fish meals are high in protein *and* fat, but fishmeal buffs still tend to add additional fats via a high fish oil content. As a guideline you are looking for a protein content of the order of 50–60 per cent, with as high a fat content as you can physically make your mix take.

The vitamin/mineral content is given more detailed consideration in this type of bait, and the list (*see* page 173) gives details of the vari-

The Tip Lake again, and this time Mark Summers displays an HNV caught fish of thirty plus. A first rate bait took Mark from the ranks of the also rans to one of the most consistent big carp catchers in Kent.

ous vitamin and mineral supplements which can be added to carp baits. Vitamin/mineral mixes are not very stable in terms of shelf life so pay special regard to this aspect. If you are really serious about HNVs you will buy a fresh supply of your vitamin/mineral supplement on a regular basis, and you certainly shouldn't carry such a mix forward from one season to the next.

Don't underestimate the importance of the vitamin/mineral content when you are planning a long term bait.

The Importance of Quality If you have ever watched a cat eat you will be aware of the importance of food quality to those creatures with a highly developed nutritional awareness. Carp have such an awareness.

There are no short cuts to successful HNV baits. Most bait dealers now go to a great deal of trouble to ensure that you get quality ingredients, but they aren't cheap. Don't buy HNV ingredients or baits on the basis of cheapness because they just won't perform as you want them to. There are cheap baits on the market; birdfood baits and attractor baits are cheaper to use than HNVs. Plan your season's bait on the basis of what you can afford to use throughout the period you are fishing. Don't duck and dive and fall between two principles.

Put together a bait you know will work, you know you can afford, then believe in it until it starts to catch for you.

Sweeteners I haven't mentioned sweeteners, but I will now. One of the most successful sweetening agents was liquid Hermesetas, a saccharin based product. Saccharin is, in turn a sodium based product. Carp have a high sodium content. Did Hermesetas attract them because it was a sodium source, or because it was sweet? Carbohydrates are starch based, starch

being sugar based. The boffins tell us carp have no nutritional need for sugars. To confuse the situation further I'm not sure that I can tell the difference between bitter and sweet. Carp love dried brewers yeast, and the earliest intentionally nutritional baits were based on the famous Phillips Yeast Mixture (PYM), a product based on dried brewers yeast. Yeast is very bitter to me, but carp love it. And yet I have been assured in print that carp love sweet things – and hate bitter substances. I guess I'll have to think it out again!

I'm only trying to make you stop and think. Every question you manage to answer about carp will raise one or two more in your mind. We can all throw up contradictions and doubts: what we have to grasp and hang on to are the principles we know are valid. They are of assistance; doubts are only negative. Nutritional baits catch: attractor baits catch.

Take your thinking from there – then concentrate your attentions on the really hard part: finding where the carp you want to catch will take a hookbait.

Bait Ingredients

The following should be considered a starting point if you are thinking of putting together your own bait. Don't be confused and think that you are looking for *the big secret* when you design a bait.

The ingredients, additives and bait recipes shown are all tried and tested in successful carp baits and what you are looking for is your own winning combination. Your best chances of success will be to team up with two or three friends to increase the chances of your bait being considered a food source. Try to make the fish dependent on your bait by ensuring them of a regular supply.

High Fat Baits

Powder Ingredients: full fat soya flour, meals made from nuts, bird foods, including Robin Red, Nectablend, PTX, Sluis CLO, High Fat Calf Foods.
Full range of seeds, and seed mixes.
Liquids: all essential oils, olive oil, sesame oil, safflower seed oil, sunflower seed oil, rapeseed oil, vegetable oil, soya oil.
Essential oils are usually highly concentrated liquids which should be used in minute quantities. Suggested dosages should appear on any bottle you buy from a bait dealer. Olive oil, safflower seed oil etc are not concentrated and can be used in larger quantities as a source of nutrition. Ideally you want a combination of a bulk food oil and a concentrated essential oil; e.g. Garlic and soya oil, or olive oil and Juniper Berry Oil. Oils are the most concentrated and readily digestible fat source for carp. The correct dosage for some essential oils is as low as *one drop*, whereas you can use up to 20–30ml of the blander bulk food oils.

Bait Binders

It isn't always enough to come up with an ideal blend of nutritional ingredients, because they may not bind together. The following will help bind the bait together: eggs, wheat gluten, caseinate, egg albumin, Nutrapro, Nutragel, CLO, ground Weetabix, semolina, wholemeal flour.

Ingredients for High Protein/HNV baits

Milk proteins: Casein (acid and rennet), caseinate (calcium and sodium), lactalbumin.
Soya Proteins: Soya isolate and health food shop soya derivatives.
Egg: egg albumin and egg powder.
Liquid: Minamino, Nutramino, Sense Appeals.

Warning: the dust from protein powders can be carcinogenic. We don't know the long term effects of constant use of these powders so they may represent a serious health hazard.

Enzyme Additives

Bengers (now being phased out), Davina Protein Foods with Bromelain, Nutrabaits' Addit-Digest, Slippery Elm Food, Health Digestion Aids and Enzymes tablets (ground up). If you are working with powders or tablets containing enzymes and aren't sure of the required dosage stick to the recommended daily human dosage per pound of bait (dry weight).

Enzymes: the required dosages are minute and the majority of anglers won't have the equipment to measure them. Stick to ready prepared enzyme foods or tablets to be sure of using safe levels. *Don't use neat bromelain under any circumstances.*

Vitamin/Mineral Additives

Pet and Health Food Shops: PYM, Equivite and Equivite Gold (horse feed supplement), Complan (for humans), SA 37 (dogs). These are just examples. You will find plenty of similar mixes designed for animals and pigeons. Compare the profile shown on the packet with the ideal profile shown in the vitamin/mineral table on page 161.

The following mixes have been designed and put together specifically for adding to carp baits, but unless the bait dealer publishes a profile you won't know how 'ideal' each one is: Vitrex (Catchum), Vitmin (SBS), Carpvit (Geoff Kemp), Nutrabaits' vitamin/mineral additive, Colne Valley Baits vitamin/mineral additive.

Recipes

8oz Red Factor
8oz semolina
10ml Nutramino Addits
1ml sweet cajouser
10ml liquid molasses
6 drops Clove Terpenes
6 drops geranium oil

———

3oz Nectablend
3oz PTX
2oz calcium caseinate
2oz Robin Red
3ml Ultraspice
6 drops black pepper oil

Attractor Baits

10oz semolina
6oz full fat soya flour
20ml Nutramino
5ml sweet mango flavour
6 drops geranium oil
1 grm methionine
1 grm lysine

———

3oz sodium caseinate
3oz wheatgerm
1oz codlivine
3oz soya flour
2ml sweet cajouser
20ml Sense Appeal
5ml chocolate malt
2 tspns Addit-Attract

Protein/High Nutritional Value Baits

(Per Geoff Kemp)
4oz casein
3oz lactalbumin
1½oz caseinate

6oz Nectablend
2oz Robin Red
8oz semolina

3ml Strawberry Jam EA
3 drops juniper berry oil

———

2oz Robin Red
½oz ground almond
2oz calcium caseinate
4oz soya flour
2oz Equivite
6oz semolina
20ml Spice Sense Appeal

(Per Clive Gibbins)
5oz full fat soya flour
5oz yellow semolina
2oz Formula S (Chemists)
1oz CLO
1oz wheat gluten
2oz Complan
5ml liquid Hermesetas
16ml Geoff Kemp evaporated milk and ice cream
Tspn Sweet Bait Appetite Stim

1oz gluten
½oz Carpvit
5 ml soya oil
Flavour as required

(Per Rod Hutchinson)
2oz lactalbumin
2oz caseinate
2oz soya isolate
4oz casein
½oz Rod's Vitamin/ mineral mix

From the author

4oz acid casein (90 mesh)
4oz rennet casein
2oz sodium caseinate
2oz egg albumin
2oz Bengers (or similar)
1oz Davina Protein food
1oz Nutrabaits vitamin and mineral addivite (or dosage)
3ml Ultraspice
1ml sweet cajouser
1 drop sage oil

3–5ml Scopex or Maplecreme for quick results or low level oil for long term results

2 drops thyme oil
3oz acid casein
3oz rennet casein
2oz soya flour
2oz egg albumin
1oz Nutragel
1oz Nutrapro
2oz caseinate
2oz 30 mesh casein
10ml liquid molasses
10ml Nutramino
1 drop garlic oil (add 3 ml blue cheese flavour to make the bait more instant)

Most of the recipes shown will mix with the addition of four or six eggs. The usual procedure is to make more than enough powder mix then add this to the eggs/liquid mix until the required consistency is attained. It isn't possible to give precise recipes because there is a variable absorption rate in the ingredients, depending on source, mesh etc. Bird food based mixes require fewer eggs than protein mixes. If you want to make boilies without using eggs add an ounce of Nutragel to your usual mix and use water or milk to make the paste.

Further Reading

If you are just entering the confusing world of carp baits and wish to know more about the theory and practise of them your best starting point is the writing of those anglers who have been making their own baits for many years now, some of whom are involved in the bait industry. The bait chapter in this book is very much a bare outline of a subject which embraces a number of sciences.

Extending your reading and your knowledge may not put more fish on the bank for you but you may find the insight into areas you previously had no recognition of exciting. To many of us the relationship between carp and their food sources is fascinating, and while ultimate understanding can only come from a total grasp of the various sciences involved, just a basic insight into what makes carp tick is a stimulating eye-opener. The following sources may be of interest:

Rod Hutchinson: 'Carp Now and Then'
                      'Carp Strikes Back'
                      'Rod Hutchinson's
                      Bait Book'
Geoff Kemp: 'Kempastini's Book of
                      Baits'
Rob Maylin: 'Fox Pool'
Tim Paisley: articles in 'Carp
                      Fisher' and 'Specialist
                      Angler', 'Carp Now
                      and Then', 'Master
                      Fisherman – Carp'
                      (Kevin Clifford),
                      Nutrabaits' 1988
                      publication 'Bait'
Dr. Lynwood S Smith: 'Introduction to Fish
                      Physiology'
Kim Jauncey: Carp section in book
                      'Recent Advances in
                      Aquaculture'

Ken Townley: Articles in 'Carpworld'.
Fred Wilton: Articles in the 'Second
                      BCSG Book' and chapter
                      in George Sharman's book
                      'Carp and the Carp Angler'
Magnus Pyke: 'Success in Nutrition'

Suppliers of Baits and Bait Ingredients

Nutrabaits, 95 Main Street, North Anston, Sheffield S31 7BE

Rod Hutchinson, Main Road, Legbourne, Louth, Lincolnshire.

Catchum 88 Ltd, 6–10 Newark Road, South Hykeham, Lincoln LN6 7HA

Geoff Kemp Baits, Pilgrims Court, Days Lane, Pilgrims Hatch, Brentwood, Essex CM15 9SL

Colne Valley Bait Supplies, 25 Blossom Way, West Drayton, Middlesex UB7 9HF

Streamselect Ltd, The Uplands, Langaller Lane, Cobham Road, Fetcham, Surrey KT22 9SP

Premier Baits, 25 Brecon Square, Ramsgate, Kent CT12 6NS

Prime Attraction Baits, 7 Sycamore Rise, Berkhamstead, Hertfordshire HP4 2JZ

Cotswold Baits, Penny Farthings, Spring Lane, Swallowfield, Reading RG7 1ST

Solar Baits, 35 Sutherland Road, Belvedere, Kent DA17 6UR

Most bait dealers publish a catalogue or price list each year. These are sometimes expensive productions which have a cover charge, which is sometimes refundable against your first purchase of goods. Watch out for details in the press, ask at your nearest specialist shop, or go to one of the carp or specialist conferences held in the close season for a fuller insight into what is available.

15 Session

Waveney D Lake in the middle of October. Anywhere October and November are magic months for carp fishing. It's getting cold and the nights are getting longer but the bigger fish are feeding, so if you've got half an idea about what you're doing the odd big carp is on the cards. I was working Saturday morning so I travelled down during the afternoon. Jim Fielding was on G Lake – and had caught fish – but did not seem very pleased with life. My confidence was sky high and was lifted even further by the news that D Lake wasn't producing. The big fish would be wide open to a good bait, which I felt certain I'd got. You've always got to have a strong question mark in your mind about flavour and presentation on the hard fished waters but wherever there are good sized fish the higher the food value of the bait the more effective it is likely to be. That part of carp fishing really is simple and is ignored by so many.

I wanted Swim One. I was starting to understand it and from the first moment I saw the water I had been drawn to the big oak. I tend to write of D Lake as though Swim One is *the* swim, but that isn't necessarily so. The majority of D devotees prefer Swim Two, and some of the locals Swim Three, but I had a gut feeling about One from the first and wasn't giving up on it.

As it turned out Swims One and Two were occupied until Sunday dinner time so I dropped into Three for Saturday night and Sunday morning. I had two bits of luck in Three which helped me a great deal during the following week. The first came immediately; the lad who was fishing One had a run just after he had recast, at about nine o'clock in the evening. I couldn't tell him but he played the fish far too hard, bearing in mind what he might have been connected to, and pulled out. It was his third run of the weekend, which did not fit in with the lake's 'not fishing' tag I'd heard from a number of reliable sources. He was chatty, which was fortunate because I rarely probe. He wasn't used to 'long range' fishing, knew he couldn't reach his hookbaits with his loose feed so had only taken about sixty boilies with him for the full weekend. As most people put their feed in from the back of D Lake (if they aren't rowing or swimming them out) I couldn't help but smile at his innocence, but what he was doing was producing action. He wasn't even casting tight to the margins.

The second stroke of luck came in the early hours, though it didn't seem lucky at the time. I'd put out two six bait stringers from Swim Three, one at about forty yards and one at sixty. At half past two in the morning the right hand indicator climbed a foot, then stopped. I was fishing two boilies tight together on the dacron rig and was fishing with the butt ring foamed. I went back to sleep, not having woken up sufficiently to query what had happened. When I came to in the morning I did query the occurrence. A foot lift on a heavily foamed set-up? That didn't make sense. The bottom bait of the two together had been 'pulled', which explained the dropped take. The carp were in a highly nervous mood. Even with a stringer the fish were taking one bait at a time, and one had picked up the bottom bait and tried to swim off with it. I fished with single baits fished tight to the hook for the rest of the week.

On Sunday afternoon I set up stall in Swim One with mixed feelings. However confident you are there are doubts hovering in the back of your mind. The reality suddenly feels very different from the anticipation. A couple of the local lads called in to watch me stick the first range-finding casts into the hedge and the oak, but I got the range sorted out pretty early by my standards, much to the disappointment of my friends. I took three different baits with me, all based on the same HNV base mix but with different smells. I took eight mixes of the main bait and two mixes each of the other two. I'd had success with all three on other waters and knew they would all catch carp, but whether the smells were valid for the Waveney carp or not was a different matter. I started out on the main bait, feeding lightly and presenting the hook bait with PVA stringers, twos, threes and fours. It's got to be said that conditions seemed ideal and the fish should be feeding.

Sunday evening was mild, windy and wet; steaming almost. I sat on the bedchair waiting for the indicators to move, fishing one rod short and one long. At half past seven I had a half way up from short. I hesitated then got up and hit it. It was a half-pound bream – which didn't over-excite me! About nine o'clock I was away for real and hit a solid feeling fish – which does not imply that it was big, but that it wasn't small. It came in without argument and I thought I was going to net it at the first time of asking, but just as I reached for the net it took off towards E Lake at a rate of knots. I back wound but the fish was high in the water and I must have put too much pressure on the hook in slowing the fish down. The hook pulled out. The long run across the surface was unusual for the water, I thought as I howled into the wind. In the early hours I landed a common of three and a half pounds (approximately).

Some time on Monday afternoon John Colgan from Bridlington joined me on the water.

If that reads as though it was prearranged, it wasn't, but I had fished with him at Roman Lakes the previous winter and considered him a friend – so he joined me. He set up in Swim Two, having made it clear that he was a Swim One man really. After he'd completed the inevitable two hours of chores setting up and getting the baits out we spent the evening rabbiting (talking, not poaching). At Monday tea time John struck a run for me, from short, while I was out of the swim for five minutes, but the fish dropped off just short of the net.

Alarm bells were beginning to ring. I'd had immediate action and knew that the bait was good enough for a build up of action to follow once they started feeding on it. Surely the flavour wasn't blown? It could have been and indications were that that was the problem. Immediate action, then two fish dropped, which suggested light hooking around the mouth, and no build up of action. But then again this was D Lake, it was supposed to be fishing badly, and I had hooked fish. No, that wasn't good enough really. It was October, the bait was good enough to really have them feeding, conditions were terrific. The flavour had got to be the problem. I'd give it one more day and see how it felt.

There was no action on Monday night; none on Tuesday. Most of my fishing was being done short, at 30–40 yards, because that was where all the action was coming from. (There is a gravel hump running across D Lake at 30–40 yards.) On Tuesday afternoon I put a three bait PVA stringer in under the branches of the oak and a five bait stringer on the action spot forty yards out. If I didn't catch from that set-up I was definitely switching to a stand-by bait. It sounds as though I was being a bit obstinate and sticking with the first version of the bait far too long but you've got to be certain you're wrong before you scrap a bait in those circumstances. I was worried about dropping it just as they really started to have it.

Swim One on Waveney D Lake in big fish weather. There is a gale blowing, the rain is coming down in sheets, and the author only emerged from the bivvy to take this picture because it was so awful. The big oak is in the background – and the big fish fed.

In the early hours of Wednesday morning I woke with a start and could hardly breathe I was so excited. Something was about to happen, I didn't sense it I **knew** it. I lay looking at the motionless isotopes, waiting for one of them to start dancing; tense. My heart was pounding like a hammer. Just five minutes after I woke up an Optonic howled – in Swim Two! My thumping heart sank and I scrambled out of the sleeping bag. John was in.

The night was pitch black and the darkness heightened under the trees of Swim Two. The fight was a protracted one and John's nerves were on edge, which soon set mine jangling, in addition to which I'd dived out of the warm bag with no regard to what I was wearing and

was soon frozen. My uncharitable disappointment at the run not being to my rods quickly vanished in the excitement of the scrap and I crouched down waiting for a chance with the net. The fish was under the rod tip and up and down the snaggy margin for a good twenty minutes before John managed to get it up to the surface, and even then it wasn't really beaten. John walked back as the carp came up on its side and I thought I'd netted it at the first attempt, but I wasn't sure and told John so. In fact I'd missed it and couldn't understand what had happened. I'd seen the fish but John hadn't and I knew it was a biggie; what I didn't know was that the landing net was a thirty-six inch one. All I knew was that I'd messed up the netting of a big fish and John was having to start over again. It was livelier than ever after it had seen the net and two minutes after I missed it it snagged itself – which made me feel great. John had never caught a twenty pounder and I knew that the animal on the other end of his line was all of that – and a great deal more.

We appraised the situation by torchlight. The line was slanting down to a raft of debris which had accumulated where the branches of the tree to the right of the swim reached down into the water about five yards out. I couldn't believe that the fish itself was snagged, it was too deep in the water for that, but the line wouldn't come free and the fish wasn't showing any signs of moving. I told John I'd go for the boat, which was usually kept in the garden to the right of Swim One. It wasn't there. I felt plenty sick. I went back to the anxious John, explained the position, and also explained that I'd got an inflatable dinghy in the back of the car. I'd quickly inflate it and get myself out onto the lake.

I wouldn't say that the inflation job was very quick, and it was worryingly incomplete because I couldn't work out how the valves for the two bottom panels worked. I had a feeling it might sink, which would involve me in a drowning, which would be a judgement on me for making a mess of landing the fish, but wouldn't help John with his snagged fish. The margins drop straight down to about twelve feet in front of Swims One and Two so I just had to chance the buoyancy bit. I hung grimly onto a bush while I did the buoyancy testing and was relieved to find I was afloat, not awash. I paddled round to Swim Two. The line was only lightly hooked round the overhang and came clear with a gentle pull. 'Came clear with a gentle pull . . .' I had a feeling of *déjà vu* as I thought the words and the idea that John was attached to Big Scale strengthened.

A highly relieved John declared that the fish was still on and I quickly beached the dinghy in

John Colgan with the first significant fish of the week – Big Scale at 31lb 6oz. I almost lost the fish for him!

the next swim. Five minutes later I slipped the net under a great deal of carp. It *was* Big Scale, the magnificent mirror I'd had the previous November at 32lb. That morning it weighed 31lb 6oz – and I'd almost lost it for John. He was over the moon with the capture and it was an emotional moment for him. Later that morning the air reverberated with the click of camera shutters as the great carp fulfilled its familiar role in the photo session. It looked superb.

It was Wednesday morning and I'd got one little common and two dropped fish to show for nearly four days fishing. I had to accept that the flavour I was using was blown and change smell and tactics. I switched to one of the reserve baits I'd taken as hookbait on one rod and kept feeding with the original bait, still fishing it on one rod. I've a feeling that at times there was another rod in all this somewhere – but we'll not talk about that, eh? The new smell was a combination of a highly effective flavour and two oils, blue cheese, garlic and soya oil. It was a smell I'd experimented with on the Mangrove with great success and a combination that went on to take a great many big fish for a lot of people. I'd no worries about the smell's effectiveness, or its having blown, just mild qualms about how soon the fish would start picking it up. The base mix was the same HNV as I was already using.

I'll follow through on smells briefly. As it turned out the Guava flavour I'd started the week on had been used by Keith Kant and Bungay Dick the previous season and had taken a lot of fish. Why I hadn't given consideration to it having been used by the locals I don't know. In terms of the pressure from a visitor on a week's fishing I wouldn't have thought a flavour could blow – and the fact that it had already been introduced might even be a slight help. In retrospect on a water like Waveney that is bad thinking. The strength of the bait (food value) did not overcome the fact that the carp were nervous of the smell with the first bait and I didn't have time to find out if protracted baiting would rebuild their confidence because of the food value. On busy waters you can rely on the curiosity aspect to get them down on a new smell or, better still, combination of smells. If the food value is high enough they will then keep having it so there is no point risking a flavour that may be blown, or which the carp are at least wary of.

Early on Wednesday afternoon I cast a single offering of the new bait under the branches of the oak. The wind had been at gale force for two days by this time and it was cold with occasional driving rain. Wednesday afternoon was slightly warmer. The single bait had been out for two hours when I was away on that rod. It was a relief giving and very welcome mirror of eighteen pounds odd. I recast to the same spot and was away again within the hour. The second fish went seventeen something. At ten that night while I was talking to Colin Pitelen I had an absolute screamer on the same rod, the run yielding another mirror of twelve pounds something.

While I was having this action on the one rod the end tackle with the original bait was lying six inches from the rushes at the back of the lake. I'd still had no action on it the following morning so I scrapped the original as a hook bait but continued to feed with it. Why? It was obvious the fish were still eating the first bait (it was to me sitting there at the water), but they were a bit nervous of it and and weren't making mistakes with the hook bait. If I'd thought that the bait was blown to the extent that they weren't even coming in over it then I would have scrapped it altogether. But because the fish were feeding warily on the original bait they were at greater risk from the second bait than they would have been if I had been relying solely on curiosity value for a take.

That's a lot of explanation to go into over the capture of three carp in a seven hour period: that can happen any time with any bait. You drop right, get lucky and have a silly few hours. I was starting a silly few days.

I concentrated on the area of the oak with both rods from Thursday morning onwards, fishing one bait tight against the margin and the other under, or just off, the branches. The ferocity of the wind blowing across from E Lake increased as the week went on and I was having to use 2¾oz leads to make the eighty to eighty-five yards to the oak. Two ounces might possibly have made it but the bigger lead holds its line better through the wind and against the pull of the water on a tightly fished line.

I dropped a fish from under the branches at about eleven o'clock. I'll not go into too much detail about how I came to lose the fish but I vaguely recall some disaster with the reel pick-up, line all over the place and the fish coming adrift while John and I were trying to sort it out. Fate works in a wondrous way . . . or something. Isn't it funny the sequence of events leading up to a moment of significance when you look back? That's why I very rarely bemoan my luck, because it isn't always possible to distinguish between the helpful hand of fate and bad luck. If I hadn't lost that fish . . .

The take came from under the branches and I cast back into the same spot – or intended to. In fact the line came off my finger a split second too soon and the end tackle flew five degrees right of the intended line. This would be the right hand rod; the left hand bait was in deeper water just off the branches. I almost stopped the cast but I watched in fascination because it looked to be *just* right for the big oak bramble. It was; it clipped some of the few remaining leaves as it went in. I reeled the left hand bait in and recast that one under the branches. Mid-afternoon I was away on the fortuitous cast rod and had a powerful scrap from a singularly un-beautiful mirror of 20lb 10oz.

That was my first fish from the actual margins – because I hadn't been casting to them. I was convinced that the season's pressure would have made them impossible to catch in the edge, so I was sticking with known haunts, but spots where they might not be too cautious. I decided to stick with the margin – if the end tackle would co-operate and the bait would end up in the right spot. You'll have to under-stand that when a carp man describes a biggish cast as being 'in the right spot' 'cast' probably means 'casts'. Across a gale force wind when the bait has to fly to within six inches of a predetermined margin target, and that target is anything up to eighty-five yards away, 'casts' can mean 'a great many casts', 'two or three

retackles', 're-tying with PVA a number of times' and so on. I'll come to one of those sessions on the Saturday. I mention all that so the sequence of casts that afternoon will appear in perspective – there was an unseen spirit on my side guiding the end tackle to a spot where it would take a fish.

Bill Whiting came round just after we'd taken the pictures of the fat, ugly twenty pounder. The fact that it was my first twenty from the lake meant that at the time the fact that it was fat and ugly went unremarked, I think. Bill and John were standing talking at the back of my swim as I prepared to make the recast to the oak. I seem to attract more than my share of wind-ups and there were plenty of them flying around at that moment. I fronted it with a broadside of bullshit and bravado.

'This is how to get the big 'uns Bill', and I whacked the end tackle out across the wind. The cast was unreal; it just isn't possible to cast to where the bait finished up. It was about eight feet past the bramble and six inches from the bank at the foot of the oak's trunk. It re-ceived the accolade from John of 'You're not going to leave that there are you?', this appar-ently being a comment reserved for ridiculously good casts by John and Brian Skoyles. While the thought didn't cross my mind at the time the bait was in almost exactly the spot I'd taken Big Scale from the previous November, although on that occasion I'd been fishing from the caravan point. But my thoughts were not of Big Scale, who'd already come out that week, but of the Leather, the biggest fish in the lake and the one I'd gone down . . . I was going to write 'hoping to catch' but I don't think that's strictly true. I'd gone down for a big fish, but was I hoping for the Leather? Yes perhaps I was. John says I was on about it all week.

I had no action during the night. John had a mirror of sixteen pounds in the four o'clock feeding spell and we took some pictures as soon

An ugly mirror of 20lb plus was part of a sequence of events of not a little import.

An early hours common of just under 20lb which picked up a stringered bait almost as soon as it hit the water.

as the light was good enough. Action for other people increases your anxiety and erodes your patience. The bait under the oak had been there over sixteen hours by the time we'd finished the photo session and I was a bit impatient to be *doing something*; but sometimes just waiting is as much as you can be doing, so I stifled my impatience and put the kettle on again. There's at least two lines of thought on how long you leave a hookbait in one position on a pressured water. You can either keep moving it to get the fish to try it again, or you can try to lull the fish into a false sense of security by leaving it there long enough for the fish to decide that it must be all right. I've had equal success with each line of thought and my decision to leave this bait put was influenced by the fact that it was in a position where the fish must be aware of it, and one I was unlikely to be able to recast to anyway! I was itching to be doing something, though, even if it was just catapulting a few free offerings out, but I resisted, after a considerable struggle. In fact I was still struggling when I was away on the oak rod. A hectic scrap under the rod tip ended with John slipping the net under a very big fish. We staggered up the grassy slope with the heavy burden and unfolded the net: the familiar sight of Big Scale greeted us! It was hooked well inside the mouth, had taken the bait confidently and was clearly feeding on baits again just two days after John had put it back.

I've got to be honest and say that at the time the fact that it was the second time out of the water that week somewhat devalued the capture. Perhaps it still does, but just to put the fish in perspective those two captures were only its second and third time out of the water that season. Not everyone's idea of fishing, I suppose, but for the majority of us it is a question of fishing for known big fish, or not fishing for big fish at all. We took a couple of quick pictures and put the fish straight back. The lovely mirror swam off strongly, apparently none the worse for the adventure. I've got a great deal of affection for that fish and felt a bit sad about the capture, somehow. Now, about this leather . . .

This was Friday morning and the weekend social event was upon us. The Burroughs brothers descended on E Lake: Brian Nunn put in one of his frequent appearances, enjoying a fruitful week on Homersfield. The engaging John Marven from Essex took up residence in the house accompanied by his equally engaging family and rather lovely wife. Neil the News took up residence in Swim Three, found the gravel bar thirty yards out, caught fish on the Friday night. The gales raged on and occasionally the rain lashed down; and it was cold. I had a fish of sixteen pounds late Friday afternoon.

We've got two Johns now (I once had this with Martins) and one of *them* was in Swim Two and the other in the big house. I love coincidences, if that qualifies as one. Essex John was in no hurry to settle down to his fishing; he was there for the week and wanted Swim One or Two. John in Two was there for another week and he was already geared for the move into One. I felt well loved – everyone was waiting for me to vacate Swim One.

There had been fish moving in the area of the join of the lakes during the hours of darkness most nights, on and off throughout the week, and I'd lost one from across there a couple of days previously. I told Essex John this and he said he'd probably have the first night in that corner. It was a wild, cold night and he decided against it. I think if I'd had the choice of being where he presumably was I'd have decided against it, too.

I had a fish of just under fourteen pounds at about four o'clock in the morning which came on the branches bait. I'd just recast that rod out towards the oak when a fish crashed out to my right. I had a strong urge to reel in and recast in that direction – towards the gap, but I didn't know whether John was fishing or not. I crept

Friday morning saw the magnificent Big Scale on the bank again – much to my confusion.

round to join him in the pitch black and was relieved to find no tackle there. I cast a six bait PVA stringer across, which was the first time I'd put any free offerings of the new bait out. It was in the air a long time and I had a horrible feeling I'd cast it into the brambles. Mercifully, it hit water, but I'd no idea where. I put the kettle on.

Less than two days to go; I'd stay awake and savour the remainder of the night and watch the new day emerging from the darkness beyond the big oak. I made a coffee and as I took the first sip the Optonic to the rod I'd just cast out sounded and the isotope started to climb. I hit the fish before the indicator had moved a foot and it came straight into the net, heavy, but no fireworks. I staggered up the bank with the heavy, wet load in disbelief; it looked like a twenty pound common.

I was getting to the stage where I didn't like telling John about each successive fish, but I wanted him to see this and weigh it. I went and woke him and we gazed at the fish in amazement. He took it well, and I couldn't have had better company for the week. The common was very beautiful, a perfect shape, unmarked, golden and really pretty. The scales proved me wrong on weight though; it went 19lb 10oz.

John went back to bed and I cast back out to the oak area, just PVA'ing one free offering to the hookbait. I sat and had a think about the common. I knew that some stock fish had been put in the water that season; 19.10 – was this one of them? I had a feeling that it would turn out to be so, which would take the edge off the capture. In fact, it was a stock fish, and I don't consider it to be my personal best common, for that reason – which makes me about as daft as everyone else in the carp world on this values thing!

The coffee I'd had one sip from was cold, and I made another cup. The sky was turning a lighter shade of pale across the lake; I reflected that the only action I'd had after first light had been Big Scale at something past eight, and the dropped fish around eleven. My thoughts were rudely interrupted. Beeeepppp. An absolute flier, which on D lake *usually* means a lowish double. This one went twelve pounds. It was beginning to dawn on me that I was getting a fair amount of action soon after casting out in the dark, which could just have been down to the fact that I was recasting at feeding time after a take, or it could have meant that the carp were investigating the splash of the cast, a not uncommon occurence on pressured waters.

Saturday morning was fine and was taken up with photographs of the common, and good-byes from Gary and his pretty wife from C lake. But Saturday afternoon was rain filled and the winds were getting stronger and stronger. I'd managed to get two casts right in there under the oak branches and was able to concentrate on trying to keep the brolly and the storm sides where I wanted them. I like the relaxation of Saturday afternoon at the back end and in winter: the soccer commentary and other bits and pieces, the score flashes and then the results. I listened to the radio and sat on the bed chair looking out at the wild, wet afternoon. They were the sort of conditions that you almost hope you don't get action in, so you don't have to crawl out for a soaking. Almost . . . But as I sat looking at nothing in particular, my eyes became increasingly drawn to a spot two thirds of the way along the right hand margin. There were fish there, I knew it, and I was getting the vibes to put a bait on them. 'Oh no', I groaned; I was all right where I was; there were fish where my baits were, they just weren't making a mistake for the minute. But I knew I'd have to do it.

About a season and a half before, I'd started following my carp fishing instincts about everything, swims, baits, moving, staying, spots to cast to, whatever; so I obeyed my inconsiderate instinct and crawled out into the downpour in my waterproof top, reeled in the right hand bait, PVA'd, which is a bundle of fun when you've got water dripping all over the place, and fired a trial cast across the rain and wind-lashed water. It was a cast that was dependent on the wind for keeping the line out of the trees for success and wouldn't have been 'on' in still conditions, because the line would snag. I thought I'd got it second cast, but I hadn't; the lead went where I wanted it, but the line held up and captured a branch.

In the next hour and a half, I retackled six times. I'd got the vibes so I'd got to have a bait in there, but it wasn't on. If I fired straight at the spot, the wind blew the end tackle left. If I made allowance for the wind, the end tackle held its line for the branches I was trying to cast round. I don't know what was out there, but its guardian angel was working overtime on the protection job, blowing, and not blowing to order. On the sixth retackle I cast back to the bramble and in it went, six inches away at the first time of asking. I had a fish on it as a sodden dusk settled in early.

The final night. The fish at dusk had deprived me of the margin bait, which sounds dumb, because I'd had a fish on it, but . . . Well, to the best of my knowledge the Leather usually fell to a margin bait, but rarely, if ever, from under the oak, which was why I'd been fishing one bait off the branches a great deal of the time. The odd thing about firing a bait right in against the trunk of the oak is that I've only had the two takes from there, and both times it has been Big Scale. I've had a number of fish from under the branches, and from the bramble and just short of it, but nothing other than the big fella from the shallow water up on the gravel. Because I'd got The Leather on my mind I wanted a bait by the bush and one under the branches, but I couldn't get one back to the margin bush after the dusk fish; there was too little light.

I booked an alarm call from the fish for my last morning and fell asleep. Truth was, I was well pleased with the week's results, but such was the consistency of the action in the morning and afternoon feeding spells that I was thinking in terms of a possible four more fish, which meant that I'd still got hopes of the Leather. I'd even started feeding some of the successful bait in, but not a lot; just enough to keep them hungry. I think I used just under half a mix of the bait I caught the fish on through the four days. That last night I put about twenty baits out off the oak, which was the area I was recasting to after early hours

action to avoid getting tangled up in the branches.

I woke up suddenly; it was dark and I had an action replay of an Optonic in my head. 'Are you in, John?' No answer. I don't see too much without my glasses, otherwise I would have noticed immediately that I'd got an isotope half way up a needle. I finally noticed, scrambled out, picked up the rod and struck. I get a great many takes like that when I'm heavily foamed, as I was all that week. I've a feeling the fish turns back against the resistance as soon as it feels the hook, which gives the appearance of the run stopping. With a heavy bomb and foam it takes the fish a while to shed the hook and it is usually still there for a while. This one was, and it was a mid-double. I carried it up to the grass but couldn't unhook it. The batteries in my torch had run out and I went to borrow John's. No need to tell him . . . 'I've got a bit of a tangle John; I'm just borrowing your torch.' The fish chose that moment to beat a tattoo on the grass with its tail.

'It's doing a lot of flapping around out there, that tangle', my friend sighed. We laughed.

I put the fish back, tied one free offering to the hook bait and recast just off the oak line. There was a faint hint of grey in the sky opposite me: I put the kettle on. Beep-beep-beep. The isotope started to climb. I struck and hit nothing and reeled in, in disbelief. I'd had a bite off. I tied a new braided hook length, baited it, tied one free offering to it and out it went again. I sat through an hour of gradually lightening sky and a couple of coffees.

Beeeeppppp. Same time as the previous morning; same flier. I smiled to myself at the speed of the run and bent the rod into the fish. It was soon coming in my direction and I presumed a smallish double – until the first time it turned over in the swim. It didn't splash, it splooshed, and at the same time I saw its flank. It looked a good fish. The scrap was heavy, but not hard and I had no anxiety until the first time I tried to lift the mesh of the net around the fish. It had picked up the line from the other rod late on in the scrap and had pulled the rod across the top of the landing net. The result was that I couldn't lift the net because of the other rod, so I had to ease the pressure off so the fish could swim out. That was a very anxious moment, letting a fish I'd already netted go again. Fortunately, the net came free and I netted the fish at the second attempt.

I pulled it up onto the bank, with the disbelief buds working overtime again. The weight felt familiar, if the fish wasn't. I was in a right pickle, and had to call John. I couldn't move further than a foot from the water because the bomb was tangled with the other line near the rod tip. I was anxious to unhook the fish, but was frightened of it slipping back down the sloping bank. John staggered out to find me virtually lying on the fish. I had a feeling it was the Leather and asked John to get Neil, for identification purposes.

After declaring that it was at least three other leathers that were all big twenties, Neil eventually inspected its tail and declared it was **The Leather**. They hung the Avons on the tree and assessed the weight of the fish as 31lb 13oz; then assessed me as a jammy rat of dubious parentage! It was just growing light and Neil set off on his rounds to inform the world.

'You talked the bloody thing onto your hook', said John, in mock disgust, as I offered him a consoling coffee. It was almost light by this time, but we had to sack the fish for a couple of hours for the pictures. Initially it didn't sack too well and I switched it to a 30 denier nylon sack; it was happier altogether. As soon as the sun was up, Neil and the two Johns took some marvellous pictures of the beautiful golden fish. I'd left it late, but it didn't seem at all odd that I'd caught the fish I'd travelled down there to catch. I think I was glad, but I always think the fish is the central character when it's on the bank: the angler is just there to

hold it. I certainly don't think it's any big deal to catch a carp, because I spend so much time not catching them. I think I enjoyed catching The Leather though; it's a lovely fish.

There is always a strong social streak to the carp fishing on D, which is great, or grates, depending on who you are, who's socialising, and whether or not you're in the mood for it. Sunday was a good day for it; the marvellous Marvens, Martin, Graham, Denis, the inevitable Bill, Derek, John and Swim Two John, at different times, or collectively. The local carp anglers were threatening to take up carp fishing again, if their women would let them: we had a game of football on the lawn with Marven Jnr, and I managed to slice a clearance into the lake. It was pleasant and relaxing and there was one more feeding time to come before I finally put the rods away and turned for home.

By early afternoon I'd put everything but the rod set up in the back of the car. I'd got both hook baits out by the oak and while I was hoping for a final flurry of action, I knew I'd done enough damage for one week. I'd moved my rods to the left hand side of the swim to allow John room to erect his bivvy and put his rod rests in. Some time during the week, when the departure of my bivvy was at its most imminent in the gale force winds, I'd found a heavy section of tree trunk and used it to anchor one of the storm sides. As I broke camp I'd rolled it to one side and, just by chance, left it behind the rods, about eight or nine feet away . . .

At ten to two I was away on the left hand rod to a bait in the open water just off the branches. It was a slow take (suggesting a fish moving parallel to the bank) and as I shut the bail arm and struck, I moved backwards to strike again and keep pressure on the fish if it moved towards me – and did a backward somersault over the aforementioned tree trunk. Have you noticed that you cannot run backwards when you are lying on your back? I waved the rod around in annoyance and glanced towards Swim Two. My discomfiture had not gone unremarked; the glamorous Carol was looking on in detached amusement, while everyone else had hysterics. What can you do but join in? I couldn't help feeling that my laughter might have been a bit hollow if it had been my only take of the week. I lost the fish.

Shortly before four o'clock I was away on the right hand rod, the bait under the branches. The log had been banished and I made uninterrupted progress up the bank behind the swim, then stopped and came back down again as the fish gave me plenty to think about. It felt as big as anything I'd hooked all week, which shows how little you can tell about the size of a fish until it is actually in the net.

It fought hard all the way in and even more powerfully once it was in the margins. The social set had heard the Optonic sound and gathered behind the swim, and I think that from the swirls and the heavy, deep scrap we all thought it was a good fish. In fact, it had suddenly had enough and revealed itself to be a handsome, lightly scaled mirror of an ounce over fifteen pounds.

I recast and shared John's bivvy with him till late evening, but there was no further action while I was there. I always enjoy clinging to the remnants of a week and we drank many a coffee and had a variety of visitors before I finally turned my back on it all. Grey reality beckoned. I was due back at work at six in the morning and had a sleep threatened two hundred mile plus drive back through the night to negotiate first.

That was the week, that was. A week at Waveney on D lake; one of my favourite waters. A week of familiar and welcome faces, and a chance to relax away from it all. And a week of pitting my wits against the thinking of those wary, pressured carp. I think the week represents one of the best sessions I've fished — because the advanced planning was wrong. The original bait hadn't worked out, my tactics had been wrong, and it took me more than half the session to think my way into the fish. The longer I was there the more my instincts took over, but whether that was because the computer had been fed enough information to produce the right formula for success, or because my sixth sense played a significant part in any of it I don't know. I think getting it right is an accumulation of pluses, supported by a fair helping of luck.

16 A List of Forty Plus Carp

Compiled by Kevin Clifford and Tim Paisley

With assistance from Steve Corbett, Chris Ball and Rob Maylin

Key letters on left-hand side indicate repeat captures.

```
m  − mirror
l  − leather
c  − common
** Weight
   estimated
```

	WEIGHT	CAPTOR	LOCATION	DATE
A	51–08–0 (m)	Chris Yates	Redmire Pool	June 1980
	46–12–0	Richard Lloyd	Surrey Pond	March 1990
B	46–08–0 (l)	Pete Richards	Erehwon	August 1989
C	45–12–0 (m)	Ritchie MacDonald	Yateley N. Lake	October 1984
B	45–02–0 (l)	Ray Stone	Erehwon	December 1986
B	45–00–0 (l)	Mark Fitzpatrick	Erehwon	June 1989
B	45–00–0 (l)	Mark Fitzpatrick	Erehwon	July 1989
B	45–00–0 (l)	Ray Stone	Erehwon	July 1987
B	44–14–0 (l)	Ray Stone	Erehwon	November 1986
B	44–12–0 (l)	Keith Longden	Erehwon	August 1987
C	44–08–0 (m)	Graham Mountain	Yateley N. Lake	March 1989
C	44–08–0 (m)	Nick Lee	Yateley North Lake	1989
	44–06–0 (m)	Ray Greenwood	Henlow Grange	June 1984
D	44–04–0 (m)	Steve Allcot	Longfield	December 1989
C	44–04–0 (m)	D Baker	Yateley N. Lake	1985
B	44–00–0 (l)	Mark Fitzpatrick	Erehwon	June 1987
	44–00–0 (c)	Richard Walker	Redmire Pool	September 1952
	43–13–8 (c)	Chris Yates	Redmire Pool	August 1972
B	43–08–0 (l)	Ray Stone	Erehwon	September 1985
E	43–08–0 (m)	Keith O'Connor	Harrow	1984
C	43–08–0 (m)	B O'Bourn	Yateley North Lake	1989
C	43–04–0 (m)	Steve Brown	Yateley N. Lake	October 1989
C	43–04–0 (m)	Adrian Tilbury	Yateley N. Lake	July 1984
B	43–04–0 (l)	Gary Morgan	Erehwon	August 1986
C	43–04–0 (m)	Sam Fox	Yateley N. Lake	September 1984

	WEIGHT	CAPTOR	LOCATION	DATE
C	43–04–0 (m)	Ray Fuller	Yateley N. Lake	July 1987
G	43–04–0 (m)	Clive Gibbins	Sandholme Pool	1984
B	43–00–0 (l)	Keith Longden	Erehwon	August 1986
	43–00–0 (m)	Graham Mountain	Trilakes	1983
L	43–00–0 (m)	Jonathan Leigh	Surrey Club Lake	July 1980
C	42–12–0 (m)	Kerry Barringer	Yateley N. Lake	1985
	42–12–0 (m)	Martin Symonds	Waltham Abbey	September 1976
C	42–08–0 (m)	Nick Peat	Yateley N. Lake	August 1988
B	42–06–0 (l)	Vic Bailey	Erehwon	June 1985
B	42–04–0 (l)	Mark Fitzpatrick	Erehwon	October 1984
B	42–04–0 (l)	Ray Stone	Erehwon	July 1986
	42–02–0 (c)	John Lilley	Mangrove	1988
C	42–00–0 (m)	M Lawson	Yateley N. Lake	1989
F	42–00–0 (m)	John Allen	Longfield	December 1987
	42–00–0 (c)	Ray Clay	Billing Aquadrome	September 1966
	42–00–0 (m)	Ken Hodder	Yateley Car Park Lake	October 1979
E	42–00–0 (m)	Z Bojko	Harrow	1984
D	42–00–0 (m)	Terry Dempsey	Longfield	September 1989
D	42–00–0 (m)	Jon Holt	Longfield	August 1987
	41–12–0 (m)	Thomas Gelston	Hainault	November 1985
D	41–12–0 (m)	Dave Whibley	Longfield	1989
C	41–10–0 (m)	Jan Wenczka	Yateley N. Lake	August 1981
F	41–08–0 (c)	David Westerman	Snake Pit, Essex	June 1988
O	41–08–0 (l)	Robin Dix	Yateley Car Park Lake	June 1985
J	41–08–0 (m)	Kevin Nash	Silver End Pit	June 1985
	41–08–0 (m)	Alan	Stanstead Abbott	December 1989
F	41–08–0 (c)	Phil Harper	Snake Pit, Essex	September 1989
C	41–05–0 (m)	Chris Riddington	Yateley N. Lake	October 1980
L	41–00–0 (m)	Jonathan Leigh	Surrey Club Lake	October 1978
B	41–00–0 (l)	Mark Fitzpatrick	Erehwon	September 1984
K	40–12–0 (m)	Dave Macintyre	Mid-Northants	October 1989
O	40–12–0 (l)	Don Orriss	Yateley Car Park Lake	October 1989
	40–10–0 (m)	Jock White	Yateley Pads Lake	1989
H	40–10–0 (m)	Jon Holt	Longfield	1982
D	40–04–0 (m)	Richard Johnson	Longfield	1985
G	40–08–0 (m)	Kevin Clifford	Sandholme Pool	1983
A	40–08–0 (m)	Eddie Price	Redmire Pool	September 1959
H	40–08–0 (m)	Colin Swaden	Longfield	1980
F	40–08–0 (c)	Zenon Bojko	Snake Pit, Essex	1988
E	40–08–0	Bernie Stamp	Harrow	July 1987
	40–04–0	AN Other	Pit 2	June 1988
G	40–04–0 (m)	Kevin Clifford	Sandholme Pool	1984
	40–04–0	Nick West	Wraysbury	1980

	WEIGHT	CAPTOR	LOCATION	DATE
E	40–04–0	Lee Jackson	Harrow	1983
J	40–04–0	Phil Harper	Essex Silver End	1984
K	40–04–0	Alan Taylor	Mid-Northants	January 1989
K	40–04–0 (m)	Kevin Maddocks	Mid-Northants	January 1990
E	40–02–0	Paul Fickling	Harrow	1985
A	40–03–0 (m)	Jack Hilton	Redmire Pool	July 1972
H	40–03–0 (m)	Colin Swaden	Longfield	1980
D	40–02–0 (m)	John Allen	Longfield	July 1988
D	40–02–0 (m)	Matthew McEwan	Longfield	July 1989
	40–00–8 (m)	Ron Groombridge	Boxmoor	June 1966
B	40–00–0 (l)	Ian Longden	Erehwon	September 1984
A	40–00–0 (m)	John MacLeod	Redmire Pool	July 1972
	40–00–0★★	Henry Weeks	East Peckham	July 1972
D	40–00–0 (m)	Clive Williams	Longfield	August 1988
	40–12	S Hale	MOD Aldermaston	1987

Footnote

The typescript for this book was submitted to the publishers during November 1989, which meant that changes to the Big Fish list were bound to occur prior to publication. The few additional big carp captures that came to my attention prior to the final proofing have been added to the list, but what I could not foresee was that the face of big carp fishing would change quite as drastically as it did during the spring of 1990. Through the winter there was talk about the closure of William Boyer's big fish water Rodney Meadow, and this close down duly took place – with the fish being moved to Farlows and Harefield. What no one could have forecast was the sudden closure of one of the greatest big carp waters of all, as happened when the shut down of Longfield was announced and carried out within the course of a week in February. At the time of writing this late footnote there are plans to move the Longfield fish to a nearby water, which will be controlled by Leisure Sport on a day ticket basis, but netting Longfield is proving difficult. How these big carp will take to their new home remains to be seen but for certain there will be no more big fish list additions under the Longfield name. The water has been a Mecca for big carp hunters for more than twenty years and its passing is a sad loss. It is also sad that the last significant capture from Longfield should be a controversial one. At the end of December 1989 Steve Allcott landed the fish known as the Parrot at 37lb plus, then caught 'The Forty' at 44.04lb within twenty-four hours. This great brace was somewhat tarnished by the fact that Steve was already banned from fishing the water, and was therefore poaching at the time!

By the time you read this, other forties will have been added to the list, but in future you will be able to keep up to date with the big fish lists in the 'Carpworld Year Book', available from early 1991.

The Big Carp List

I've always found lists of big fish exciting, especially the carp lists. Big carp lists are comparatively new, but they have been appearing since the early fifties – one of the first, if not the first, being in Faddist's book '*Memorable Coarse Fish*'. I'm sure the most comprehensive list ever attempted was at the back of Jack Hilton's book '*Quest for Carp*', that being a list of twenty plus carp up to the beginning of the seventies. There was a list of forty plus carp in the '*First*

BCSG' book, and a number of up-dates have been published, the latest I have seen being in Kevin Clifford's book '*Carp*'. The list reproduced here was compiled by Kevin, with alterations and additions being carried out by the author.

As this book is about fish over twenty-five pounds I suppose this list should, ideally, be of 25lb plus fish, but such a list would probably fill the whole of this book. The growing lists are an indication of the spread in popularity of carp fishing, and the growth in the average weight

The first English forty, and the fish that captured the imagination of would-be carp anglers, Dick Walker with his marvellous Redmire common of 44lb.

Kevin Nash with a Silver End mirror at 41lb plus.

of carp in the last twenty years. On second thoughts perhaps it isn't quite accurate to suggest that the average weight is higher; it could just be that the carp population is higher, with a proportionate increase in big fish. Whatever the reason there are now more big fish being caught than ever before. Or are there? Let's have a closer look at the list published here and put the number of forties put on the bank into perspective.

Obviously the fish listed are not all different fish. In fact the eighty plus entries represent just twenty-eight different fish from twenty-four waters. Only three waters have produced more than one forty, these being Redmire, which is top of the list with three; Longfield, which has produced two; and Yateley Car Park Lake, which has also produced two. The key letters down the left hand side of the list identify the repeat captures. Those fish with no

letter against them were only caught once (or only once at forty plus), and for the most part they are not still around for the catching. A great many of the fish listed are no longer with us, or aren't showing even if they are. Both Chris Yates's forty plus fish are dead, as are Dick Walker's 44, the Harrow forty – fish E, Ray Clay's Billing fish, Kenny Hodder's Yateley Car Park Lake forty, the Silver End mirror – fish J, Jonathan Leigh's mirror – fish L, the first of the two forties Longfield has produced – fish H, Ron Groombridge's Boxmoor forty, and the Aldermaston fish.

In addition there are a couple of fish which are considered to be dubious qualifiers for a list of this type because they come from small 'domestic' waters which could be classified as stock ponds. These fish are Kev Clifford's Jumbo – the Sandholme Grange fish – and Martin Symonds' 42, which was caught from a holding

Phil Harper with the Essex Silver End mirror which weighed exactly 40lb when Phil caught it after two years of concentrated effort.

Clive Gibbins with Kev Clifford's Jumbo at 43lb plus.

pond. The latter fish was later transferred to Homersfield and either died in transit, or lost weight and now comes out as a mid-twenty to mid-thirty. There is no carp fishing snobbery in the suggestion that these fish 'don't count'. There has long been a fear in carp fishing circles that the record could be eclipsed by a big carp stocked and brought on specially for the purpose. I think the test of a carp's validity is if it would be accepted for record purposes, and I don't think anyone would dream of claiming the record if they caught Jumbo, magnificent as the fish undoubtedly is.

The East Peckham forty has to be considered doubtful, in view of the fact that the weight was estimated. The fish was later caught at weights well below forty and never made its original claimed weight again. Nick West's Wraysbury forty is also thought to be dead by Pete Springate and Kenny Hodder, who spent many years watching and fishing the water, although this is a very big lake and fish could possibly disappear for long periods. I have no definite confirmation that Ray Greenwood's Henlow Grange fish died but Rob Maylin thinks it did, and from the pictures this looked to be a heavily spawnbound fish with a limited future.

That's the gloom and doom over with, what

Mark Fitzpatrick with a growing Pinky at 35lb. He has caught the fish five times at 40lb plus.

Ray Stone with Pinky at 45lb 2oz.

about the fish that are still alive and well, and those that look as though they may well make it onto this list in the future? Happily two of the biggest fish on the list are still going strong, these being the Yateley North Lake fish which made 45lb 12oz when Ritchie Macdonald caught it (Fish C), and the 'Erehwon' Leather called Pinky, which topped out at 46lb 8oz in August 1989. Both fish are caught fairly frequently and the pressure they are under no doubt limits their potential for making fifty pounds. That's a shame because both fish are naturally very big. They have also made a great many carp men very happy, their combined

capture total on our list accounting for twenty-seven entries – and I'm perfectly sure *all* their captures haven't been recorded. Incidentally, the mystery fish Pinky lives in a water of eighteen acres and is a completely natural fish.

One of the captures of the Erehwon fish requires comment because when it came out in August 1986 it formed half of the biggest brace yet landed in this country (to my knowledge). On that August night Gary Morgan – just fourteen and a half years old at the time! – was fishing with his father, Dave. As a rule the father and son team took it in turn to strike runs to their rod set-up but on this occasion Gary had just come back from holiday and had

Father and son Dave and Gary Morgan pose with Gary's incredible brace of 43lb 4oz and 36lb 6oz. Gary was just fourteen and a half at the time.

some catching up to do with dad, who had been enjoying a successful streak while Gary was away. It was therefore agreed that Gary could take the first two takes, which just happened to come from the two biggest fish in the water, Pinky, at 43lb 4oz, and Perky at 36lb 6oz. The runs came within three quarters of an hour of each other, between four and five o'clock in the morning, the date being the 28th of August. A remarkable achievement brace.

According to my records five men have caught two *different* fish over forty pounds, these being Chris Yates, the first man to

achieve such a feat, Jon Holt, Graham Mountain, Phil Harper and Zenon Bojko. Of these the last three named have caught forty pluses from different waters, the talented Zenon being the first to reach this coveted target. Both Jon Holt's fish came from Longfield and both Chris Yates's from Redmire. There does seem to be some slight controversy about Graham Mountain's first forty plus capture, which was the Tri Lakes fish of 43lb, but I think the carp was definitely confirmed as a forty-three, and it certainly looked that big in the pictures.

In the final analysis the list breaks down to

Jon Holt with the first of his Longfield forties, a fish which later died.

just seven forty plus fish that have already been caught and are still alive and well. What are the prospects of catching one of them? Well, Erehwon is a private water, so you can cross that off your list. Yateley is the best bet at the moment with a definite two forties, and a number of other big fish at the venue. Yateley Car Park Lake has already produced two forties, the North Lake one, and the Tri Lakes, just across the fence, one, which makes the area God's little acre in the forty plus stakes.

Longfield has also produced two forties, and currently holds at least one, together with a number of other big fish. Stanstead Abbots, is being whispered about, has produced at least one forty and again has other biggies. I think

this water is still something of an unknown quantity.

The Snake Pit common is a lovely fish, but this is an ultra hard, very frustrating water. Mid-Northants is Duncan Kay's lake, which is a private syndicate with a limited membership. According to the grapevine Duncan is on the verge of losing the water, which is a great shame because he has carefully developed one of the best carp waters in the country here. The other surviving forties include the Hainault fish, which fluctuates in weight and has, I think, only gone over the forty barrier once, and the Pit 2 fish, to which the same comments can apply.

In terms of existing fish I suspect the forty

Lee Jackson with the Colne Valley forty which later died in slightly controversial circumstances (the fish developed a disease and was put to death by a club member). At the time of writing this no publicity water is on the verge of producing two more 40lb plus fish.

Ritchie with his huge fish, the Yateley mirror at 45lb 12oz.

plus total is lower than it was two or three years ago, but on the evidence of this season the big fish ranks look set to grow in the near future. Savay Lake, Harrow and another gravel pit in the Colne Valley could well produce a forty this season or next. While I was actually finalising the list Alan Smith from Kent rang to tell me he had landed a fish of 39lb 15oz that afternoon. The fish was from a no-publicity Colne Valley water which has already produced one forty, and is obviously on the verge of housing at least one new one, possibly two. The steady flow of good bait into Darenth Tip Lake has pushed the weights of these old fish through the roof, and the water could well do a forty this winter or next season, an unforeseeable prospect until this season. No doubt other waters have benefited from the two mild winters and the hot summer just passed and could add new fish to the forty list in the not too distant future.

Let's hope so, but the major problem is the one Rod emphasises in his chapter (Chapter 5).

The potential for growth is there, but the biggest limiting factor is angling pressure. A big thirty or forty is caught and it is immediately put under pressure by the bounty hunters after its scalp. That is a fact of life we have to live with, and it means that only genetic freaks like Pinky and the North Lake mirror – or uncaught fish – can make it into the upper forty sphere. In the case of previously uncaught fish it means that the first capture could be the biggest, so the giant you want could be an unknown fish. If you can find such a fish it is likely to be catchable. Don't just think in terms of known fish when you think big. There can be no greater pleasure than getting on the list

On the way to forty? Chris Ball cradles his Wraysbury 36lb mirror which was caught on a floater.

with an unknown fish, as David Westerman did with a huge unknown common from a known Essex water as recently as 1988. Other parts of the country are under less angling pressure than Essex and could well turn up a biggie.

The list makes fascinating reading, but don't get the mistaken impression that landing a forty will just be a question of going and sitting it out on the right water. The captures are the tip of the iceberg and each successful angler represents scores of very capable carp men who have failed in their forty plus objective. On the other hand don't be daunted by the list; big carp are only human, and if you get your sums right your name could appear on the next version of the forties list.

17 Afterthoughts

I'm back where I started really. I've put together what feels like a smashing book, but I've not really managed to say all that I wanted to say. I think I've finally realised what the problem is. Carp fishing is changing all the time, and each session and each new book adds a new dimension. The new knowledge might not change *my* mind about things, but unless the reader has the full range of carp fishing alternatives at his disposal the vital piece may be missing from his particular jigsaw. As a result a chapter that feels more or less complete at the time of writing suddenly has a couple of glaring omissions when I read the final typescript. But there comes a time when you have to cry 'enough', and as a rule that time is when the publisher had got tired of promises and wants the typescript! In the case of this book ninety per cent of it has already been sent, and I'm working on borrowed time to dot any i's that haven't yet been dotted.

It's always the technical material that causes the last minute doubts, in particular chapters on presentation and bait. My thoughts on presentation are influenced by practical experience and the teachings of others. I tend to lay emphasis on the thinking required to meet the subtle differences in the carp's approach to suspicious baits, encouraging the reader to experiment with different lengths of hooklink and different materials for the vital bottom few inches of line. Other writers lay greater emphasis on the actual relationship between the hook and the bait, rarely mentioning the length of the hooklink – which surprises me slightly. It's not the bait/hook emphasis that surprises me but the omission in not discussing the length of the hooklink. The latest book to be published is Rob Maylin's '*Fox Pool*'. There is a brilliant rig chapter in it that is compulsory reading for any big fish man, but in it Rob restricts himself almost exclusively to discussing the hooking arrangement, the last few inches of line. Now Rob is an ex-match angler and will understand all the subtle nuances of fine tuning in presentation. It's possible that he doesn't discuss hooklink length because he takes his readers' understanding of such matters for granted, or perhaps he doesn't think it's as vital in carp fishing as in match fishing. For whatever reason readers could get the impression that Rob and I view the question of presentation very differently. If we do, and it's not really an area we've discussed, it is because we are fishing for different fish which have been subjected to different pressures over the last few years. I agree entirely with what Rob has to say about rigs, and I can relate to the thinking behind the bent hook rig – but then again I also have to relate to what Ken Townley has to say about presentation in his chapter 'Looking in on Carp'.

What you are looking for in presentation is a marriage of the most effective hooking arrangement and the hooklink (length and material) that is most likely to take the carp off guard. There must be an element of surprise, and even with a bent hook rig other considerations have equal importance as the hook itself. I do like the bent hook rig, and I've caught fish on it, but I'm not clear in my mind that they were fish I wouldn't have caught with a different hooking arrangement. That may read as a cop out, but it isn't. The bent hook rig is most effective when fish are suspicious and testing baits in a certain way; I've been prebaiting the water I'm fishing and I'm not sure presentation is of great significance with these carp – within reason.

The other area I'm not sure I've dealt with adequately is fish meals – in the light of the tremendous success they have had this season. I've used fish meals in the past, I like them very much, and they undoubtedly catch carp. Their success on Darenth in particular has been staggering, but I don't know whether the success is due to the baits themselves, or the fact that they are in common usage. The inflated success rate that occurs when a bait becomes *the* bait in general use on a water is proven, the most recent examples being tiger nuts, fish meals and Richworth boilies. But in the context of what has happened over the last fifteen or sixteen years fish meals have got a lot of catching up to do on milk/egg protein and bird food bait results.

It is dangerous to jump to hasty conclusions about any occurrence in carp fishing until time has put in it perspective. Is it a one-off – a seven day wonder – or does it occur often enough on enough waters to suggest that there is a predictable principle at work? Are fish meals and fish oils working so well at the moment because they are what they are, or because of the saturation method of baiting that is being used to fish them? I'm not going to try to answer that one. What I will reiterate is that where everyone on a water is on one bait it is very difficult to establish your own. But watch for the trends. When a bait starts to get best results when fished as hook bait only that bait is open to attack, and it should be possible to establish another bait in those circumstances. Baits that are catching on a hook bait only principle are on the wane because there isn't the compensating introduction of free baits to maintain the carp's confidence in the food source. A single is a bait, a supply of bait is a food source.

In '*Carp Fishing*' I looked at what it takes to make a successful carp angler, and quoted Dick Walker's suggestion that determination is a big asset. '*It must matter tremendously*' were his words, and that is especially true of fishing for big carp. I think that if I had to pick one attribute to make someone successful in any sphere it would be determination, guts, bottle. If it hurts like hell to fail you will become determined to succeed – succeed in getting admission to the right waters, to get the bait and the presentation right, to put up with the travelling, the loneliness and the frustration. You can spend a long time waiting for a big carp to take and you need determination to stick it out.

I think *determination to catch* is the biggest factor you can have going for you. You will all think you are determined to catch, but you're wrong. About five per cent of carp anglers have this determination all the time, and the rest of us perhaps some of the time. There is a big difference between wanting to catch and being determined to catch. It is very easy to think that sticking it out behind the rods is being determined, but very often it is a form of self-deception. Re-read Jan Wenczka's chapter about Burton (Chapter 3). One comment Jan made stopped me in my tracks. Very few of the Burton fish he and Andy caught came to full-blooded runs. I've long accepted that a percentage of 'takes' are less than full runs, but Jan's observation that they tend to be only a low percentage took me by surprise, particularly as his chapter goes back some time. My set-up is geared to register small movements of the indicators, but most of my lakes are night feeding waters, and night is when I do my sleeping. The fact is I struggle to stay awake when it's dark, so I get in the bag and go to sleep. Now I know it usually takes two or three bleeps from the Optonic to wake me, and one bleep can be very significant in registering a small movement of the indicator. And I'm likely to be asleep while this is going on and might not even hear it! No determination there.

The waiting game.

Stalking carp is another area in which I don't exactly shine. I say it's because I'm not a good stalker, but I know that in truth it is because I don't have the patience for stalking. I wish I had the stalking application of Elliot Symak, or Martin Herbertson, or Brian Skoyles, and I am working at it, but not determinedly enough I think.

Can you honestly say you move pitch as often as you should? I don't. I tend to think that two or three days is a minimum in a swim, mainly because I've got so much gear that it takes me half a day to move. But moving is the key to location, because you very often don't know exactly where the carp are when you first get to the water. How often is your first choice of swim based on inspired guesswork? It often has to be because you get to the water so late in

the day that you can't spend any time locating fish before it gets dark. What happens then is that you pinpoint the fish during the first night – through hearing them – or next morning, through observing them. You then kid yourself that they will move onto your baits, and stay put. Then pack up two days later annoyed with yourself for getting it wrong.

The trouble is there has to be a compromise between being determined to catch, and wanting to enjoy the fishing; I think this is the main reason my determination wavers on a number of points, and on many occasions. I enjoy carp fishing, so I tend not to burn out. Being at the water is my main relaxation, and at times I am a dedicated camper rather than a dedicated carper. In fact I recently saw an article which was critical of carp men, suggesting that there is now more camping than fishing. Why not? It's a magical escape and a terrific pleasure. A great many of us do nothing but carp fish and work, so we can't really be criticised for treating the carp fishing as a relaxation occasionally. Carp fishing has always been a compromise between spending as much time as possible at the water and trying to catch carp while you are there. For some fish you can only work at getting it right in advance, set up the trap, and *wait*. The combination of camping and carping is not an eighties trend, it was a way of life for the Carp Catchers Club at Redmire in the fifties.

I'm not a patient waiter because to me blank periods mentally spell ineptitude, when very often they aren't actually anything of the sort: sometimes you have to wait. Set yourself sensible objectives and work towards achieving them and you will find carp fishing exciting and enjoyable. One aspect of the sensible objectives should be to give yourself a reasonable time limit for catching a big fish. Too many carp men get all fired up with enthusiasm in the close season, carry out an exhaustive pre-baiting campaign, then become discouraged when they don't catch their biggie immediately. Big carp fishing is not like that. It takes time and in June you have to keep reminding yourself that it could be October before they start feeding heavily enough on bait to make a mistake. Will you still be there in October, or will the whole struggle have got to you by then? Don't let it. Soldier on. All but one of my eight twenty-five plus fish have been caught after the end of September.

It is difficult to be realistic about the time element involved in fishing for big carp. I don't think any of the anglers who write about fishing for big carp give an unrealistic impression about the difficulty of catching the big ones but the reader can easily get a distorted impression, nonetheless. Rod in 'Carp Strikes Back', Yatesy in 'Casting at the Sun', Rob Maylin in 'Fox Pool' and some of the chapters in this book spell out

the fact that you can go for long periods without fish. The blank spells are inevitable, however good a carp angler you are. If you don't read between the lines, or pick up on the references to long periods without catching and just look at the pictures, you can fool yourself into thinking it is easy to catch and that some of the big fish southern waters are easy – when they are nothing of the kind. If you want to catch big fish you may have to travel south, but be mentally prepared for how hard it is going to be when you do go down there. In 'Fox Pool' Rob refers to having found the secret of Savay, the secret being time. That is true of a great many waters, and of all big fish waters for all but the most gifted of carp men.

I'll warn you in advance that one of the biggest difficulties in switching from just carping to fishing for biggies is one that sounds a bit silly. When you are used to catching numbers of fish and your objective becomes a handful a season, at best, you will find the questions of your friends putting you under pressure to start with. 'What have you caught this season' can become an irritating question, and a source of some embarrassment, when you have to answer 'Nothing' for long periods. There are a handful of known liars in the big carp world. Don't be tempted to join them as a sort of defence mechanism. The boys who spend their lives fishing for big fish know full well that no one needs excuses for not catching them, so be reassured by that. The carp world instantly recognises a liar; don't make the mistake of becoming one.

Don't start fishing for the big carp until you have caught enough carp to satisfy your appetite, and to give you a good insight into carp behaviour. I still remember very vividly that 7lb 14oz fish I referred to earlier. I well remember being quietly envious of a 13 pounder John Curry caught at dawn one Snowberry morning. I never, ever thought that there would come a time when I would think of a

It isn't all hard work. Here Fred J Taylor, Colin Dyson of Coarse Angler, *Len Arbery and the author relax over a celebratory meal in the car park at the historic Redmire Pool.*

low double as a small fish, or that I would be slightly disappointed by the capture of a big double, or a low twenty. In some ways all those things have happened to me, but in another way it doesn't matter. My biggest thrill is still the movement of the indicator and the surge of power through the rod when your mind says 'carp'. The disappointments are born of the need to prove yourself in the eyes of others, or because your objectives mean more to you than they need do. In one respect I am very fortunate; I am never envious of others because of what they catch. Occasionally it can hurt a little bit when someone lands a biggie you are hoping for while you are on the water. But we've all got the same hopes and dreams, and

I've caught my share of big fish. Not as many as I'd like, certainly and I've had my share of disappointments and heartbreaks, but they are as much a part of the big fish game as the occasional elation at landing the fish of your dreams. Dream on, fish for objectives that are meaningful to you as fish, not as status symbols, and enjoy it. If you can combine the enthusiastic expectation which comes of expecting a fish at any moment, with the world weary knowledge that it may be five years rather than five minutes before you catch the fish you are after you will be able to keep going back for more until it all makes sense to you.

And if you do learn anything along the way don't be afraid to pass it on. In *'Death in the*

Afternoon' (a book about bull fighting, not carp fishing) Ernest Hemingway wrote: '*There are some things which cannot be learned quickly, and time, which is all we have, must be paid heavily for their acquiring. They are the very simplest things and because it takes a man's life to know them the little new that each man gets from life is very costly and the only heritage he has to leave.*'

If you have learnt anything from this book reflect that the contributors have all paid very heavily with time in acquiring their knowledge, and even more heavily in trying to understand that knowledge and going to the trouble of passing it on. Non-carp fishing anglers tend to be surprised at the number of books there are about carp fishing, a surprise that comes from failing to recognise the depth of the carp fishing mystery.

We read about carp partly to be entertained and partly in the hope that what we read will go some way towards solving the mystery for us. I'm far enough down the road to recognise that it will always be a mystery – because the combination of the vicissitudes of nature and the carp's ability to learn means that the terms of reference keep changing. Occasionally the innovators give us a partial, temporary solution to the mystery; then, almost as quickly, the carp out-think the thinkers and innovators and the mystery becomes even deeper. I rarely try to give solutions in my own writing. Rather I encourage thinking because if you can't think for yourself you will always be fishing with yesterday's solutions, which may be a day too late.

Therein, I think, lies part of the great ongoing beauty of carp fishing. It always will be a mystery because however brilliant a temporary solution may be the carp always manage to get back on terms and drive the thinkers back to the drawing board.

That is why there is no definitive work on carp fishing, and there never will be. 'Mystery is too involved, it can't be understood, or solved,' was Dylan's explanation of something else altogether. It can be enjoyed, though, and if this book has given enjoyment, or gone some way to giving an insight into the mystery, it is as much as I can ask of it.

My thanks again to the contributors who have given me so much pleasure from their writings, both in this volume and elsewhere. I hope their writings here will encourage you to go away and read their other works. They have given many of us great inspiration down the years. Long may they, and the carp, continue to do so.

Other fishing books published by the Crowood Press